Making Corporate Social Responsibility a Global Concern
Norm Construction in a Globalizing World

LISBETH SEGERLUND
Stockholm University, Sweden

ASHGATE

Published by
Ashgate Publishing Limited
Wey Court East
Union Road
Farnham
Surrey, GU9 7PT
England

Ashgate Publishing Company
Suite 420
101 Cherry Street
Burlington
VT 05401-4405
USA

www.ashgate.com

British Library Cataloguing in Publication Data
Segerlund, Lisbeth, 1959-
   Making corporate social responsibility a global concern :
   norm construction in a globalizing world. -- (Non-state
   actors in international law, politics and governance
   series)
   1. Social responsibility of business. 2. Social
   responsibility of business--International cooperation.
   3. International business enterprises--Social aspects.
   4. Human rights and globalization. 5. Social responsibility
   of business--Case studies.
   I. Title II. Series
   658.4'08-dc22

Library of Congress Cataloging-in-Publication Data
Segerlund, Lisbeth, 1959-
   Making corporate social responsibility a global concern : norm construction in a globalizing world /
by Lisbeth Segerlund.
       p. cm. -- (Non-state actors in international law, politics, and governance series)
   Includes index.
   ISBN 978-0-7546-7707-9 (hbk) -- ISBN 978-0-7546-9414-4 (ebk)
1. Social responsibility of business. 2. International business enterprises--Social aspects. 3. Human
rights and globalization. 4. Social responsibility of business--Case studies. I. Title.
   HD60.S44 2010
   658.4'08--dc22

2010006284

ISBN 9780754677079 (hbk)
ISBN 9780754694144 (ebk)

Mixed Sources
Product group from well-managed
forests and other controlled sources
www.fsc.org Cert no. SA-COC-1565
© 1996 Forest Stewardship Council

Printed and bound in Great Britain by
MPG Books Group, UK

MAKING CORPORATE SOCIAL RESPONSIBILITY A GLOBAL CONCERN

Non-State Actors in International Law, Politics and Governance Series

Series Editors
Dr Math Noortmann, Oxford Brookes University, UK
Dr Bob Reinalda, Radboud University Nijmegen, The Netherlands
Professor Dr Bas Arts, Radboud Wageningen University and Research Centre
(WUR), The Netherlands

The proliferation of non-state actors in the international system over the last three decades has increased the need for a broader theoretical analysis and empirical validation. The series explores the capabilities and impact of non-state actors, such as privately-based transnational corporations, non-governmental organizations (NGOs), international criminal organizations, and liberation movements, as well as intergovernmental organizations (in which NGO's often participate). The series seeks to address this need and to deepen the knowledge and understanding of non-state actors by scholars, practitioners and students in the fields of international law, politics and governance. By emphasizing legal, political and governance aspects of non-state actors' activities at the international (global or regional) level, the series intends to transcend traditional disciplinary and organizational boundaries.

Also in the series

Partners in Peace
Discourses and Practices of Civil-Society Peacebuilding
Mathijs van Leeuwen
ISBN 978 0 7546 7743 7

Civil Society and Nuclear Non-Proliferation
How do States Respond?
Claudia Kissling
ISBN 978 0 7546 7300 2

Closing or Widening the Gap?
Legitimacy and Democracy in Regional Integration Organizations
Edited by Andrea Ribeiro Hoffmann and Anna van der Vleuten
ISBN 978 0 7546 4968 7

Choosing the Lesser Evil
Understanding Decision Making in Humanitarian Aid NGOs
Liesbet Heyse
ISBN 978 0 7546 4612 9

Contents

List of Figures

List of Tables

Preface

There can be little doubt that Lisbeth Segerlund's contribution to this series is addressing one of the most controversial issues of the past few decades. Social Corporate Responsibility has not only inspired multiple discourses in a variety of disciplines (law, social and political sciences, and management), it has also stirred societal and political debate as evidenced by such well known anti corporate campaigns as the 'boycott Shell' campaign, the 'Nike anti-sweatshop' campaign or the anti-whaling campaigns.

Represented by Naomi Wolf's turn of the century bestseller 'No Logo', anti-corporate activism has become a respectable civil society force to reckon with. NGO efforts to 'changing the standards by which TNCs [transnational companies] are judged' are increasingly successful and the multi-stakeholder initiatives increasingly popular as the UN Global Compact initiative has demonstrated.

The content of the rules and norms that NGOs seek to impose on TNCs or the Codes of Conduct that TNCs adopt are not uncontroversial. The reports of John Ruggy, the UN Secretary General's Special Representative on human rights and transnational corporations and other business enterprises, makes it clear that neither every advocated CSR standard is a norm of international law nor that every corporate conduct is socio-politically acceptable. SCR is indeed, as Lisbeth Segerlund puts it: 'a contentious issue, where different world views and perspectives on the working of the international system are at odds in a contest for legitimacy'.

The question as to how this 'contentious issue' came to dominate academic and societal discourses is one of the main questions in this book. However, it not only provides the state of the art on the development of SCR, it also seeks to offer a comprehension of this process by seeking the 'middle ground' between 'understanding' and 'explanation'.

Adhering to a constructivist approach, Segerlund applies the 'Norm Cycle Model' as the conceptual vehicle to perceive the development on norms and rules in an increasingly transnationalizing world in which a variety of non-state actors, with various values and interests, cooperate in matters of particular socio-political concerns.

Having said this, it is not only the issue and the involvement of multiple non-state actors that makes Lisbeth Segerlund's book so valuable for our series, but also the explicit acknowledgement of and engagement with the relationship between international relations and international law. Chapter 2 starts with an exposé on 'Norms and International Relations', while near the end of her analysis, Lisbeth Segerlund addresses the normative development 'Towards Binding International Law', in particular the 'UN Draft Codes'.

Lisbeth Segerlund brings law and politics, values and interests, and procedures and processes together, and thereby adheres to an important momentum of the recognition of the interdisciplinary relationship between international relations and international legal scholarship. The appreciation of that relationship dates back to the heydays of regime theory, spilled over into neo-liberalism and is now an important element in the dual agenda of international law and international relations, be it in the (neo-)liberal, the constructivist or the international society approaches to IR/IL cross cutting themes. Captured in the various concepts of appropriateness and compliance, the process of global norm formation is a recurring and central theme in these multidisciplinary discourses.

In her conclusion, Lisbeth Segerlund stresses the importance of the interdisciplinary character of the future research agendas: 'research by legal scholars and others is important to further understand the content and implications of various developments in the area of CSR and the role of non-state actors'. This conclusion is reflected in the consideration of a forthcoming publication in this series with the title *Non-state Actor Dynamics in International Law: From Law-takers to Law-makers*, which opens with two articles on SCR as the empirical context for the theoretical assessment of the position of non-state actors in international law.

The SCR discourse and indeed Lisbeth Segerlund's book are prime examples of the ongoing scholarly crossing of those disciplinary boundaries between international relations and international law in the field of non-state actors and thereby serves the larger objective of this series and the interdisciplinary research agenda set by the editors of the series.

Math Noortmann
Oxford
January 2010

Acknowledgements

In the journey that has led up to this book, there are many persons whom I feel grateful to in one way or the other for their contribution to the process. They include colleagues in my department, students in courses I have taught, discussants of papers presented at seminars and conferences, scholars I have met in other circumstances, informants and other staff members of the organizations I have studied, institutions providing me with grants, and not least, friends and family. I would, however, like to mention two persons in particular that have been important for this project. They are Ph.D. Elisabeth Abiri, School of Global Studies, Gothenburg University, who has been an inspiration both for my research and for me as a scholar, and Jo Levy, Write by Design, who has performed wonders language editing the text under severe time pressure – professionally and politely suggesting clear, elegant solutions to the language. Thank you both! Any omissions and errors that remain are all mine.

Lisbeth Segerlund
October 2009

List of Abbreviations

ATCA	Alien Torts Claims Act
CCC	Clean Clothes Campaign
CSR	Corporate Social Responsibility
ECOSOC	United Nations Economic and Social Council
EU	European Union
FLO	Fairtrade Labelling Organizations International
GSP	Generalized System Preferences
IBFAN	International Baby-food Action Network
IBLF	International Business Leaders Forum
ICC	International Chamber of Commerce
ICCR	Interfaith Center for Corporate Responsibility
ICFTU	International Confederation of Free Trade Unions
IGO	Intergovernmental Organization
ILO	International Labor Organization
ILRF	International Labor Rights Fund
INGO	International Non-governmental Organization
IOE	International Organization of Employers
IR	International Relations
ISEAL	International Social and Environmental Accreditation and Labelling
NAALC	North American Agreement on Labor Cooperation
NAFTA	North American Free Trade Agreement
NGO	Non-governmental Organizations
OECD	Organisation for Economic Co-operation and Development
SOMO	Center for Research on Multinational Corporations
TNC	Transnational Corporations
UDHR	Universal Declaration of Human Rights
UNCTAD	United Nations Conference on Trade and Development

UNCTC	United Nations Center on Transnational Corporations
UNDP	United Nations Development Programme
UNGC	United Nations Global Compact
UNIDO	United Nations Industrial Development Organization
USCIB	United States Council in Business
WHO	World Health Organization

Chapter 1
Introduction

If in the late 1980s, someone had declared that in 20 years time, we would have an international social labelling scheme for coffee that would give millions of small coffee farmers and their families a guaranteed price so that they could support themselves in spite of fluctuating world market prices, very few would have believed such a claim. If, furthermore, it had been claimed that this scheme would involve thousands of actors all along the supply chain, including big coffee roaster companies and retail chains, and that consumers and institutional buyers would be prepared to pay a higher price for the coffee, the idea would have been seen as yet another utopian dream by someone trying to make this place a better world. Yet today, this has all become reality. What is more, several other current initiatives are accompanied by claims that companies have social responsibilities, initiatives that were not in existence just a decade ago or so.

The origins of this development can to a large extent be linked to three major events that occurred in the 1970s: the UN negotiations on a code of conduct for transnational corporations (TNCs), efforts targeting companies in apartheid South Africa and the boycott of Nestlé for its practices in marketing breast-milk substitutes. The subsequent fall of apartheid, the successful boycott of Nestlé (which led to the adoption of an international code of conduct by the World Health Organization (WHO)), the unsuccessful (terminated) UN negotiations, the advent of the era of economic liberalization in the 1980s, and the collapse of communism in the Soviet Union and Eastern Europe weakened the criticisms of TNCs heard in the 1970s. However, in parallel with these events, a new wave of concerns related to TNCs began to gain momentum in the late 1980s and cascaded into the establishment of numerous new organizations and initiatives, mainly under the umbrella of corporate social responsibility (CSR).

These developments involved a variety of actors in the international system, but non-governmental organizations (NGOs) were the main advocates. These NGOs are seen in this study as norm entrepreneurs, engaged in international norm construction aimed at changing the standards by which TNCs are judged. The TNCs themselves (including their associations), the prime targets of this advocacy, have as a result increasingly adopted codes of conduct, created new organizations to address CSR issues, and entered into dialogue and cooperation with their critics in so-called multi-stakeholder forums. Governments have become part of, or contributed to, the creation of multi-stakeholder initiatives and have also undertaken other measures related to CSR. A number of intergovernmental organizations (IGOs) have begun to address the issue, among them the European Union (EU), the UN Industrial Development Organization (UNIDO), the UN Development Programme (UNDP), the UN

Commission on Human Rights (UNCHR), and the World Bank. Some of these IGOs are now part of the UN Global Compact, which developed out of the well-known call upon businesses to take action in this area that was made in 1999 at the World Economic Forum by the UN Secretary General, Kofi Annan. The establishment of and interest in the UN Global Compact confirms the increasing importance of CSR internationally and, at the same time, provids legitimacy to the issue of CSR.

This development has been driven mainly by NGOs and is occurring in the context of the transformation of the international system defined as globalization, with changes taking place in technology, international institutions, and the roles of actors, among other things.[1] The development of CSR also draws our attention to the issue of global governance, in particular the role that civil society and NGOs are playing in shaping the content of present and future international regulatory frameworks in various issue areas (see, e.g., Rosenau and Czempiel 1992, O'Brian et al. 2000, Wilkinson and Hughes 2002). Although governments are found among the actors who have taken the initiative in the area of CSR, the majority of actors and activities centre around non-governmental voluntary regulation, agreed to mainly between TNCs and NGOs, often within multi-stakeholder processes. This private authority constitutes an interesting challenge to the idea of the sovereign state and the international system as a whole in terms of opportunities, limits and dilemmas. Some interpret this challenge as the effect of a new transnational solidarity that empowers previously neglected individuals (Sassen 1998), with corporate power being checked. Others regard the very same developments as acts of misguided virtue (Henderson 2001), with well-intentioned NGOs wrongfully intervening in and adversely affecting the functioning of the market. Thus, CSR is a contentious issue, where different world views and perspectives on the working of the international system are at odds in a contest for legitimacy.

Focus of the Book

In view of the expansion of CSR within the context of globalization, there are two questions in particular that I find to be of special interest:

- Why is there renewed interest in CSR in the 1990s?
- How can we understand the process that made this development possible?

The changing role of the state has long been the focus of analyses of globalization, among other things in relationship to the growing importance and influence of 'new' actors and issues in the international system. In particular, the role of TNCs is seen by some as problematic, since they are perceived as more powerful than governments elected by the people. Lately, however, interest in civil society has

---

1   For an overview of the arguments on globalization, see, e.g., Sassen (1998), Held et al. (1998, 1999), Scholte (2000), Held and McGrew (2003) and Rossi (2007).

increased and is seen as a counterbalancing force, not least to multilateral institutions but also in relation to TNCs. The emergence of CSR can be seen as an element of this transformation. The issue encompasses the complexity and tensions produced by the different and intersecting dimensions of actors, processes and structure that provide the setting within which CSR is negotiated, involving principles such as sovereignty, democracy, legitimacy, transparency and representation.

In view of this, I am particularly interested in the role of NGOs in the effort to bring CSR to the international agenda. Which NGOs are involved, and what were their reasons for involvement? Who do the NGOs represent, and how is this representation played out? What are their aims, and how do they go about achieving them? What is the content of the initiatives advocated by the NGOs, and what is the basis for their construction? How does this relate to the already existing body of international instruments and procedures concerning the relationship between TNCs and human rights? The answers to these questions will contribute to further the understanding of the actors, motives and social processes that are part of the development of CSR. They will also help explain the reasons for the revival of CSR and the process involved, as well as illuminate problematic aspects linked to globalization.

The study will only cover CSR as related to human rights, in which I also include labour rights.[2] One reason for this is that human rights are normally seen as the prerogative of the state, a situation that has been challenged through the implication of certain non-state actors in human rights violations and the issue of humanitarian intervention, among other things. Another reason is the growing tension between the free trade and the human rights regimes as human rights become more established in the international system. Furthermore, human rights have been frequently used for the 'framing' of various issues or causes, and thus are also of interest in the case of CSR.

This study is restricted to the period from 1960 until the first half of the 2000s, with a focus on the period from the second half of the 1980s on. This is the period when TNCs and the international production of goods and services develop and the criticisms of both begin to surface.

The discussion here will not deal with the question of whether or not CSR is a good and desirable norm or with the logic of CSR per se (i.e., deontological or teleological), although a discussion of the logic of consequence and logic of appropriateness of norms in general will figure in the discussion of norm construction. The focus on CSR in this study is instead a part of what is called descriptive or comparative ethics, where the emergence and development of CSR as such, not its content, is the main interest. This study is about changes in

---

2   Although the responsibility of TNCs for the environment has become an important international issue and may be included in the concept CSR, I have chosen to focus on human rights in this study. The responsibility of TNCs for human rights is a fairly new topic on the international agenda, which motivates the present research to further an understanding of this development.

international norms regarding the perception of the appropriateness of the activities of TNCs and about the process involved in this change.

Theoretical Approach in the Study of Corporate Social Responsibility

The theoretical approach applied in this study is based on the developments in IR theory labelled social construction or constructivism and, in particular, the 'norm life cycle model' (hereafter the norm cycle model) developed by Finnemore and Sikkink (1998, see also Chapter 2). The point of departure for the norm cycle model is an interest in how current 'standards of appropriateness', at one time seen as immutable, change into new standards of appropriateness. The assumption is that material and rational considerations are not sufficient to explain such changes, and that therefore other considerations must also be influential. The identity of the actors, their actions, the social processes involved, and the context within which they unfold also have to be considered. The use of the norm cycle model is seen as appropriate in view of the aims of the study – i.e., interest in CSR as a new standard of appropriateness and the role of NGOs as important norm entrepreneurs.

The main purpose of the study and applying the norm cycle model is to provide empirical evidence to the research on both constructivism and norms, in particular research concerning the development of CSR. Although theory development or theory testing is not the primary objective here, applying a theoretical model to an empirical case has led me to adjust some parts of the norm cycle model.

Brief Overview of Constructivism

The term constructivism is difficult to define because of conflicting positions on various issues, e.g., whether or not to include post-structuralism, apart from its already debated position in IR in general (Adler 2002, Wight 2002). This internal discord is of course also related to conflicting positions on the philosophy of social science in general. As a result from this, constructivism may appear to be very heterogeneous. However, an effect of the introduction of constructivism is that it has led to an undermining of the conventional positivist view in IR and to disagreements on the merits of scientific explanation.

Even though the constructivist field within IR is 'in construction', so to speak, and the constructivists might be divided internally, there are three elements of common interest (not necessarily common agreement) (Reus-Smith 2001):

- the value of material *and* normative/ideational structures;
- the interconnection of identity, interest and action; and
- the mutual constitution of structures (material and non-material) and agents (practice).

Taken together, they constitute the difference in views on actors, interests and society that distinguish constructivism from, for example, rationalism, as well as cause differences within constructivism itself.

Another way to distinguish constructivism, also based on ontological and epistemological considerations, is to define constructivism as occupying the middle ground in IR theory between explanation and understanding. One strand of IR theory is mainly involved with explanation, i.e., aspects of positivism and rationalism. The other strand of IR theory is involved mainly with understanding, with post-positivism and reflectivism in focus. Here, explaining is understood as putting things in context, whereas understanding involves interpretation (hermeneutics) of human awareness or consciousness (see Figure 1.1 below).

Explanation		**Understanding**
Positivism		Post-positivism
	The middle ground Constructivism?	
Rationalism		Reflectivism

Figure 1.1   Situating Constructivism between Explaining and Understanding
Source: Wight (2005: 36).

Occupying the middle ground would then suggest a combination of both of these strands within IR, i.e., of both explaining and understanding. The middle ground is sometimes also referred to as constituting a bridge between the two.

An important contribution to constructivism is the introduction of the much-debated theory of 'structuration' by Anthony Giddens, involving a complex argument about the interconnectedness of action (agency) and structure. Ontologically different from both functionalism and structuralism, structuration theory claims that social phenomena are linked to a context and are open-ended (non-deterministic), and it seeks to bridge the division between action/agency and structure. The theory of structuration represents a rejection of functionalist and evolutionary (and similar) theories in favour of a focus on social practices – it is the activities of agents that 'reproduce the conditions that make these activities possible' (Giddens 1984: 2). There is thus a circular aspect to social practices. These conditions or structures, reproduced by agents over time and space (i.e., the temporality of the process, not 'history'), are manifested as rules and resources, structures thus being at the same time both the medium and the outcome. From this argument follows the idea of the duality of structure (not to be confused with dualism). In the duality of structure 'the rules and resources drawn upon in the production and reproduction of social action are at the same time the means of system reproduction' (Giddens 1984: 19).

The constructivist approach applied here in the form of the norm cycle model represents a 'pragmatic' position between realism and postmodernism as well as between the rationalist and relativist approaches. In brief, this approach involves the study of the ways in which actors shape and in turn are shaped by context, and the process by which their identities and interests originate and change – the process of mutual constitution.

The Norm Cycle Model

The norm cycle model is based on the idea of transformation as a social construction project driven by a normative agenda (Finnemore and Sikkink 1998). In this social construction project, norms and institutions are defined as regulative, constitutive (creating new actors, interests and categories of action) and evaluative and/or prescriptive. The development of a norm is furthermore understood as consisting of three separate stages: norm emergence, norm cascading and norm internalization, which are all affected by different social processes and logic of action. Each of these stages is characterized by the different actors, motives and mechanisms of influence (or what I have chosen to define as the dominant social processes) involved. An important element of the model is the 'norm tipping' that takes place between the first and second stages. Norm tipping consists of a process in which a certain number of states (one-third or one-fourth), including key states, are required to support the norm before norm cascading can take place. The first two stages may develop into a 'prevailing standard of appropriateness against which new norms emerge and compete for support' (Finnemore and Sikkink 1998: 895) although this is not a given.

In brief, the arguments of Finnemore and Sikkink on strategic social construction combine both rationality and norms. That is, norm entrepreneurs are rational in means-ends calculations (making rational choices) in order to achieve normative commitments from other players (social construction of the normative context). Thus, the common knowledge (or intersubjective understanding) used as the bases for the calculations made by actors is not static; it is the object of the game. Thereby, a process emerges where the actors are creating the 'rules of the game' by playing it.

The norm cycle model takes its point of departure from an assumption of the central importance of states as well as state action and involvement in the process of norm construction. However, as CSR is mainly regarded as a phenomenon of private authority and regulations and also involves multi-stakeholder processes, the implications of this for the norm cycle model suggest that the dominant status of the state needs to be modified. If new actors are more influential in the international system, and the traditional role of the state is undermined as a consequence of globalization, these phenomena should be reflected in the working of the international system. I will therefore explore whether by bringing other actors into the model, the norm tipping can be understood in ways other than by referring to the legitimacy and prominence of the states involved.

A further discussion of the norm cycle model, including reformulation of parts of the model, is found in Chapter 2.

✓Key Concepts

The central concept in this study, corporate social responsibility (CSR), is a broad term that can encompass almost any responsibility that a company might have towards society. This may include simply making a profit and abiding by the laws, regulations and customs of a country, which is a responsibility advocated by market liberals. At the other end of the spectrum, a considerably more extended view of the responsibility of a company would include aspects such as environmental conduct, the working conditions at foreign affiliates and subcontractors, and protection of human rights in general. The latter interpretation is advocated by the UN Sub-Commission on Protection and Promotion of Human Rights, in its proposal for norms for TNCs (the UN Draft Norms) made in 2003 (discussed later). CSR is also defined by other concepts such as corporate citizenship, corporate accountability, corporate responsibility, etc. However, I will use CSR as the overarching and analytical term to denote all of these concepts. My interest lies in what the organizations themselves include in their perception of CSR, given my delimitation, rather than in trying to establish a definition of my own. In general, CSR is understood as going beyond the minimal social responsibilities of a company, i.e., adhering to laws and regulation and customs, and thus rejects the idea of treating the negative aspects of a company's activities as 'externalities'. There are, however, different views on the limits and scope of CSR.

I will also be referring to CSR organizations and CSR initiatives. CSR organizations are organizations that in view of the present delimitations meet the criteria used to select the organizations for this study (see below). This definition does not claim to be the only or best definition of a CSR organization, but it is a relevant and useful definition in view of the aims of this study. CSR initiatives are the initiatives taken by these organizations as well as by other actors (such as governments, IGOs and TNCs) to address the issue of CSR. CSR initiatives are mainly, but not necessarily, initiatives taken in support of CSR.

By the international system, I mean the traditional understanding in IR of a system of sovereign states and their interactions, mainly as inter-state relationships. However, I will view the international system as mixed-actor in character, with importance also given to IGOs (and not just as extensions of their member states), TNCs, NGOs and multi-stakeholder organizations. By transnational, I mean aspects that are both 'cross-border' and 'cross-level' in character at the same time, involving partial detachment from the state and the national but with an attachment to a local context. The local context, thus, is seen as connected both to a national and an international context, as well as to a transnational sphere. In the case of a TNC, the TNC has a local attachment through its headquarter and its relationships with the home country government and other domestic actors, as well as with IGOs and similar institutions. The TNC furthermore conducts its foreign activities in other local contexts, involving interrelationships with host country governments and other host country actors, NGOs, and multi-stakeholder organizations. A similar argument would hold for NGOs.

Other concepts applied in this study will be discussed as they feature in the text when necessary.

Selection of Organizations Covered and Data Collection

Focusing on the role of NGOs as international norm entrepreneurs, I began by making an inventory of selected NGOs involved in the advocacy of CSR (see the criteria used below). Five focus organizations were later selected from this inventory for an in-depth study. Although no geographical demarcations were made at the outset, the focus organizations covered are all located in Europe and North America.

Selection of Organizations

The selection of organizations was based on the following criteria: (1) organizations whose primary aims or an explicit part of their aims are concerned with CSR, (2) organizations claiming to be international, having an international orientation and being involved in activities in other countries on a regular basis, (3) organizations that were NGOs or so-called multi-stakeholder organizations, and (4) organizations that were not trade unions, employer organizations, trade associations or the like, except for the major organizations involved in the three events in the 1970s discussed elsewhere.[3] The criteria serve the purpose of limiting the number of organizations to a robust selection of organizations that can be said to have an influence on the development of CSR and that are neither only the few large established international NGOs nor the myriad of local grassroots NGOs involved in globalization issues. I have identified 75 organizations that according to these criteria are involved in the advocacy and norm creation of CSR. The organizations are listed in Appendix 1.

One result of my research and the initial inventory of CSR organizations is that I discovered apparent distinctions between the organizations that led me to define and divide them according to the following three categories:

- Activist Organizations, or 'traditional' social change organizations with neither company nor government or IGO participation.
- Business Initiatives Organizations, or organizations with only company membership.

---

3   The reason for excluding trade unions and employers' organizations is that they are usually seen as part of industrial or labour market relations and thus more connected to matters related to the workplace or employment. Exception is made for international bodies of trade unions, i.e., the international trade secretariats and the International Confederation of Free Trade Unions (ICFTU) in relationship to the events of the 1970s.

- Multi-stakeholder Organizations, or organizations whose membership includes at least two of the following groups: NGOs, companies, governments, IGOs, or other groups or individuals.

The different categories are based on the membership of or support basis for the included organizations, with the understanding that this difference has consequences for the ways that the organizations in question address CSR. The NGOs involved in CSR are not a homogeneous group, and the organizations in the different categories influence the process in different ways.

The selection of the focus organizations concentrated on 'first movers' from each category in order to study specific cases of NGOs in-depth that from an early stage engaged in CSR. This in-depth study is mainly based on printed material and reveals the particular characteristics of early 'norm entrepreneurs' in these categories. The in-depth study also attempts to capture variations in geographical locations, types of CSR initiatives, organization size, and organization aims and activities. Inevitability, the selection has been restricted by the accessibility of the individual organizations.

This selection does not intend to be exhaustive or representative of the CSR movement as a whole. However, it claims to cover fairly well the more important organizations involved in CSR, given the limitations stated above. Furthermore, the characteristics of the focus organizations taken together are intended to show the more important aspects of the CSR movement as a whole.

Data Collection

This section will account for the kind of sources that are used, as well as the methods that have been applied in the collection of information. The choice of sources and methods is mainly guided by the research questions and of pragmatic considerations, since a constructivist approach does not prescribe particular methods. I see NGOs as important actors (norm entrepreneurs) and a way to gain a grasp of the social practice of norm constructing concerning CSR. Therefore, their background, aims and activities have been seen as important sources for understanding this practice.

The data collection is based on three kinds of sources: printed material, interviews and Internet websites. The printed material consists of literature studies in the subject field of CSR, published and unpublished material mainly collected from the focus organizations. The purpose of the literature study is to mainly cover the early stage in the development of CSR, i.e., the 1960s and 1970s, with the three major events of this period discussed in the study. The printed material collected from the organizations consists of mostly published, but also unpublished material, and varies in scope depending on the extent of publication activity, as well as the state of the archives of each organization. In general, the printed material concerns public information on the organization, its aims and activities, and statements on various issues, in the form of annual reports of activities, newsletters, press releases, and books and reports.

As for interviews, these were initially made with representatives of some of the selected CSR organizations (some 20 interviews) with the main objective to obtain a general knowledge and an overview of the field as well as access to the organizations. A semi-structured interview method has been applied based on a checklist of thematic questions or matters to be covered in the interviews with each informant. Later interviews were organized so as to mainly deal with issues not covered in the printed material or information on the Internet website collected at the organization. This was seen as the optimal choice for obtaining maximum information from informants often pressed for time and approached by many other researchers.

I have also made use of Internet websites, which represent the main source of information for the large group of selected CSR organizations and a part also of the information collected from the focus organizations. Through the use of Internet websites it was possible to gain an efficient overview of the movement as a whole regarding the total number, the organizational character (limited to the type of organization, year of establishment, location of main office), and their aims and activities in brief. Internet today has become important for information and communication in general and also for NGOs to present themselves, carry out activities and frame issues; it represents an important source for data collection on and tracing of the process. However, as Internet websites change and are seldom found in archives or in libraries, I consider them to be equivalent to public speech and interviews.

Most of the material is produced by the organizations themselves. As such, it can only be considered to represent the self-image the organizations want to portray of themselves. However, this also represents a manifestation of the framing strategies undertaken by the organizations that are of central interest for understanding the process of international norm construction and thus also key to an understanding of the development of CSR. In case others have made relevant writings on these organizations, this has been considered as well.

When combined, the data obtained from the printed material, the interviews and the Internet websites covers a lot of ground and compensate for shortfalls in each source of data.

Previous Research

I have not been able (nor did I intend) to delineate specific fields of research in my review of the literature on CSR, although literature abounds on the topic. A study of library catalogues can be illustrative, and it reveals that publications on the 'social responsibility of business' (the index terms used for cataloguing by libraries) appeared already in the 1960s. However, the issue is partly covered by other index terms, mainly the social aspects of industries and business ethics. Publications on these topics date back even further.

It is notable that the number of publications indexed under 'the social responsibility of business' increases considerably from 1990 onwards, when some 80–90 per cent of the titles under this heading were published (as of 2004). This preponderance of literature can be taken as evidence in support of TNCs emerging as powerful actors in the international system as well as attracting attention to the responsibility that this entails, reflected in the norm cascading of CSR organizations and initiatives from the mid-1990s and onwards.

At present, apart from the Business and Management Schools and related academic institutions, where a large part of the research on CSR is carried out, research in this area in Sweden (and presumably in other countries as well) is dispersed over many disciplines, such as Sociology of Law, Political Science, Bioethics, Peace and Conflict Research, Natural Geography, Economics and Management, Industrial Environmental Economics, Media and Communication, Economics, and Sociological Anthropology.

Apart from more recent writings on industry self-regulation, new forms of social regulation or specific CSR initiatives such as the UN Global Compact, the issue of CSR has not attracted any considerable attention from mainstream IR in the past. A more general approach to questions of private international authority and the role of non-state actors in global governance can of course be found, related to the debate on transnational actors and globalization that has been active since the 1970s.

Norms in international relations, on the other hand, is an area of research that has attracted greater interest, which is briefly discussed in Chapter 2. However, this research has not addressed the issue of CSR in general.

This study aspires to contribute to filling the gap in research in this area.

Chapter Overview

In the next chapter I will elaborate further on the idea of norms and other concepts that relate to the theoretical approach chosen for my study, in particular concerning international human and labour rights and globalization.

Chapters 3–9 will deal with the different stages and key elements of the norm cycle model as applied to the development of CSR.

Norm emergence is covered in Chapters 3–6. In Chapters 3 and 4, the early phase of the development of CSR is discussed in relationship to three major events of the 1970s – the UN negotiations on a code of conduct for TNCs (Chapter 3), efforts targeting companies in apartheid South Africa and the boycott of Nestlé for its practices in marketing breast-milk substitutes (Chapter 4). These two latter events mark a break with prevailing standards of appropriateness at the time and are a point of departure for this study.

The later phase of norm emergence, with the creation of norm entrepreneurs for CSR, is the focus of Chapter 5 (on Activist Organizations) and 6 (on Business Initiatives and Multi-stakeholder Organizations). On the assumption that actor identity affects interest, choice and outcome, the background, aims and activities of these actors are explored so as to better understand the actors, motives and social process of persuasion involved in this stage of norm emergence.

The norm tipping and norm cascade, with its mushrooming of CSR organizations and initiatives that occurred in the mid-1990s, are discussed in Chapter 7 and 8. The shift in the set of actors, their motives and the social process is demonstrated through specific topics significant to the development of CSR in this stage. In particular, the targeting of the US company Nike by Activist Organizations (Chapter 7) and the development of voluntary standards, exploration of legal accountability, and the role of good practice and partnership (Chapter 8) are discussed.

The possible development of norm internalization will be the focus in Chapter 9, with a discussion of empirical cases supporting the arguments for norm consolidation. A summary and concluding discussion is found in Chapter 10.

Chapter 2
Norms, Globalization and Human Rights

The diffuse, shifting and intersubjective character of social norms in general presents challenges for the study of international norms in particular. The manifestation of a norm is usually implicit in the behaviour of individuals and in their mutual understandings of reality in a known social setting. The existence of norms is made possible because they are part of an intersubjective process, produced and reproduced in the social practices of everyday life. Norms therefore have a taken-for-granted quality that in a sense makes them invisible and absent, yet present, at the same time. However, in spite of their taken-for-granted nature, norms do not appear out of thin air. Norms change and new norms appear, sometimes due to implicit advocacy by someone for specific motives. This implies that norms are part of a locally (re)constructed process, a process that changes through the social practices of the participating individuals. The process of norm construction, thus, by definition, is difficult to transfer into an international context. Who are the individuals/actors in the process of international norm construction? Which are the international social settings where this process takes place? What forms does the intersubjective process of norm construction take in an international context?

In view of the complexities involved, I will give a brief overview of norms in general and of norms in international relations. The purpose is to point out some of the distinctive issues raised and the ways that they affect international relations, with a focus on issues pertaining to the process of globalization and to human rights. This will be followed by a discussion of the norm cycle model applied in this study so as to clarify my point of departure and to put CSR in the context of a discussion of norms.

Norms and International Relations

There are various definitions of what a social norm is. The definitions generally include the presence of an expectation (an 'oughtness' distinct from one's own preference) under a certain condition as well as the behaviour, beliefs or attitudes of individuals or collectives of individuals. Furthermore, norms are also often seen as shared (intersubjective) and involving a likelihood of sanctions in the case of non-compliance.

Emergence and Effectiveness of Norms

The emergence of norms often involves a discussion of instrumentality or instrumental rationality (considerations of the consequences), functionality, socialization and culture. Whereas the instrumentality, functionality and socialization of norms may seem fairly straightforward, culture may not. In cultural explanations, norm emergence takes a broader approach to norms in which defining and expressing identity are included in the conceptualization of a norm (Lapid and Kratochwil 1996). From these different aspects it follows that norms may emerge spontaneously, appear as the effect of strategic actions and may or may not involve some form of enforcement through positive (incentives) or negative (penalties) sanctions. Few norms, however, are likely to be maintained through only internal or external sanctions. In practice, norms often work through a combination of both mechanisms – i.e., through internal *and* external sanctions.

The ways that norms are effective may involve the roles that individuals take on in social interaction, the effect on choices that individuals make (relating to internal or external sanctions), the influence on habit, or the practice of conformity. Norms may of course also have indirect and unintended effects, at least until these effects become monitored and reflected upon – after that they can no longer be seen as unintended.

In general, one can therefore say that norms involve the patterned behaviour of actors, including their expectations and normative reflections (of oneself and others). This involves both perceptions of the present (what 'is') and the reflexive monitoring of day-to-day social interaction, as well as ideas about the future or a distant and idealized appropriate behaviour (i.e., normative, what 'ought' to be). Although patterned behaviour is central to discussions of norms, different emphasis is put on whether it is the regularities of the behaviour or the standards of the patterned behaviour that is the focus.

When *regularities* of behaviour are seen as the main interest, it is the (external) sanctions or the material incentives that are seen as the most important features. The choices that actors make are dependent on these sanctions or incentives. From this perspective, norms are more or less equal to (distribution of) power or to interests involving cost-benefit calculations and utility maximization. On the other hand, if it is the *standards* of the patterned behaviour in question that is the most important feature, then the obligation and the internal sanction stand out. Norms are here seen as embedded in social practices and intersubjective, involving an element of legitimacy that shapes goals and means and therefore determines preferences and interests. This also regulates behaviour, perhaps in even a more powerful way.

A norm may also be seen as a 'cognitive energy-saver' and time-saver in providing guidance for decision-making when bounded rationality and uncertainty about the future is considered (Florini 1996: 366). These latter two perspectives on norms, norms as standards or guidance, stand in contrast to realist and traditional rational choice theories. In international relations, the issue of sanctions is particularly interesting, as this presents challenges to international organization in the absence of a centralized governance or authority structure. Although sanctions in the international system may also originate from dispersed centres of authority or power, the expectations from such a situation could be unclear as to what the outcome will be. Patterned behaviour is therefore of specific interest and supports the claim of norms not only being based on external sanctions, as such sanctions may be difficult to construct in an international system of sovereign states. Norms as guidance and as standards for patterned behaviour are of most interest in this study (see also the discussion on the norm cycle model below).

Norms in International Relations

Turning to norms in international relations, there has been a significant revival in the study of norms in IR in recent times. The reasons for this include a questioning of the alleged artificial divide between international and domestic politics and of the uniqueness of international politics, as well as a questioning of positivism in the social sciences in general. Furthermore, the debates among political theorists on individualist versus communitarian liberalism or cosmopolitanism have been part of this renewed interest. The recent pressing global issues and the question of global justice have also contributed to the interest in norms (see, e.g., Hurrell 2005, Florini 1996 and Björkdahl 2002a, 2002b).

In spite of the challenges to the understanding of (international) norms, ideas and norms have been shown to play an important role in international relations, and not just a causal one (see, e.g., Goldstein and Keohane 1993, Wapner and Ruiz 2000, Clark 2007). Issues relating to culture and identity have, since the emergence of globalization and the end of the Cold War, reappeared in both mainstream and critical theories in IR. However, the focus on aspects of sovereignty, predictability and 'manipulability', entities rather than process, as well as a tendency toward isolationism and parochialism has made and still makes it difficult for culture and identity to enter the field of IR (Lapid and Kratochwil 1997: 5). Recent research has begun to tackle the questions raised above, and in spite of the illusive nature of norms, they have been shown to be very powerful in their taken-for-granted quality. This can be seen in the discussion of norms related to apartheid (Klotz 1995), chemical weapons (Price 1995), national interest (Finnemore 1996), humanitarian intervention (Finnemore 2003), and human rights (Risse, Ropp, and Sikkink 1999, Thomas 2001). As for human rights, these norms serve to further reinforce other norms and legitimize new normative claims, as in the case of CSR discussed here.

At the same time, there is wide debate about certain topics relevant to any discussion of norms, such as whether they exist, their importance, role and effect in world politics, and in the moral evaluation of different and competing norms. This is often due to the diverse ontological perspectives on which these differences are based, which tend to be confused with debates on the substance of a particular norm or normative claim (see, e.g., Checkel 1998, Krasner 1999, Zehfuss 2002). To appreciate some of the arguments involved, a brief discussion of different approaches within IR to the study norms will be made next.

Norms in International Regimes   When norms in international relations are brought up, reference is often made to the discussion of norms in international regimes theory. The brief and now well-known definition of international regimes states that they are: 'principles, norms, rules, and decision-making procedures around which actor expectations converge in a given issue-area' (Krasner 1983: 1). In brief, international regimes are about rule-governed activity in the absence of a central government or authority in the international system. Some examples of international regimes involve activities that are now taken for granted, such as the international communication regimes (postal, aviation, maritime and other similar systems) and the international human and labour rights regimes. The existence of other international regimes, such as international environmental or security regimes, may be more contested.

The early definition of norms made in international regimes theory states that: 'Norms are standards of behaviour defined in terms of rights and obligations' (Krasner 1983: 2). Norms, as defined here, together with principles ('beliefs of fact, causation, and rectitude'), rules and decision-making procedures are treated as *one component* of what makes up international regimes, where norms and principles constitute the defining characteristics of these regimes (Krasner 1983: 2). Changes of norms and principles lead to change *of* the regime itself, whereas changes of rules and decision-making procedures only constitute changes *within* a regime.

In the discussion that followed on international regimes theory (Kratochwil and Ruggie 1986), contradictions of the ontology of international regimes theory (intersubjectivity and convergence of expectations) and the foundation in an epistemology based on positivism have been pointed out. Since norms are neither causal (rather, norms guide behaviour) nor subject to counterfactual evidence (violations or formal non-existence of norms do not refute norms), norms create a problem in positivist-oriented research – norms may exist even though they are not formal. Norms can therefore not be seen as variables; instead, it is the communicative dynamics involved that are of interest. This critique of the view on norms in international regimes theory turns the attention more to a discussion of the social practice and the communication related to norms. Consequently, later studies have focused more exclusively on norms on their own terms.

Norms, State Interest and State Identity   The traditional assumption of national interest as given in relation to matters of national security has been questioned in various studies. Rather, interest is to be seen as socially constructed. Hence, security interests also depend on who the actors are, their definitions of security and of related issues, and the cultural setting within which they are found. Although power is not to be rejected altogether, it cannot only be seen as material. Also other forms of power are important, such as norms. Therefore, the meanings that actors attach to power and security need to be analysed. From this follows greater attention to the cultural-institutional context and the construction of identity of international political actors – states, governments and others.

Norms can from this perspective be defined as 'collective expectations for the proper behaviour of actors with a given identity' (Katzenstein 1996: 5) – i.e., they simultaneously define the identity of these actors (constitutive) and act as standards of appropriate behaviour (regulative). Here, norms emerge as a process of communication, a process that can emerge spontaneously (through social practice), be consciously promoted (political strategy), and/or be deliberately negotiated (e.g., in mechanisms of conflict resolution).

When applied to the issue of national security, the argument is that the structure of the environment of states (global or domestic) influences national security interest or security policy as well as state identity. For example, this can be seen in that certain technologies are regarded as more accepted for killing people than others (compare chemical weapons to other equally destructive weapons), and also in how these perceptions can change, as was the case in the successful campaign against antipersonnel landmines (Price 1995, 1998). Another example is seen in the changes in the reasons for and the manner of military intervention over the last 150 years in the cases of debt collection, humanitarian military intervention, and threat to international peace and security. This change cannot be ascribed to material factors or change in number or scale alone. Although large states continue to make interventions in smaller and weaker states, they do not do this whenever it suits them. 'What have changed are state understandings about the purposes to which they can and should use force' (Finnemore 2003: 3). This is so because 'actors consciously set out to change the perceptions and values of others' (Finnemore 2003: 5) involving different mechanisms at both the collective and individual level.

Norms, Legitimacy and Socialization   As was mentioned in the introduction to this chapter, norms may be seen as mainly related to incentives and constraints on behaviour (liberal/rationalist perspective), or as constituting identities and interest (constructivist perspective). In the case of identities and interest, discussed below, the emphasis is on aspects such as legitimacy and socialization for explanations of norms.

Legitimacy as a motive for an actor to abide by rules is put forward in rejection of material power or self-interest as the only or main explanation of international order in the absence of a centralized power (Hurd 1999). It is argued from this perspective that the normative structure also affects actor behaviour, not just physical capacity (sanctions/coercion) or incentives (self-interest). Legitimacy evokes the actor's *perception* of the institution (the rules) in question based on the content of the rules or how the rules were constituted (the procedure or source). Legitimate institutions are in this case seen as based in authority. Therefore, the existence of authoritative international institutions is not due to coercion or mere self-interest, but because of legitimacy (see also the discussion on moral authority below). Furthermore, although international authority currently is decentralized – a consequence of the institution of sovereignty – sovereignty only represents one form of international governance without a government. This does not rule out the possibility of other forms of international authority. Viewing the international system as governed by various 'institutions of legitimate authority' would open up the discussion for alternative explanations (including community norms and shared beliefs as segments of authority in the international system).

Caution should be urged before focusing narrowly on either liberal/rationalist or constructivist perspectives, since norms may involve both constraining and constitutive effects. An alternative explanation focusing on the diffusion of norms into a domestic setting (diffusion seen as distinct from and necessary for compliance) involves two mechanisms: *societal pressure dynamics and elite learning* (Checkel 1997). Here, also, success in the diffusion of a norm is important, as it contributes to empower the norm. Which diffusion will prevail in a domestic setting depends on the political institutional structure (liberal, state-above-society, corporatist or statist) that predicts when norms are going to constrain and/or constitute agents. Here, both incentives and constitution in combination with the intervening variable of the domestic political institutional structure can help explain the various ways of norm diffusion and empowerment of norms, as well as the many roles of norms.

Norms, Language and Communication   Norms may also be linked to the function of language in social interaction and the importance of language for social action as such. Human beings do not primarily act on stimulus and therefore need to resort to choice in their pursuance of goals; rules and norms help reduce complexity in choice situations. In the process of attaining goals, human beings interact with others and need to communicate through different communicative acts using 'action words' (Kratochwil 1989). According to speech-act theory, these action words are of different kinds; some refer not only to an independent action (e.g., riding) but also to actions that are performed as the action words are uttered (e.g., I promise). It is the latter action words that are of interest in the relation between norms and language. These kinds of action words are partly normative, as they also refer to certain rules and norms (a social practice) that constitute the action that is performed with the utterance of the actual action word – such as keeping one's promises. An example of where speech-act theory is applied in IR is in the field of securitization studies.

In general, human actions are rule-governed as rules give meaning to actions such as 'pursue goals, share meanings, communicate with each other, criticize assertions, and justify actions' (Kratochwil 1989: 11). This brings the discussion of communication beyond the referential dichotomy of 'is' and 'ought' as well as the instrumental rationality of a goals-means context. Instead, the speech-act theory of language distinguishes between statements that are about (1) saying something, (2) doing what is said, e.g., promise, and (3) the impact this has on the listeners. Through these different aspects of speech-act it is possible to distinguish the effective conditions of communication. These conditions should not be confused with whether the action word or performance is appropriate or not; this is often a confusion found in the discussion about for example regimes in security studies.[1]

In this brief overview of norms support is found to the arguments in IR against power or interest to be seen as givens. It also indicates that identity influences the understandings and choices made by actors – consequently affecting the outcome. Furthermore, the institutional settings and social processes within which these understandings and choices occur also contribute to the outcome. They influence the constitution of identity, which is important for the meanings actors attach to various phenomena. This will affect interest and, hence, which choices are actually made. In particular, the communicative actions demonstrate how this social practice takes place in more detail (see also the discussion below on civil society and 'framing').

Globalization as a Context for Norm Construction

As was mentioned in the introduction, norm construction is not an easy project in an international system of sovereign states; a system that recently has been challenged by the advent of new actors and new forms of governance. Furthermore, with IGOs no longer seen only as an extension of state authority, but also as partly independent centres of authority (the EU being a case of its own), the complexity of the transformation process increases. The transformation of this system has also given rise to conflicting situations when changing trade and production patterns have become detached from a nationally based protective structure of labour rights. Simultaneously, the emerging trend is that this protective structure is being detached from the domestic to balance the negative aspects of globalization.

The key driving force behind these changes is the actions of committed individuals, whether acting independently and simultaneously as part of social movements, or as leaders, members or supporters of particular organizations. They form part of the civil society[2] that plays an important role in putting new issues

---

1   As unauthorized threats do occur (although not permitted), it has been concluded that norms do not exist, that norms are insignificant, that norms are not involved in making threats or that threats cannot lead to normative expectations. One here needs to distinguish the validity of a threat, i.e., the conditions under which a threat is effective (the expectations from this 'negative promise'), and whether the same threat is allowed. The same argument holds when obligations are to be established (Kratochwil 1989).

2   There are two major conceptions of civil society (Ehrenberg 1999). The first is concerned with the importance of the state for maintaining order and liberty, but where political freedom and economic activity are seen as the cornerstones of civil society. The other, dealing with the idea of civil society as an intermediating body, combines individual interest and an objective common good. In the first conception, companies are seen as part of civil society and represent freedom from state control. In the second, civil society takes on the role of a third force distinct from both the state and companies; this is the view of civil society adopted in this study.

on the international agenda. They thereby constitute a channel other than the existing political system or the economic sector through which to voice opinions and interests. The idea of a civil society in the international system is somewhat of a paradox, as there is no equivalent to the domestic centralized state authority at the international level apart from the fragmented formal authority structure of IGOs. However, the international trade and production systems do constitute a global economy accompanied by international regulation relating mainly to economic matters. The actions of civil society organizations thereby have become more complex, having to relate to a structure organized at two 'levels' (domestic-international) as well as a supranational level (the EU) and in a transnational (cross-border/cross-sector) sphere – see Figure 2.1.

Emergence of New Actors and Forms of Governance

At the centre of the transformation discussed above are the changing role of the state, the emergence of new actors and their interrelation. In particular, this has concerned TNCs as dominant actors in trade and international production and the negative aspects of TNC activities at focus here (see, e.g., Holton 1998, Sassen 1998, Held et al. 1999, Gilpin 2001, Phillips 2002; on the role of the TNCs see, e.g., Vernon 1971, Dunning 1997, Henderson 2001). Since the 1960s, the total number of TNCs has increased tenfold. Today, there are over 79,000 TNCs and more than 790,000 affiliates/subsidiaries, with the largest TNCs mainly found in the automobile, pharmaceutical and telecommunication industries. About 75 per cent of all TNCs are found in developed countries, a majority of them in Western Europe (UNCTAD 2006, 2008).

In general, the transformation of the international system has mainly been seen as influenced by the interrelation and dynamics between TNCs and states. But this view has lately been challenged by the effect of the activities of civil society and especially NGOs. Even more spectacular growth than that of TNCs can be seen in the development of NGOs, although their total number still does not compare with that of TNCs. Since the early twentieth century, the number of INGOs has increased, from less than 200 to an impressive 28,500 in the early 1990s. A large majority of these were established from 1970 on. INGOs at present still tend to be mostly European-based, but participation in NGOs is growing faster in developing countries. Furthermore, the changing role of NGOs has also changed their position vis-à-vis the IGOs, and the distinction between them has blurred. This means that not only have the NGOs become directly involved in some of the operations of IGOs, the NGOs have also become more professional in their own operations and, as a consequence, their relationships with IGOs have changed (UIA 2003, Braithwaite and Drahos 2000: 497, Boli and Thomas 1999).

In spite of their main bases in 'soft power', the NGOs have been ascribed increasing influence and, together with the scientific community, are seen as a major influence on new regulatory ideas for international regimes as well as norms and practices in international relations in general. In the last decades, they have also developed different working methods, facilitated partly by new information technology, such as the Internet, which can even be considered a political tool (Braithwaite and Drahos 2000, Warkentin and Mingst 2000, Khagram, Riker and Sikkink 2002).

Since the end of the Cold War, efforts to establish a governance system for sustainable development have been particularly prominent in world politics. In combination with increasing demands by and coherence of ethnic groups, economic globalization, growth in social movements, shrinking political distances (due to information technology) and greater global interdependence (due to economic crises, pollution, terrorism, drug trade, and HIV/AIDS), these changes have led to shifts in sites of authority toward the development of governance functions that do not always originate with governments. Rather, that governance exists somewhere between anarchy (the international system) and government (domestic context) and in circumstances where different international regimes overlap, conflict or otherwise require adjustments between competing interests. Anarchy, then, can be seen in a different light – still meaning lack of government, but not necessarily a complete lack of governance (Rosenau and Czempiel 1992).

Global governance carries with it different frame of references for the development of governance forms, involving a 'reconfiguration of authority between various layers or infrastructures of governance' (Held and McGrew 2003: 10). This rather points in the direction of a 'new medievalism' (Friedrichs 2001, see also Hedley Bull), with overlapping and multiple authorities and loyalties held together by the competing claims made by the nation-state system and the transnational market economy.

Although many might agree on a shift in world politics, from post-war multilateralism to more 'complex multilateralism' (O'Brien 1999), there is less agreement on whether this actually means a qualitative shift towards a global governance structure, or even on the potential and desirability of some of the new issues of global governance. From a sceptical and critical perspective, the arguments of both realists and Marxists are that geopolitics in global governance can never be ignored. Non-reflective views on global governance are furthermore seen to ignore the power dimensions involved in the development of 'new constitutional frameworks' relating to the tensions that arise from the changing orders of production and social reproduction as a result of globalization (Bakker and Gill 2003). Other scholars maintain that although they are well aware of the risk of certain global governance structures becoming ghettos for specific issues (as in the case of gender), these structures still constitute important spaces for activities (see, e.g., Meyer and Prügl 1999, Gilpin 2001, Callinicos 2002, Held and McGrew 2003, Barnett and Duvall 2005).

Civil Society and the Role of Non-governmental Organizations

Lately, renewed attention to civil society has brought up transnational relations from another perspective, now referred to as global civil society and seen as a 'third force' (Florini 2000) in the interplay of the powerful actors in the international system. The third force is simultaneously the source of a challenge to TNCs as well as a contributor to the undermining of state sovereignty with the development of private regulation, seen in areas such as CSR. The undermining of the traditional role of the state and the growth of private regulation promoted by the activities of this so-called third force raises a further related issue, namely, that of global governance.

The debate on civil society from an international perspective (Pasha and Blaney 1998) reveals some of the paradoxes involved in what has also been termed *global* civil society. One view is that global civil society is autonomous vis-à-vis the state or the state system and has developed mainly due to the loss of state sovereignty; global liberalism (the universalization and fragmentation of identities resulting from the consumer culture) is seen as the enabling factor for its development. Other perspectives emphasize the governance side of global civil society more strongly, and although still separate from the state, it is regarded as part of an emergence of formal institutions and a global constitutionalism. Yet others favour the relational approach of global civil society and the state, involving not only the negotiation of interests but also the development of a common language and common values. Global civil society in this view develops simultaneously with governmental institutions to establish the accountability of the latter.

Some reject the idea of a global civil society altogether, and rather perceive an international civil society of interlinked national civil societies, where national loyalties are still dominant. Civil society in this view is not global and at best transnational, with emphasis on the 'border-crossing nature' of its activities. The argument here is that the supposedly global society in fact lacks representation for the majority of the people of the world, due among other things to the use of English and modern technology (one-third of the world's population does not have telephones) (Naidoo 2000, Florini 2000: 7), although village phones to some extent address this problem and the number of mobiles in developing countries is growing. This is the view of civil society that I support and that forms the basis of the discussion in this study.

The critique of an ahistorical and disembedded view of civil society (Hahn and Dunn 1996, Colás 2002, and Naidoo 2000) as well as an idealized view of the role of civil society as always furthering the right standards of appropriateness and their alleged superior representativeness is, in my opinion, justified. Civil society is somehow seen as representing a universal justice and democracy, the voice of the people (demos) or humanity as a whole. A genuinely global deliberative process seems very difficult to picture, when the scale and scope of such an undertaking is considered. This tends to reify civil society and makes (per the definition) any questioning unjustifiable. On the contrary, the activities of civil society also could be seen as circumscribing the democratic order when this is manifested in the form of traditional political representation. The voice of the people also tends to be the voice of a small number of dedicated individuals or groups resourceful enough to become influential, whatever the initial intentions might have been.

Powers of Civil Society: Moral Authority, Legitimacy and Persuasion

The influence of civil society is generally based on the assumption of a hierarchy of power instruments in international relations. This includes, in order of importance, (1) military power, (2) economic resources, and (3) soft power, such as moral authority and persuasion (Florini 2000: 10). Governments are seen to make use of all three of these power instruments and companies mainly use the second and third, but civil society groups most often use only the third. I will focus here on this last category of power instrument – soft power.

Soft power can be employed and effective in different ways (Florini 2000). This includes persuading policy makers and business leaders to change their goals, changing the public's perception of what these actors should be doing, conferring legitimacy on a decision or an institution (such as social labels), threatening to disclose embarrassing information (a form of coercion, dependent, however, on the persuasion of the general public), diffusing credible information and achieving a perception of moral authority. The effects of this soft power are according to Florini (2000) both real and considerable and manifested as:

- Increase in the number and effectiveness of civil society organizations.
- Getting neglected issues onto the agenda (e.g., anti-personnel land mines).
- Determining how to solve problems (influence the discussion and the resulting agreements (e.g., non-violent end to the Cold War through the 'Helsinki effect' (Thomas 2001)).
- Monitoring compliance to agreements.
- Providing direct services to governments and IGOs (policy implementation and roles as 'subcontractors').

Although these powers are real and considerable, there are also limitations following from the fact that the participants in civil society often are heterogeneous and divided over issues, and that there is no single, coherent transnational civil society agenda. This follows from having to work through the instrument of persuasion, with the need to achieve voluntary compliance. This often means obtaining support from influential actors and thus involves some form of dependence. The task of remaining credible can also be a difficult one, as too close cooperation with governments, inaccurate or misleading information and how representation is handled, can have an undermining effect on the status of the organization. Overestimating the reach of soft power and the willingness to accept the moral authority of NGOs, e.g., resistance to greater access of NGOs in the UN, are other limitations (Florini 2000: 213).

Opportunities and Limits of Non-governmental Organizations

The changes discussed above have led to the need for new skills among activists, an understanding of and ability to play by the rules of the game. NGOs have therefore become structured so that they can continue with national activities and deal with the intergovernmental level at the same time (Smith 1997: 43, 51).[3]

The methods of influence used by NGOs generally involve information, persuasion and moral pressure (or socialization of other actors). Also important here are the symbolic politics pursued; i.e., 'to call upon symbols, actions, or stories that make sense of a situation for an audience that is frequently far away' (Keck and Sikkink 1998: 16). They often make use of competing justifications, which thereby become part of the political process with the justifications used as a source of political power. In this process, key individuals and organizations become important as 'transnational moral entrepreneurs' (Nadelman 1990: 482) who campaign on specific normative demands motivated by a search for meaning and their principled beliefs. Often powerful actors are used in strategies of leverage politics (Khagram, Riker and Sikkink 2002, Keck and Sikkink 1998).

Certain core concepts (Smith, Chatfield and Pagnucco 1997) have been identified as common to and important for an understanding of social movements (including NGOs): among these are strategic framing processes and repertoires of contention that are of special interest in relation to a discussion on norm construction.[4]

Strategic Framing of Issues   Framing can be defined as 'conscious strategic efforts by groups of people to fashion shared understandings of the world and of themselves that legitimate and motivate collective action'. More specifically, the framing results in 'specific metaphors, symbolic representations, and cognitive cues to render or cast behaviour and events in an evaluative mode and to suggest alternative modes of action'. The frames are therefore not simply ideas but also ways of packaging and presenting ideas and involve a meaning-creation process. Movements use these frames in their persuasive communications (mobilization of consensus); the communication can be seen in their choice of tactics and the connection between their actions and rhetoric (McAdam, McCarthy and Zald 1996: 6, 262 and 354).

However, persuasive communication is also important to mobilize people for concrete action in order to draw the attention of the media and domestic and international public (Khagram, Riker and Sikkink 2002). Therefore, framing is considered a condition for broad mobilization, which in turn is dependent on both timing and the social location of mobilization. As framing is a context-specific process, it takes time to develop (having to be contested and debated) and is therefore more difficult to transfer to a transnational level with cultural differences as well as a difference in scale and scope.

---

3 Naturally, national institutions also affect the opportunity structure of social movements and NGOs. If the national environment is oppressive; the need to reach out across borders for support becomes more important. I will here focus on the international aspects of opportunities and other aspects relating to NGOs.

4 Other concepts not discussed here include activist identities, mobilizing structures, resource mobilization, and the political opportunity structures of a country.

One way to achieve framing is to locate an international forum or institutions where the frames can be lodged and then leave written traces of frames. These traces can then be discussed in proceedings from international conferences, in international agreements and in media reporting of the traces. The discourse that evolves from this process can be shaped to fit the mobilizing frames of the activists. The actors who become involved in the process in this way may include TNCs, multinational religious bodies, states, etc., which means that the context and the scope of the framing process is very wide and not just limited to actual IGO meetings. The most successful framing is perhaps the conception of human rights, 'the mother of all successful transnational framing efforts' (McCarthy 1997: 246). Several case studies have been shown to draw on this framing (Smith, Chatfield and Pagnucco 1997); trying to expand the notions of human rights as seen in the cases of conscientious objection and in the framing of CSR discussed in Chapters 4–8.

Repertoires of Contention   The strategies and tactics of organizations (here referred to as repertoires of contention) have generally been seen as independent collective initiatives. However, the view increasingly is that they are dependent on framing choices, i.e., on how the organizations within a movement are structured, and on political opportunity structures. The repertoire is often a mix of activities such as public education, direct aid and change of structures, including a mix of orthodox and unorthodox methods, although uncontrollable or disorderly tactics are usually less common (Khagram, Riker and Sikkink 2002). Uncontrollable and disorderly tactics are perhaps what is often reflected in media reporting.

Important spaces where meetings take place are the IGO forum, where interaction between governments, business and non-governmental actors occurs. Most notable have been the large UN conferences, but smaller meetings are also involved. The interactions at these meetings can be conflictual and involve 'battles of justice', due to the different characteristics and aims of the participating organizations, but they can also constitute arenas for consensus mobilization. These interactions become a combination of struggles over meaning and power politics and 'are not divorced from power politics, but are rather enmeshed in them' … 'the struggle cannot be understood if we use only the lens of state power and interest to analyze it. Nor are issues of individual or collective self-interest unrelated to struggles for meaning' (Khagram, Riker and Sikkink 2002: 11).

Usually, social movements are explained as emerging from mobilizing structures in communities, families, friendship networks and schools, churches, etc. – i.e., from informal structures of everyday life (in a local context). These local contexts do not exist in the transnational arena, at least not in the same way. Thus, truly transnational collective identities are few. One way of achieving a mobilizing structure in the transnational arena is the creation and enforcement of international norms (Khagram, Riker and Sikkink 2002), traditionally seen to develop in cooperation between states within the context of international organizations.

Since norms are held by communities and not independently by individuals, they are intrinsically intersubjective. Thus, when a broad range of actors accepts principled ideas (about right and wrong), the ideas eventually become norms. Of interest then is how beliefs in the form of individually held principled ideas are transformed into 'collectively held principled ideas' (i.e., intersubjective beliefs) – in other words, norms.[5] This is particularly complicated in an international context and will be the focus of the following chapters regarding the development of CSR as an international issue. Next, a social constructivist model for approaching the study of norms will be discussed.

The Norm Cycle Model

A constructivist approach that directly relates to the study of norms in international relations is the 'norm life cycle' model (Finnemore and Sikkink 1998). The model contains arguments regarding the origins of international norms, which norms will be influential and how these norms influence actors' behaviour as well as the conditions needed for this influence to take place. The normatively driven social construction project in the form of the norm life cycle (hereafter the norm cycle) is explained as consisting of three distinctive stages: *norm emergence*, *norm cascade* and *norm internalization*. Each stage involves 'different social processes and logics of action' (Finnemore and Sikkink 1998: 895), which are characterized by different *actors*, *motives* and what I choose to define as *dominant social processes* of influence. The first two stages may develop into a 'prevailing standard of appropriateness against which new norms emerge and compete for support' (Finnemore and Sikkink 1998: 895), although this is not in any way automatic and the process can be overturned at any stage.

Figure 2.1 below illustrates a situation where a prevailing standard of appropriateness (or a norm) is questioned through the introduction of new normative claims by norm entrepreneurs driven by an ideational commitment and applying a strategy of persuasion – the first stage of norm emergence occurs.

Norm Emergence

According to Finnemore and Sikkink (1998) two elements are found to be common to successful norm creation: norm entrepreneurs and organizational platforms.[6] In order for norms to emerge, it is vital that key actors with strong convictions

    5   Principled ideas are distinguished from *causal ideas*, which concern beliefs about cause and effect that are supported by evidence, often of a scientific kind. Distinction made by Goldstein and Keohane (1993).

    6   A particularly illustrative example of an early norm entrepreneur with an organizational platform is Henri Dunant and the Red Cross, leading to the adoption of the Hague Conventions on the laws and customs of war in the early twentieth century.

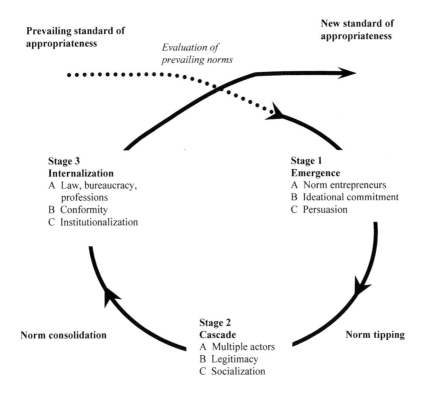

Prevailing standard of
appropriateness

*Evaluation of
prevailing norms*

New standard of
appropriateness

Stage 3
Internalization
A Law, bureaucracy,
    professions
B Conformity
C Institutionalization

Stage 1
Emergence
A Norm entrepreneurs
B Ideational commitment
C Persuasion

Norm consolidation

Stage 2
Cascade
A Multiple actors
B Legitimacy
C Socialization

Norm tipping

Figure 2.1   The Norm Cycle Model

Note: A: Actor, B: Motives, C: Dominant social processes.

Source: Reformulation of the norm life cycle model developed by Finnemore and Sikkink (1998: 898).

about what represents good behaviour raise awareness about or create issues for this purpose. This is done through a process of framing and in contestation with already existing norms and interests, which can take many forms (as was shown in the discussion on framing above). Often, this involves efforts to 'take what is seen as natural or appropriate and convert it into something perceived as wrong or inappropriate' (Finnemore and Sikkink 1998: 900). For norm entrepreneurs to engage in this process they need to be highly motivated and therefore empathy, altruism and ideational commitment are important motives for their engagement.

The platforms used by the norm entrepreneurs are often those of already existing international organizations (such as the UN and the ILO) where it will be possible to promote the norm. The expertise within and diffusion of information from these organizations are important sources of influence in international relations. At times, independent organizations are also created for the purpose of norm promotion, which is common in the creation of new NGOs.

If and when the normative claim gathers enough support in terms of the number of actors, including authoritative key actors, as well as legitimacy, norm tipping occurs.

Norm Tipping   For norm tipping to occur, a certain critical mass of actors who support the norm is needed, i.e., who become norm entrepreneurs/leaders and also adopt the norm themselves. In the case of the ban on anti-personnel land mines, about one-third of all states were needed before a change occurred.[7] However, not all actors have equal weight. Critical actors are more important than others, i.e., actors without which the norm will not be secured. In the case of anti-personnel land mines, states producing them were seen as critical actors to win for the cause, and so was South Africa, with Nelson Mandela (for the symbolic importance to other African states). The fact that the US in the end did not support the land mine treaty proved not to hinder norm cascade, which indicates that material power alone cannot determine the outcome in every situation.

What is the role of other actors in norm construction apart from states? I make a parallel of states to other actors in the international system, such as IGOs, TNCs and NGOs, when it comes to defining a critical mass of actors for norm tipping to occur. Similar to the argument of states, certain key actors has more influence in the international system than other actors, and which actors may vary from situation to situation. In general, one would expect large, established and acknowledged actors to be more influential. However, arguments on the power of moral authority of an actor partly contradict this claim.

When norm tipping occurs, many more actors join in who might not have shown an interest in the issue previously, but the motives of the participating actors now will differ. Therefore, a process of socialization replaces that of persuasion by norm entrepreneurs.

Norm Cascade

During norm cascading, norm adoption occurs more easily among different actors and there is a demonstration effect, where international or transnational influence is more important than domestic. A process of socialization takes place where those violating the norm are pressured to comply by other participants, and compliance is achieved by means of identification with those who have chosen to conform.

This can take place through diplomatic channels, combined with sanctions or incentives, the adoption of certain policies, including laws, and the ratification of existing instruments. Norm entrepreneurs who have formed networks as well as international organizations can take part in pressuring for socialization. Monitoring of compliance with existing international instruments is another way to achieve

---

7   In international law, this is formally stated in that a certain number of states are required to ratify a convention before it is considered to have entered into force.

socialization. Socialization here works through a process of identification where actors 'relate to their identities as members of an international society' (Finnemore and Sikkink 1998: 902). The understanding is that the cultural-institutional context shapes state/actors' identity and that identity affects behaviour. In this process, legitimation plays an important part. International legitimation of state behaviour enhances domestic legitimation by citizens of the state. The same is true for esteem, where the relationship to state 'peers' is of importance, relating to the perception of individual state or business leaders of the opinion of others as well as their self-esteem.

Norm Consolidation   If norm tipping is needed for a norm to pass from norm emergence to norm cascade (i.e., the support of a sufficient number of important actors), I argue that a similar element needs to be introduced for norm cascade to pass to norm internalization to account for the dynamic that contributes to the continuation of the process into the third stage.

What is needed, then, for a norm to make this passage? I suggest that a process that can be characterized as consolidation needs to take place. This involves a convergence of the competing claims and definitions of the new norm involved in the previous norm cascade. It involves a converse process to that of norm cascading, i.e., the creation of new organizations and initiatives slows down and actors converge around certain existing organizations and initiatives. This would involve a significant transformative change in substance also, and thus the concept of norm consolidation would be adequate.

In the case of norm consolidation, the transformation would be more subtle and prolonged than is the case with norm tipping, where there is a sudden surge in support for the new norm for different reasons. It would involve a continuation of the processes involved in the norm cascade, but the process is intensified slowly. Norm consolidation should manifest the transformation from a conscious approach to the norm to one where the norm over time obtains its taken-for-granted quality (i.e., the general characteristics of a norm). This would require a consensus around a common definition of the norm and its content as well as increasing compliance in the behaviour of the actors concerned.

This consolidation need not necessarily involve precisely the norms that the norm entrepreneurs originally advocated in the emergence stage. The involvement of other actors in the norm cascade stage should by necessity have made an impact on the norm construction process and the content of the developing norm.

Norm Internalization

In this third stage, what previously was considered controversial becomes accepted as resistance fades with time and persistent activity by norm entrepreneurs. Here one sees agents (rather than actors) of internalization in the form of impersonalized law, bureaucracy and professions (including professional training),[8] and conformity and institutionalization represent the motive and dominant social process, respectively.

Norms that previously were a matter of socialization have now become generally accepted and internalized by actors and are more or less taken for granted. They are thereby simultaneously the prevailing standards of appropriateness and difficult to actually perceive. They are no longer seen as controversial in that conformance is automatic, and the norms are not questioned nor the focus of debate and, thus, are mostly ignored. This stands apart from the previous stages of the norm cycle, in particular the norm emergence stage. The norms are part of what is seen as ordinary everyday activity. Examples of such norms are seen in such social practices as market exchange, sovereignty and individualism, which however in recent research have been deconstructed and problematized.

An important social practice for internalization, or rather the maintenance of internalization, is habit. Through repeated interaction and cooperation, 'habits of trust' may be built, which may become internalized and change the behaviour, identity and identification of participating actors as well as lead to a change of norms. A similar argument can be made for confidence-building in international negotiations. There is a 'gradual and inadvertent normative, ideational, and political convergence' involved in the process (Finnemore and Sikkink 1998: 905).

Successful Norms and Favourable Conditions

It is not only the processes involved in the norm cycle that constitutes norms, also other aspects are central. Aspects of importance in the above model for defining which norms and under what conditions they will be influential in world politics are suggested to include the need of legitimation of an actor, prominence of the actor promoting the norm, intrinsic characteristics of the norm itself, historic efficiency and functional institutionalism (Finnemore and Sikkink 1998).

In the case of *historic efficiency/functional institutionalism* the relationship between new normative claims and existing norms such as international law is brought to mind. The weapons taboo on chemical warfare was partly achieved by managing to link weapons with poison and the ban on land mines through linkage to images of bodily harm. Changing the use of the concept 'female circumcision' to 'female genital mutilation' is another example of this aspect, showing how new concepts contributed to a change in the understanding of the difference between this practice and male circumcision as well as facilitating mobilization of support. World historical events and 'world time' (such as wars or the end of wars), and the fact that the speed of normative change has accelerated are also important aspects

---

8   Professions represent not only a specific set of knowledge or expertise but also a socialization of certain values and normative perceptions, seen e.g., in professions such as doctors, soldiers, and economists. As different professionals staff the decision-making bodies, these bodies and their policies are influenced by the corresponding values and normative perceptions of the professionals in question.

of norms. This can be seen in the 'ITT-Affair' in Chile of the 1970s and football manufacturing by child labour of the 1990s in Sialkot, Pakistan, both creating 'world news' and spurring action.

In conclusion, the arguments of this model and its relation to strategic social construction combine both rationality and norms. That is, norm entrepreneurs are rational in means-ends calculations (decisions of rational choice) in order to achieve normative commitments among the other players (social construction). Thus, the common knowledge (or intersubjective understanding) constituting the bases of the calculations made by the actors is not static; it is the object of the game. This common knowledge is created and recreated in a process where the actors are creating the rules of the game by playing it.

Changing the Norms on the Responsibilities of Transnational Corporations

Taken together, the globalization process, the growing importance of civil society and NGOs as the third force, and the development of new global governance frameworks, constitute a complex dynamic important to an understanding of CSR. Thus, CSR can be said to represent one issue area where the debate on globalization is played out. Among other things, this has led to a situation where demands for accountability in the area of human rights are now increasingly made on actors other than the states. Among these are the TNCs.

Different Perspectives of Globalization and a Restatement of Human Rights

Sometimes globalization is referred to as corporate-led globalization or 'from above', restricting the rights and freedoms of individuals. The global market forces, with their perceived priority on efficiency, are seen to dominate societies and citizen demands for justice by many involved in stakeholder activism (Cavanagh et al. 2002). On the other hand, globalization can also be seen as having great potential to liberate or empower the individual; i.e., globalization 'from below', either through increasing free choice (the liberal standpoint) or creating possibilities for transnational solidarity (globalization critics). However, it appears that in spite of the promises of globalization, some people find themselves in a situation where they still suffer from the oppression of the state and at the same time are exposed to new denials of rights due to transnational forces (Brysk 2002). An open economy market system and migratory flows do not seem to go well together with an international human rights regime based on implementation by the sovereign state. From this perspective, the (deterritorialized) free trade regime and the (territorially dependent) human rights regime are not compatible. At the same time, the very same globalization process presents opportunities through increased awareness, facilitating information technologies and transnational social movements.

This has led to increasing interest in human rights issues, especially in how they are applied and adhered to in real life, including an attempt at linking these rights to other actors and contexts. Human rights are no longer seen only as the responsibility or obligation of an individual state towards its citizens, or something that can be reduced to a question of domestic or internal affairs. Human rights have also become an issue at the supra-national level and for non-state actors on different levels (armed groups, IGOs, companies, NGOs, etc.). In particular, TNCs are increasingly seen as implicated in this responsibility (see Figure 2.2). Furthermore, economic and social rights are now also given greater importance in this context, rights that in the past have been overshadowed by political and civil rights. The division on these rights, linked to the Cold War, has been replaced by a view of them as being mutually reinforcing.

These arguments are closely related to discussions within CSR, with the conflict between and overlapping of the free trade and human rights regimes taking as their points of departure the different views of human experience. From a perspective of the arguments on global governance, this causes a need for adjustment between competing interests. This regime conflict contributes to a stakeholder activism with the aim of redefining corporate mandates. This activism targets and challenges TNCs to not only consider obligations to *share*holders, but also to expand to include *stake*holders in a broad sense.[9]

The perceived lack of accountability of TNCs in the area of human rights has put in motion a whole set of initiatives to counteract the negative consequences of TNC activities. A 'CSR movement' has evolved, and possibly a new system of governance is emerging in this area. The concern over TNCs often highlights the enormous power of these companies with regard to their large revenue, which is often larger than the national budgets of states.[10] However, it is not only the economic power of the companies that raises concern, but also the changing ways of organizing their activities. In particular, the concern on the consequences of the changes to the organization of production and the influence of TNCs in national and intergovernmental decision-making bodies, which is not open to scrutiny of the general public.

Activists have begun pointing out more specifically the many risks and dilemmas that TNCs may face when conducting business in countries where the respect for human rights is weak or absent. Amnesty International has framed this in maps showing the risks companies may face in countries where human rights violations are frequent, calling this 'the geography of corporate risk' (Frankental and House 2000). The list of risks is fairly extensive, involving torture, 'disappearances', extra-judicial executions, hostage taking, harassment of human rights defenders,

---

9   For an overview of issues of concern regarding the responsibilities of TNCs, see, e.g., Addo (1999).

10   In 2008, WalMart Stores was the largest company in the world, with total revenue of 379 billion US dollars, which is equivalent of the GDP of the 30th wealthiest country in the world. It is almost four times the total revenue of Sweden (810 billion Swedish Cr. or approx. 100 billion US dollar) (Fortune 2008, Government Offices of Sweden 2008).

denial of freedom of association, forced or bonded labour, forcible relocation, systematic denial of women's rights and prisoners of conscience.[11]

Although TNCs have justified their corporate presence in countries with human and labour rights violations by arguing that their activities will improve the economy of the country as a whole and eventually lead to respect for human rights, this has not been considered enough. Increasingly, demands have been raised that companies also should undertake *active* measures to contribute to the advocacy of social issues and human rights. Measures suggested to companies are, e.g., to adopt and implement guidelines, monitor and promote respect for human rights, influence government policy, increase transparency, publicly protest against violations, and, in general, provide support for the development of the community where the company is active.

Transnational Sphere of Norm Construction

Below, I illustrate the arena of norm construction (and negotiations) in the area of CSR. The focus here is on the relationship and demands for human rights obligations between the TNC based in a developed country and the individual worker of a developing country. Those directly involved in norm construction are mostly non-state actors in developed countries, such as NGOs, TNCs, IGOs and others (state presence is, of course, found in the IGOs). Although NGOs in developing countries also address issues of concern relating to human and labour rights, the political opportunity structure in the domestic setting and their relatively weak position internationally make them less influential. The influence of other domestic actors in developing countries is also less prominent, but for different reasons. In this process, state obligations for human and labour rigts that may exist and be manifested in national legislation are overridden, complemented, or exchanged for mainly transnationally constructed private and non-binding regulation.

The basic situation here is that a TNC headquartered in a developed country (home country) conducts activities in a developing country (host country) through subcontractors[12] (a common situation referred to in the debate on CSR). There is no direct contractual link between the workers involved in the export production and the TNC, only between the TNC and the subcontractor. This represents a standard case for new international production resulting from globalization (global supply chains). Any obligations for an individual employee's human rights are the responsibility of the host country government (implemented through

---

11   Similar concerns also appear in the reporting of other NGOs (notably trade unions) and of the ILO, but seem to receive a different type of attention when associated with human rights, see, e.g., the annual reports of Human Rights Watch, the annual surveys of the ICFTU, and ILO.

12   In a case where activities are conducted through affiliates, there is a direct link of responsibility, which represents another matter. This situation may also be covered by concerns of CSR, but the case with subcontractors takes the problem to its extreme.

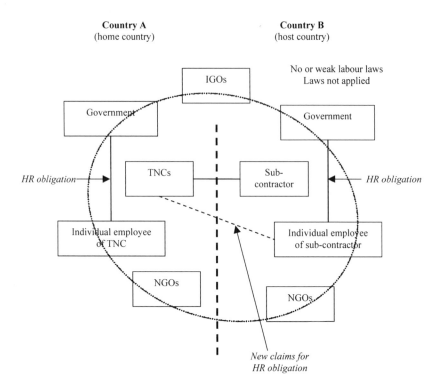

Figure 2.2   Transnational Process of Norm Construction Concerning CSR
Source: Based on author's findings in this study.

national legislation). The host country government may not have adopted any such legislation, adopted inadequate legislation or the existing laws may not be implemented (waived or lax implementation). The responsibility to abide by the existing laws of the host country thus lies with the subcontractor and not the TNC. A subcontractor may furthermore be in a position where abiding by the laws might increase costs compared to less scrupulous competitors and jeopardize the ability to obtain contracts with the TNCs. There are no international laws to regulate this situation, and the only remedy is to address the host country government. However, the political opportunity structure in host countries has often made such a solution less probable.

This situation has attracted attention from various parts of the international system, particularly from the NGOs in developed countries (often in cooperation with or at the request of developing country NGOs), giving rise to what may be labelled a CSR movement. What has happened is that these NGOs attempt to establish a direct link between the employees of the subcontractor and the TNC. These efforts in turn have involved other actors, such as the TNCs themselves, governmental organizations, governments and IGOs, but not in the intergovernmental interaction that categorises the traditional international system of sovereign states. In this interaction, a 'boomerang effect' (Keck and Sikkink 1998: 13) occurs where less powerful NGOs (in countries where the political opportunity structure is working against activism) can mobilize support from actors in other countries that put pressure on governments, TNCs or subcontractors. These efforts have given rise to a complex setting of actors and initiatives at various levels and sectors of the international system, mainly in the form of private voluntary frameworks in a transnational sphere. It is in this transnational sphere that the norm of CSR is currently being negotiated.

In the following chapters the development of CSR is explored making use of the norm cycle model.

Chapter 3

Emergence of Corporate Social Responsibility in the 1970s

Three major events in the 1970s focused the attention of the international system on the responsibilities of TNCs for a sustained period of time. The events in question include the attempt by the UN Center on Transnational Corporations (UNCTC) to develop an international code of conduct for TNCs, the Nestlé boycott and the development of the WHO International Code on the Marketing of Breast-milk Substitutes, and the anti-apartheid campaign. Together these activities represent the early emergence of CSR. I argue that the emergence stage of the CSR norm cycle has an early phase represented by these events, which is the focus of the present chapter and the next – this chapter will deal with the negotiations on the UNCTC Code of Conduct.[1]

I see the development of CSR as an emerging new norm, based partly on the former international labour rights standard but also on human rights standards that developed later. These collections of rights represent standards of appropriateness, i.e., a body of instruments and procedures generally accepted (although not always complied with), but with CSR reaching beyond the ILO tripartite setting of states, TNCs and trade unions, and the international law setting of human rights (general principle of state sovereignty). CSR also introduces new issues, new actors and new working methods, including elements of inappropriateness that all point towards a transnational sphere of relations.

The point of departure for the discussion in this chapter is the earlier advocacy by the international labour movement that led to the establishment of the international labour rights standards that I see as a successful norm cycle. One can view the later development of human rights in a similar manner, although these rights were not yet established international norms when the UNCTC Code of Conduct became an issue on the international agenda. Thus, in the 1960s and 1970s, human rights principles were quite a novelty in international relations, which explains why human rights are not really part of the debate on CSR in this early period as will be shown below.[2]

---

1   The second phase of norm emergence, beginning in the second half of 1980s with the emergence of the focus organizations mentioned earlier, will be discussed in Chapter 5.

2   In spite of the fact that the UDHR was adopted in 1948, the two conventions that resulted were not adopted until in 1966 and did not come into force until in the 1970s.

Past Responses to the Negative Effects of Economic Activity

In spite of the great amount of attention given to CSR today, the idea of justice and fairness in economic activity is not a recent concern, but rather dates as far back as the thinking of the ancient Greeks. The discussion continued throughout the centuries until the different social sciences started to distinguish themselves from each other. When the idea of the self-regulating market appeared in the eighteenth century, a disembedding of economic activity from the social sphere also emerged. In this study, one can speak of a re-embedding of economic activity in the social – what we today call CSR. These past concerns laid the foundation for modern issues and debates, and a closer examination will demonstrate what changes have occurred there.

Opposition to the Slave Trade and Foundation of International Labour Rights

Two early examples of organized opposition to what at the time were considered to be negative aspects of economic activity are the abolitionist and the international labour movements. A need for labour in the former colonies led to the practice of a system of forced labour, in which the transatlantic slave trade had a dominating role. The movement towards the abolition of the slave trade and slavery did not emerge until the second half of the eighteenth century, set in motion by earlier slave rebellions and influenced later by the French revolution. The first organizations within this movement were established in the second half of the eighteenth century, starting with the Pennsylvania Society for Promoting the Abolition of Slavery in the US in 1775, the Society for Effecting the Abolition of the Slave Trade in the UK in 1787 and the Societé des Amis des Noirs in France in 1788. Opposition continued into the second half of the nineteenth century before complete abolition was achieved. The movement towards the abolition of slavery can be explained as part of modernization and of the evolution of free labour and industry, meaning that slavery and its abolition can be seen as a combination of both ideological and historical complexity (Engerman 1981). From this perspective, the abolition process is also part of a new attitude towards labour, property and society, not simply a debate over moral or economic explanations.

It is not until somewhat later that concerns over labour issues began to take on an international dimension. In the 1840s, the first attempt at creating an international labour movement was made with the establishment in London of the organization called the Democratic Friends of All Nations. The aim was to achieve 'cosmopolitan intercourse' and 'universal brotherhood'. In the process, differences arose regarding the use of moral or physical force and nationalism versus internationalism. For example, the use of the strike as a campaigning method is said to have had a mobilizing effect both on the development and breakthrough of the international labour movement (Knudsen 1988). The strike, however, also mobilized the capitalists. This campaigning method gave the general impression that the movement was more concerned with social revolt than with political class struggle, which caused concern in parts of society. Eventually, the International Association for the Protection of Labour was created in 1900, which in turn led to intergovernmental conferences and the establishment of the ILO in 1919 (including the international labour rights standards in the form of ILO conventions that followed). The ILO also formed part of the new League of Nations, created the same year. Note that at the time, there was no equivalent organization for employers. The International Organization of Employers (IOE) and the International Chamber of Commerce (ICC) were not established until 1920. These two organizations did not, however, form part of the League of Nations.

Other examples of organized opposition that occurred simultaneously with the development of the international labour movement were the growing populist and progressive movements in the US towards the end of the nineteenth century. The main concern of these movements was the corruption and economic power of large companies. This led to the creation of public interest watchdogs and regulatory agencies, as well as to intervention by the US government in the business of large companies, represented by the regulation of business that occurred during this period.

The churches were also involved in the issue from an early stage. As early as in the 1920s, the following statement was made in connection with a church conference: 'Alongside of the work of individual conversion and simultaneously with it an effort must be made to Christianise the corporate life of mankind in all its activities' (COPEC 1924: v). These concerns were related to recent developments and the effects of the industrial revolution (social conflict and difficult conditions of life), the increase in population, the growth of cities, the creation of mass production, the specialization of work – an unsatisfying system and methods that could even be regarded as antagonistic to a Christian life. The ethical nature of the teachings (of God), being not only of a spiritual nature but also referring to material conditions, legitimized the Church's dealings with material conditions, specifically with industry and property issues. The solutions were seen as substituting the motive of service for the motive of gain, organizing industry as a cooperative effort to supply the needs of all and giving people an effective voice, providing sufficient remuneration, removing causes of unemployment, and evaluating the right to property according to the degree to which ownership contributes to the development of personality and to the good of the whole community. Concerns also related to issues of inherited wealth or position. This represents a fairly revolutionary stance that resonates well among some CSR organizations even today. The churches have also been an important and active actor in the advocacy for CSR, as will be shown below.

As can be seen in the anti-slavery and labour movements as well as the concerns among churches, moral considerations related to economic activity had surfaced in various ways in the international system prior to the 1970s. One can therefore say that some of the roots of today's CSR advocacy can in fact be found in these two examples: one connects with the civil rights and anti-apartheid movement, and the other with the ILO and the international labour rights standards expressed in the ILO conventions. Both of these are in my opinion examples of successful norm construction and norm cycles resulting in changing attitudes towards slavery and labour, respectively. In the next section I will turn to the new norm cycle that was to begin in the 1960s and 1970s.

Modern Era of and Debate on Corporate Social Responsibility

Apart from issues of CSR concerning the employer-employee relationship, the views on corporate responsibility that had been debated up until the 1950s had mainly revolved around the role of companies as social institutions and their relationship to society in general (Heald 1970). These concerns had been expressed explicitly in discussions on whether or not companies should engage in philanthropy, and if so, to what extent. Initially, the issue of philanthropy focused on the power relationship of management towards shareholders and employees, but the discussion later expanded to cover the responsibility of companies in certain social activities such as social welfare, education, etc., i.e., the role of companies in these activities in addition to the state. Even though some controversy still existed on the issue, in the 1950s there was a shift towards seeing this responsibility as linked to the 'preservation and progress of democratic society itself' (Heald 1970: 271), and with this shift came an increase in and a legitimacy for the involvement of business in society. It is worth noting that this shift coincided with both the appearance in the US of Senator Joseph McCarthy and his targeting of communism and the political strategy of the US government on 'containment' of the Soviet Union's expansion and of communist aggression. Companies in this way became part of a very concrete national and international struggle for democracy at the same time that the role of companies in society in general was being debated.

Although most of the formal writing on CSR emerged in the twentieth century, the modern discussion of CSR is said to have started in the 1950s with the work of Howard R. Bowen, the 'Father of Corporate Social Responsibility' (Carroll 1999: 270). Bowen stated that 'by virtue of their strategic position and their considerable decision-making power' the social responsibility of businessmen is 'to pursue those policies, to make those decisions, or to follow those lines of action which are desirable in terms of the objectives and values of our society' (Bowen 1953: 4, 6), i.e., not being guided by profit motives alone. It is interesting to note that Bowen's independent work appeared in a series called 'Ethics and Economic Life' under the auspices of the Study Committee of the Federal Council of Churches in the US as part of a larger study on the issue of economic life and its relation to spiritual and moral values conducted by the Council in the late 1940s. The series demonstrate the ongoing discussion in the churches on this issue at the time.

In the 1960s, the concept of CSR in general was beginning to be formalized in literature and with this development a more critical discussion followed (Carroll 1999). Arguments were made that certain business decisions on social responsibility could be justified on the grounds of leading to economic gains in the long run, the expectations of the public, the enhancement of the total socio-economic welfare, or the obligations to society in general. Most famous among the critics at this time is probably Milton Friedman (1970), who argues that the social responsibility of the corporate executive is to increase profits and conform to the basic rules of society (laws and ethical customs). Friedman had in fact already approached the issue with similar arguments in his work *Capitalism and Freedom* (1960).

In the 1970s, the idea of stakeholders also started to emerge, as social responsibility was related to the need for companies to balance the interests of different groups. Here the company was seen as part of a socio-cultural system (with certain norms and business roles) and as responding to what was happening within that system. Attempts were furthermore made to integrate the profit motive of companies and their mainly economic nature with the idea of social responsibility. The survival of the business system was seen as dependent on the social order in society as a whole, and therefore there was a role for business in society. Corporate social performance is a definition that comes into use more during this period, as does the idea of public responsibility of a company. There was also discussion of a change in 'the social contract' between society and business, that society was demanding more of companies than just a supply of goods and services (Carroll 1999).

Not only was the idea of CSR new at the time, the concept of the TNC was also emerging in the 1960s. Although large international companies had appeared early in history and the discussion of ethics in business had emerged even earlier, in the 1960s these phenomena seemed to need new expressions. No agreed-on definition of a TNC existed during this time. The preferred term seems to have been multinational corporations (MNCs) rather than TNCs; the latter concept came into more common use later. In a UN report at the time (United Nations 1973), a discussion of the various definitions in use covers terms such as multinational corporation, international corporation, transnational corporation, supranational firm, global corporation and cosmocorp. The UN Economic and Social Council (ECOSOC), however, used the concept of TNC when establishing the UN Center on Transnational Corporations in the 1970s (see below). The ILO (1973) also discusses the absence of an agreed definition, but uses the term multinational enterprise. The interest in CSR that developed at this time was very much directed towards TNCs.

This apparent shift in attitudes towards large companies and their social responsibility coincided with other changes in societies in the 1960s; i.e., the era of new social movements, which would contribute to the development of CSR. Human rights and other political issues, such as the protests against the Vietnam War and the apartheid regime of South Africa, and the development of the civil rights movement in the USA (including activism directed towards companies), represent some of the topics that were high on the list.

As mentioned in the introduction to this chapter, there are three major events in the 1970s that directed international attention towards the development of CSR for a sustained period of time. The events in question are the work of the UNCTC to develop an international code of conduct for TNCs, the Nestlé boycott and the development of the WHO International Code on the Marketing of Breast-milk

Substitutes, and the activities of the anti-apartheid movement targeting TNCs with operations in or business relations with South Africa. These events represent examples of both the 'success' and 'failure' of early attempts to establish CSR as an international norm. Success was in fact achieved in the establishment of the WHO code and in achieving a change in company behaviour regarding the apartheid in South Africa (including a change in attitudes towards companies on this issue). But there was less success in developing a general code of conduct for TNCs by the UN. Whatever the outcome of these events, they are examples of the initial emergence of new actors and initiatives involved with CSR. These events illustrate the different aspects involved in the emerging international norm construction in the area of CSR and will be the focus of the remaining part of this chapter and the next.

UN Negotiations on a Code of Conduct

The negotiations within the UN took place in a situation in which the (formal) institution of colonialism was being dismantled, but the remaining de facto elements of this institutional structure were still reflected in the proposed text of the UNCTC Code. Several other international events also affected negotiations within the UNCTC: the demand for change from developing countries (the so-called G77), resulting in UN resolutions such as on a New International Economic Order and the Economic Rights and Duties of States; the creation of the United Nations Conference on Trade and Development (UNCTAD); the effects of the Cold War; and the economic crises of the Bretton Woods institutions. In spite of the overall aims of the UNCTC Code, the whole endeavour actually came to focus on regulating states and their relationships to TNCs – in particular, the role of the newly independent states – and less on the conduct of TNCs per se, as had been intended initially. The negotiations were also primarily an intergovernmental affair, with little formal involvement of other actors.

The immediate beginning of the creation of the UNCTC was a decision made in 1972 by the ECOSOC to initiate actions 'on the role of multinational corporations and their impact on the development process and on international relations' (ECOSOC 1972). The decision was prompted by the Chilean government, with reference to the so-called ITT-affair (revealed by the *Washington Post* the same year), in which the US-based International Telegraph and Telephone (ITT) Corporation, with the support of the US government, had attempted to interfere with the election in 1970 of the socialist Chilean President Salvador Allende and allegedly was involved in the later military coup in Chile in 1973 (Sethi 1974).

At the time, concerns in relation to development and international relations were also noted in several UN resolutions passed on matters such as permanent sovereignty over the natural resources of developing countries, transfer of technology, foreign private investment and its relationship to development, the economic rights and duties of states, and export promotion. Concerns over TNCs had also been raised at that time in other parts of the UN, e.g., in the annual

World Economic Survey for 1971 (concerns relating to the international economic system following the breakdown of the Bretton Woods Monetary System), by the ILO at a conference in 1972 and by the newly established UNCTAD (United Nations 1972a, 1972b, and ILO 1973). Documents reveal a turbulent time in the international system that certainly created concern.

A 'Group of Eminent Persons', consisting of representatives (all of whom were male) from the governments of both developed and developing (including socialist) countries, the business sector, and academia, was appointed to carry out an initial study and put forward recommendations for future work. Note that no trade union representative was included in the group. Apart from this formal representation, an informal strategy group made up of a small number of corporations, including Nestlé, is said to have been created with the purpose of 'infiltrating' the UN to ensure that its findings were not too critical (see Chetley 1986: 46, Baade 1980: 418). The Group of Eminent Persons issued a report in 1974 recommending that the ECOSOC create a permanent machinery to deal with issues related to TNCs (United Nations 1974b).[3] The specific issues raised in the report mainly concerned ownership and control, financial flows and balance of payments, technology, employment and labour, consumer protection, competition and market structure, transfer pricing, taxation and information disclosure and evaluation, i.e., issues of mainly an economic nature.[4] As a result of the report, the UNCTC was created by the ECOSOC the same year. The issue of a code of conduct was given top priority, and an intergovernmental working group was established, scheduled to start working in early 1977. It can be noted that a new organization was seen as necessary, even though the ILO, with its unique tripartite constitution, probably could have undertaken the work. However, the ILO was regarded as 'politicised', due to the re-entry of the Soviet Union (which mobilized other socialist countries) and the increased membership of newly independent countries, with the consequence that the majority of the ILO membership was found in countries with no free and representative labour market organizations. As a result, the US government left the ILO in 1977 (Ghébali 1989).

---

3   Hearings were conducted with representatives of corporations, governments, IGOs, NGOs (including the International Council for Social Welfare, International Organization of Consumers Union, and the International Chambers of Commerce), the US trade union The American Federation of Labour-Congress of Industrial Organizations (AFL-CIO), the World Federation of Trade Unions and Ralph Nader, a well-known US activist. Note that the International Confederation of Free Trade Unions (ICFTU) was not called to the hearings; see discussion on ICFTU in Chapter 4. Most of the representatives were from developed countries and were also, at this time, almost all men (United Nations 1974a).

4   The employment and labour section covered differentials in employment and wages, labour relations (respect of trade unions and trade union rights and bargaining matters) and labour standards (TNCs acting as spearheads of good labour practices), whereas consumer protection dealt with false and misleading publicity, price differentials of identical products, and implications of differentials in consumption patterns, quality and safety (United Nations 1974b).

Existing International Regulation on Transnational Corporations in the 1970s

As was mentioned earlier, a number of international labour rights conventions followed the establishment of the ILO in 1919. The first so-called ILO core convention, 'Forced Labour' (No. 29), was adopted in 1930. The other core conventions that were to follow did not appear until after the Second World War, including:

- 'Freedom of Association and Protection of the Right to Organise' (No. 87) in 1948;
- 'The Right to Organise and to Bargain Collectively' (No. 98) in 1949;
- 'Equal Remuneration' (No. 100) in 1951;
- 'Abolition of Forced Labour' (No. 105) in 1957;
- 'Discrimination (Employment and Occupation)' (No. 111) in 1958;
- 'Minimum Age' (No. 138) in 1973;
- 'Worst Forms of Child Labour' (No. 182) in 1999.

The ILO had also adopted a number of conventions prior to the first core convention concerning various issues such as hours of work (the first in 1919), unemployment, maternity, night work for women and children, minimum age for work in different sectors, right of association and compensation in agriculture, working conditions in specific sectors, safety and health care, etc.

Other international standards related to TNCs that developed were oriented more towards economic aspects, such as the International Convention for the Settlement of Investment Disputes (adopted in 1965), the OECD Convention on the Protection of Foreign Property (adopted in 1967) and similar regulations adopted by individual countries. One example of a host government's effort to regulate or control TNCs in developing countries on a regional level was Decision 24 (a common regulatory framework for foreign investments) of the Andean Pact for the Andean Common Market. Together with the previously mentioned UN resolutions and ILO Conventions, these were the *appropriate standards* in place at the time and reveal a focus on international labour rights as well as on the issue of investments and development in an era of decolonialization and the Cold War (United Nations 1986, Tharp 1976).

During the course of the negotiations on the UN Code from the 1970s onwards, other regulations were adopted (Baade 1980, United Nations 1986) including (in order of adoption):

- ICC Guidelines for Investment (1972);
- ICFTU Charter of Trade Union Demands For the Legislative Control of the Multinational Companies (1975);
- OECD Guidelines on Multinational Enterprises (1976);
- ILO Tripartite Declaration of Principles Concerning Multinational Enterprises and Social Policy (1977);
- UNCTAD Set of Multilaterally Agreed Equitable Principles and Rules for the Control of Restrictive Business Practices (1980);

- WHO International Code of Marketing of Breast-milk Substitutes (1981);
- UN General Assembly adoption of international guidelines for consumer protection (1985);
- Convention for the Establishment of a Multilateral Investment Guarantee Agency (MIGA) (1985).

Of these, only the ILO Principles, the ICFTU Charter and the later WHO Code (limited to a specific issue) represented the initial introduction of CSR issues into the international system. The others dealt more with economic or other aspects of TNC activity. It can furthermore be noted that the ICFTU Charter, the ILO Declaration and the OECD Guidelines (dealing to a minor extent with labour) were adopted just as the UNCTC was about to start negotiations on the UN Code and could be seen as a positioning before the UNCTC negotiations. It could be said that the ICC guidelines by the International Chamber of Commerce might also be partly a positioning gambit, although the guidelines had already been adopted at the time the ECOSOC decided to develop measures applying to TNCs.

It is also worth noting here that the first two central treaties on human rights (civil and political rights, and economic, social and cultural rights) were not adopted by the UN until 1966 (in force in 1976).[5] On a regional basis, the European Convention on Human Rights (adopted in 1950) represents a general approach to international human rights regulation, but with a limited geographical scope. The two conventions, on civil and political rights and economic, social and cultural rights, were initially intended to be one document; however, due to disagreements between the US (supporting civil and political rights) and the Soviet Union (supporting economic, social and cultural rights), two separate conventions were eventually developed. Thus, the concept of human rights was introduced into the international system in parallel with negotiations on the UN Code and therefore did not influence the debate on the social responsibilities of TNCs until later. International labour standards (also part of human rights) had of course already been introduced through the work of the ILO. In all, the ILO had adopted an impressive number of conventions on international labour standards – 115 conventions – by 1960, including most of the core ILO conventions.

As can be seen from this brief overview, existing international standards at the time mainly dealt with TNCs in relation to economic matters, with some exceptions. This bias in issues was also to be the case with the UN Code, as will be seen.

Trade Union Activity on the Issue at the Time

Although the formal decision to undertake activities on TNCs was a political decision by an IGO (the ECOSOC) initiated by a government (the Chilean

---

5   Treaties on genocide (1948), refugees (1951, 1967) and racial discrimination (1965) had already been adopted, but these were specialized human rights conventions that had been put on the international agenda due to specific events.

representative) – i.e., the traditional view of how the international system functions – issues of this kind had already been addressed outside of the UN system for some time. In the late 1950s, foreign investments and development were important concerns on the ICFTU agenda (ICFTU 1959a).[6] An ICFTU study from this period, however, also reveals a firm trust in foreign investments and the improvements that industrialization would provide. There are only minor direct criticisms of 'foreign firms', that they are expected to give a lead on certain issues and that previous investment had not been aimed at economic development but at the utilization of minerals, raw materials and cheap labour and developing transport and communication for this utilisation only (ICFTU 1959b, Gumbrell-McCormick 2000a).

The International Metalworkers' Federation (an international trade secretariat created in 1893), and the US national trade union, the United Automobile, Aerospace and Agricultural Implement Workers,[7] had also started working on the issue of TNCs in the 1950s. Their views on the issue were less optimistic than those of the ICFTU due to the growing concern among US workers about the loss of jobs when production started to move to low-wage countries (although the move created new jobs for workers in the automobile industry in developing countries). The International Metalworkers' Federation saw the need to adopt an 'enlightened attitude' toward structural changes and recognition of free trade (not least for developing countries that might otherwise start trading with communist countries), but not at the expense of the workers involved. Trade liberalization and exploiting labour were seen to undermine the living standards of *all* workers. The need was identified to induce a sense of obligation and responsibility in investment policies and to prevent 'economic cannibalism', where workers are moved around like 'chessmen'. Individual automobile industry workers in developed countries, experiencing the concrete effect of structural changes, called on their respective trade unions to act. At the same time, their trade union representatives were

---

6   The ICFTU was created in 1949 when trade unions of Western countries within the World Federation of Trade Unions (WFTU), created in 1945, broke off. They considered WFTU a communist organization, as the national trade unions of the socialist countries were not seen to be independent of their home governments. The American Federation of Labor (AFL) had from the start been opposed to the formation of WFTU after the Second World War for fear of communist influence, but the British Trade Union Committee (TUC), with the support of the US trade union the Congress of Industrial Organizations (CIO), participated in the creation of the WFTU. AFL and CIO merged later (Trade Unions of the World 2001).

7   The creation of the United Automobile, Aerospace and Agricultural Implement Workers (in 1935) is closely linked to the history of the American Left, which contributed to its formation and activities. Its influence diminished over time. The Left influence, however, was still felt on issues such as the support for collective bargaining in the 1950s and 1960s, civil rights legislation and the opposition to the Vietnam War (Buhle, Buhle and Georgakas 1992).

constrained by support for free trade and 'containment' policies, limiting the choice of action (Trade Unions of the World 2001, Gumbrell-McCormick 2000a).[8]

One strategy opted for by the International Metalworkers' Federation to counteract the powers of TNCs was to create world company councils for international collective bargaining purposes. The first councils were established in 1966 in two US companies – Ford Motor Company and General Electric. Other international trade secretariats were to follow this initiative; however, these councils did not turn out to be successful. This lack of success was due to, among other things, the reluctance of the national trade union to give up power, counter-attacks by journalists and academics, and tensions within the world labour movement (between anti-communist and communist-influenced unions in the same workplace). It has been pointed out that it was not accidental that these councils emerged in the automobile industry, that industry being a highly concentrated, capital intensive, unionized industry and male-dominated as compared to the textiles and clothing industry, even though the latter also attempted similar activities (Gumbrell-McCormick 2000a: 379, 381). The clothing industry has only fairly recently been addressed more extensively by activities of CSR organizations such as the Clean Clothes Campaign, discussed later.

More active work on issues concerning TNCs within the ICFTU was to begin in the late 1960s. In 1968, the ICFTU made a statement to the ILO calling for the first time for a study on the social aspects of the operations of multinational companies. The ICFTU appears to have been influenced by the activities of the International Metalworkers' Federation and some of the other international trade secretariats, not only to take a somewhat stronger stand on the issue of TNCs, but also to gain control of the various trade union activities relating to this issue. In a joint statement following an international conference in 1971, an appeal was made to the trade union movement to intensify activity in international and regional organizations for the adoption of an international agreement on a code of conduct for TNCs. In April 1972 (one month after the 'ITT affair' had been made public), this statement is followed by a more confrontational address made by the ICFTU at the Third Session of UNCTAD taking place in Chile (ICFTU 1968: 34, ICFTU 1970: 14, 38, and ICFTU 1972).

It is apparent that trade unions played an important role in advocating international action on the issue of the TNCs prior to the actual decision of ECOSOC to establish the UNCTC. Yet the ICFTU was not directly involved in the negotiations.

Issues and Differences in the Negotiation of the UN Code

The negotiations on the UN Code were primarily a intergovernmental process, in which the differences in perspectives and motives between the countries involved would turn out to be considerable. Two purposes were stated for the development

---

8   See the Bulletin of the International metalworker's federation for the years 1959, 1960, 1961 and 1962.

of the UN Code: the positive role of TNCs in development in both developed and developing countries, and the need to formulate guidelines to control TNC activities (United Nations 1986). Thus, the UN Code was simultaneously to *prescribe* standards of conduct for TNCs (seen by developing and socialist countries as the main objective of the code) and to charter principles for the *treatment* of TNCs (the main objective according to the developed countries). These purposes were stated by the UN in the following way:

> further the understanding of the nature of transnational corporations and of their political, legal, economic and social effects on home and host countries and in international relations, particularly between developed and developing countries; to secure effective international arrangements aimed at enhancing the contribution of transnational corporations to national development goals and world economic growth while controlling and eliminating their negative effects; and to strengthen the negotiating capacity of host countries, in particular the developing countries, in their dealing with transnational corporations (United Nations 1986: ii).

As can be seen, the purpose stated above represented quite an ambitious agenda, and invoked considerable contention. The overall concern shared by most countries was that although there had been increasing internationalization of economic activity, this had not been followed by development of an international regime of standards concerning FDI as had been the case for trade, money and finance, such as with the General Agreement on Trade and Tariffs and the International Monetary Fund. When it came to more specific issues, however, there was less agreement. The *developing and socialist countries* were mainly concerned with issues such as tax evasion, restrictive business practices, illicit payment, and abusive transfer pricing, consistency with national laws, and disclosure of information, and environmental and consumer protection. These measures were seen as necessary in order to increase the flow of capital to developing countries. For the *developed countries* (often both home and host country at the same time), the purpose of the code of conduct was to obtain a favourable climate for FDIs as a means of advancing and promoting economic development through standards of fair and equitable treatment of TNCs as well as through their conduct (United Nations 1986).[9] This division proved to be insurmountable as negotiations continued. It is interesting to note that some of the arguments and controversies of the time still hold today.

---

9   In the ILO conference of 1972 (ILO 1973), mentioned earlier, five groups can be identified among the participants (an almost complete domination by men and developed country representatives): the diplomatic but cautiously TNC positive *developed country governments*; the TNC hostile *socialist country governments and socialist worker representatives*; concern over conflict between national policies and remote control of TNCs by *developing country governments*; a generally positive attitude to TNCs on the part of *developed and developing country employers*; and the TNC-critical (while admitting their beneficial contributions) *developing and developed country workers' representatives*.

Ten years after work had started on the UN Code there were still a number of unresolved key issues. The draft at this point consisted of six main areas, and contrary to what perhaps might be expected, the most controversial area was not the *activities and conduct of TNCs*[10] (agreement existed on most provisions, except on the exercise of permanent sovereignty over natural resources and wealth), but *the treatment of TNCs* by host countries. Instead of regulating TNCs, it was the behaviour of host countries that came into focus. The controversy concerned issues such as nationalization of property and compensation, 'national treatment', and jurisdiction. The developed countries wanted to see a flexible provision, so that the general national treatment standard could be waived when necessary, whereas the developing countries referred to the importance of the sovereign discretion of each individual country. The issue of free transfer of earnings and other payments also caused disagreement; the host governments were unwilling to give up their power to regulate the use of foreign exchange resources. Yet the most difficult issue concerned nationalization and compensation, i.e., whether standards of compensation should be stated explicitly in the UN Code and, in particular, whether international law should govern these matters (the view of the developed countries).[11]

Not surprisingly, in view of the many unresolved issues, the efforts of the UNCTC never led to the establishment of a code of conduct. The UNCTC was eventually dissolved in 1992, and the work on TNCs continued in another, less ambitious form under the UNCTAD. The dissolvement of the UNCTC should be viewed in relationship to the initiatives seen in the UN Draft Norms and the efforts by former Secretary General, Kofi Annan, to launch the UN Global Compact only a few years later (these initiatives are discussed further in Chapter 9). In the late 1980s and early 1990s, the issue of TNCs was not yet of sufficient importance to warrant the continuation of the activities of UNCTC.

---

10   Issues concerned national sovereignty (and issues related to the effects of decolonialization), human rights, apartheid and the occupation of Namibia, non-interference in internal affairs or in intergovernmental relations and corrupt practices. Also, economic, financial and social issues, e.g., ownership and control, balance of payments and financing, transfer pricing, taxation, restrictive business practices, transfer of technology, consumer protection, and environmental protection, disclosure of information.

11   The reference to international law in general, and whether the international law reflected the changes in the composition of the international system after the decolonialization, created further disagreement. The developing and socialist countries accepted treaties and conventions (as they were binding to the signatories), but not customary international law. The latter, being developed by the OECD countries and therefore unrepresentative of developing countries' views and practices (most of them under colonial rule when developed). International obligations meant different things to different governments. The disagreement on international law in combination with the issue of jurisdiction of states over TNC, and of corporate law in an international setting, further complicated the matter (United Nations 1986).

Chapter 4

New Issues of Corporate Social Responsibility Introduced

Whereas the negotiations on the UN Code had been limited mainly to economic aspects and involved state actors, IGOs and certain trade unions, other issues attracted considerably more attention in the 1970s and engaged other kinds of actors. The process that characterizes the anti-apartheid movement's targeting of TNCs is different than the process that characterized the evolution of the UN Code. The Nestlé boycott (described in the next section) illustrates yet another process. Both the anti-apartheid and the Nestlé boycott cases represent a change to the international order; a transformation of the international system is beginning to occur with the appearance of other actors, activities and issues on the international agenda. The discussion of these cases that follows will demonstrate this point.

Anti-apartheid and Transnational Corporations

A number of initiatives contributed to raise the profile of the anti-apartheid issue internationally. Among these was the early concern raised by the Indian government in the UN in 1946 over the treatment of the Indian population in South Africa. In addition, the African states (many of them newly independent from colonial rule) criticized the apartheid regime in the UN General Assembly and achieved adoption of limited sanctions in 1961. Furthermore, the internationalization of the boycott campaign first initiated in South Africa, and the concern of the US about the political developments in South Africa related to its 'containment policy' also contributed to putting the anti-apartheid issue on the international agenda. The internationalization of the anti-apartheid movement that had started in South Africa evolved more or less simultaneously with that of the civil rights movement in the US, and the two were linked in various ways (Massie 1997, Gurney 2000). The two issues reinforced each other; the attention paid to civil rights enhanced the amount of attention paid to anti-apartheid and vice versa. The groups involved in the anti-apartheid movement outside of South Africa that targeted TNCs were also drawn from different parts of society; the main groups were the churches, trade unions, and student organizations. This should be compared with the UN Code case, which was limited mainly to governments, TNCs and a few trade unions.

Support for apartheid by the Dutch Reformed Church and the growing anti-apartheid position (influenced by new theological ideas) of the Protestant churches and the Roman Catholic Church in South Africa brought increased attention to the apartheid issue among churches within the World Council of Churches (WCC) in the 1950s. In spite of earlier fears that the organization would disintegrate, the effect of the so-called Sharpeville killings[1] in 1960 led to an official criticism of apartheid by the World Council of Churches. As a consequence, the Dutch Reformed Church of South Africa chose to withdraw from the World Council of Churches. At about the same time, the American Committee on Africa (ACOA) had started to campaign in the US for disinvestment (withdrawal of corporate operations) from South Africa – the campaign was carried out together with Martin Luther King Jr. In the course of time, King and other civil rights activists began to link the civil rights movements to the anti-apartheid movement, which proved advantageous for both issues and movements. However, it was not until the 1960s that the issue of apartheid caught the attention of a broader audience (Massie 1997, Sethi and Williams 2000b). This was most certainly spurred on by the spread internationally of the oppressive conduct of the South African government in connection with the events of the Sharpeville Killings.

The International Confederation of Free Trade Unions (ICFTU), which was in a formative stage after leaving the World Federation of Trade Unions (WFTU) in 1949 (see also the discussion in Chapter 3), was already involved in the apartheid issue. At its first General Council in 1952, criticism was directed towards the apartheid regime, and in 1959, a call was issued for a boycott. Apart from solidarity with the black South African workers and trade union members, the issue was unique and vital to the ICFTU in other ways. It represented a way of uniting the international labour movement and avoiding the South African apartheid opposition to obtain support from communist countries. However, the situation was complicated due to the policy of no contact with communist organizations, activities to counteract the moves of the WFTU within the UN, and the fear of non-independent trade unions linked to the liberation movement taking government office after independence. However, in the 1970s, ICFTU increasingly targeted the activities of the TNCs by, among other things, compiling and updating a list of around 3,000 TNCs operating in South Africa. ICFTU also demanded sanctions against South African business interests, reduction/elimination of pension fund investments in companies with interests in South Africa, and pressure on companies to improve labour relations and recognize black workers' trade unions. The ICFTU also supported the various codes in existence at the time, but considered their attempts as limited and as a way only of putting additional pressure on the South African government by

---

1 The Sharpeville killings came about during demonstrations against the apartheid regime's passport laws. Demonstrators were attacked by the police and some 90 people were killed and 180 injured. This was documented by the international media, who happened to be in South Africa at the invitation of the government for the purpose of giving the world a more just image of apartheid.

giving publicity to the cause. These activities continued into the 1980s, with new programmes of action in which ICFTU emphasized mandatory sanctions and disinvestment by TNCs and which included targeting individual TNCs (Gumbrell-McCormick 2000b)·.

The US student involvement in the anti-apartheid struggle (and most likely students in other countries) can be described as three progressively larger waves, starting in the mid-1960s and lasting until the end of apartheid (Voorhes 1999). In 1965, a newly established organization in the US, Students for a Democratic Society, initiated a protest against loans by Chase Manhattan Bank in New York to the South African government and later targeted university administrations to divest themselves of (sell) their South African holdings. Although many US universities resisted the demands of the students, the universities were at least forced to examine the issue (publishing the results), develop guidelines and establish committees (one of the first was Harvard University in 1972). The second wave of protests appeared after the Soweto uprising in 1976, with the arrest of some 700 students in the US in 1977 alone. Some US universities decided on divestiture, but others chose to demand that companies ameliorate their labour practices and undertake other actions in line with the Sullivan principles (see below), just launched. The third wave came in the mid-1980s, as part of an increasing international mobilization, and called for a total divestiture of South African holdings.

Companies with operations in South Africa or involved in business indirectly related to apartheid consequently met both resistance from various groups in society and new initiatives. The strategies among the companies varied. Some disinvested. In some cases, this meant a commitment only to the letter of the law, e.g., decreasing ownership in subsidiaries from a majority ownership of 50 per cent or more to 49 per cent or less. Others decided to work for reform from within, retaining their operations in South Africa but adopting measures against employee discrimination. Others adopted codes of conduct and joined new initiatives such as the Sullivan Principles, discussed below. What effect these measures had is debatable, and the argument has been made that in fact the effects were insignificant in comparison to the effects of the sanctions later adopted by governments. This issue will not be discussed here; of interest rather is the development of the new initiatives that are part of the emergence of CSR as a new norm.

Development of New Initiatives

There are two specific initiatives that were prominent at the time, which also represented two somewhat different approaches to the issue of CSR. First, there were the activities of what is called shareholder activism, which mainly consisted of obtaining shares in a particular company and filing shareholder resolutions at the annual corporate meeting demanding divestiture (selling off direct ownership of a company) or disinvestment (selling off shares). Although the initial purpose might have been to actually influence the company's board, in time the resulting publicity became just as important. These shareholder resolutions were seldom adopted but managed to attract attention to the debates that they sparked, both at the actual meetings and outside of them.

Second, there was the approach of seeing companies as agents of change, where the companies were asked not to withdraw from a country, but to actively contribute to change; e.g., by adopting codes of conduct in order to counteract racism. The latter was the approach chosen by those companies that decided to join the initiative called the Sullivan Principles.

A third approach (not treated here) is the adoption by IGOs, governments and local governments of laws and policies directed at companies, such as sanctions, selective purchasing laws, and the like. This approach become more prominent in the later phase of the anti-apartheid struggle in the late 1970s and even more so in the 1980s (such as the legislation adopted in Sweden in 1978 to ban investments in South Africa and Namibia).[2]

Shareholder Activism   An important actor in the development of shareholder activism at the time was the US-based Interfaith Center for Corporate Responsibility (ICCR), an international coalition of 275 (as of 2009) religious institutional investors of Protestant, Roman Catholic, and Jewish beliefs. The ICCR was created in 1971 as a consequence of certain members of the clergy starting to question whether religious institutional investors should profit from war (Oden 1985). This led to further questioning of the military industry as a whole and also to criticism of apartheid, an issue closely related to slavery and racial discrimination in the US, to which religious communities had been opposed.

Among the first shareholder resolutions to be coordinated by the ICCR concerned the US automobile company General Motors in 1971 (see also the Sullivan Principles below).[3] These resolutions sought to make companies withdraw from or cut their ties with South Africa, end or prohibit sales to South Africa's security agencies, become signatories to the Sullivan Principles, disclose information on operations in South Africa, or prohibit loans to South Africa (Sethi and Williams 2000a). Shareholder resolutions were also used as a strategy in the campaign against the marketing practices applied to sell breast-milk substitutes by US companies in connection with the Nestlé boycott, which will be discussed later.

The initiative of Leon Sullivan and the Sullivan Principles that developed somewhat later partly challenged the shareholder activism of the ICCR. The Sullivan Principles advocated a different strategy than that of divestiture or disinvestment, which the ICCR favoured. Although the ICCR never openly criticized the Sullivan

---

2   In the 1986 UNCTC draft for a code of conduct, there was a provision with an explicit requirement that TNCs refrain from operations and activities that contributed to maintaining the system of apartheid and illegal occupation of Namibia (United Nations 1986).

3   A decision by the US Securities and Exchange Commission (SEC) in 1970 made it possible to submit public-interest resolutions at annual meetings (Sethi and Williams 2000a: 281).

Principles, and even called for companies to become signatories, there were criticisms of what the initiative represented (Sethi and Williams 2000a).

The Sullivan Principles   The Sullivan Principles is an example of one of the early CSR responses that developed in the second half of the 1970s. The principles served as a code of conduct for companies with operations in apartheid South Africa, with the overall purpose of achieving equal opportunity for employees in a particular company.

The key individual behind this initiative was Reverend Leon Sullivan, a Baptist pastor in the US who was active in civil rights issues and who had also started organizations for campaigning and developing programmes to counter employment discrimination. In 1971, he was elected to the Board of Directors of General Motors, as the first African-American board member. This followed the General Motors Campaign conducted by Ralph Nader,[4] who had criticized the company for not having any African-American representatives on the Board of Directors during General Motors' 1970 Annual Meeting, a meeting attended by some 3,000 shareholders. Coincidentally, at Sullivan's first board meeting in 1971, following the Annual Meeting that same year (where for the second time some 3,000 shareholders attended), Sullivan, in opposition to the rest of the board (and much to their dissatisfaction), expressed his support for a shareholder resolution that had been put forward calling on the withdrawal of all companies (including General Motors) from South Africa (Massie 1997: 285, 292, Sethi and Williams 2000a: 7).

The turbulence that surrounded Sullivan's election to the Board of Directors, his statements on the shareholder resolution and his later visit to South Africa, eventually led to the development of the Sullivan Principles. According to these principles, companies were to remain in a country as agents of change by committing themselves to a set of principles on non-discrimination instead of withdrawing their activities from a country all together. This represented a change in his previous position in support of withdrawal. In 1976, Sullivan, together with the chairman of IBM and the chief executive officer of General Motors, hosted a meeting for a group of top executives to muster support for the principles. In 1977, the Sullivan Principles were launched (Sethi and Williams 2000a: 10).

In order for the Sullivan Principles to be effective in South Africa, they needed support not only from the companies that were to be future signatories, but also at least tacitly from the South African government and the anti-apartheid movement. This support was not evident. Some regarded the Sullivan Principles unfavourably (South African activists and the business community), others were sceptical but supportive (like the ICCR, having themselves chosen another strategy, and the

---

4   An attorney by profession and a well-known consumer advocate in the US, opposed to the power of large companies. Ralph Nader is the author of *Unsafe at Any Speed: The Designed-In Dangers of the American Automobile* published in 1965, especially critical of General Motors.

ICFTU). Support eventually came from the US Carter administration, the South African government (as a strategy to guard against criticism), and various pension funds (university teachers and administrations, state and local employees, etc.). In 1979, over 100 companies had committed themselves to the Principles and were also subject to independent monitoring, the first of its kind (Sethi and Williams 2000a: 15, 18, Massie 1997: 448).

The apartheid regime of South Africa ultimately came to an end; however, both of the initiatives discussed above (shareholder activism and the Sullivan Principles) have continued as part of present-day activities of CSR. Shareholder activism has spread and is now used by other organizations as well. A subfield of CSR defined as socially responsible investment (SRI) has even emerged, consisting of other initiatives such as ethical investment funds, investment indexes, etc. The Sullivan Principles constitute the first attempt at implementing codes of conduct including monitoring schemes, independent monitoring, etc., in a multi-stakeholder forum. The Sullivan Principles were relaunched in 1999 as the Global Sullivan Principles in the presence of the UN Secretary General, Kofi Annan. On that occasion the Secretary General referred to the Global Sullivan Principles as important for the UN Global Compact (United Nations 1999). The UN Global Compact Principles that developed shortly after the launch of the UN Global Compact also bear strong resemblance to the Global Sullivan Principles.

The Nestlé Boycott and the Establishment of the WHO Code

Parallel to the activities of the UNCTC and the anti-apartheid movement, another concern related to the activities of TNCs was growing stronger and finally surged onto the international agenda. In contrast to the UN Code, the efforts of the Nestlé boycott case, discussed in this section, proved successful, with the adoption of an international code of conduct on the marketing of breast-milk substitutes by the World Health Organization (WHO).

Although breast-milk substitutes only became an international issue in the 1970s, the product itself had a much longer history. Breast-milk substitutes were actually introduced simultaneously in the US and Europe in the second half of the nineteenth century, although they were developed through different techniques. Condensed milk for infants was first developed in the US in the 1860s, partly due to the conversion of a milk surplus into new products through advances in technology and innovation. The growing number of women workers also contributed to this development, as did the increase in hospital deliveries, where doctors were able to advise the (often affluent) mother on the use of breast-milk substitutes. From this developed a medical-commercial relationship, with companies being interested in getting doctors to legitimize their products and doctors being interested in controlling the quality of baby food (criticized at the time for low nutritional content). The colonies were an important market for breast-milk substitutes, due to increasing participation by women in plantation work (equivalent to the effect of industrialization on women in Europe and North America). Later, aid and development organizations contributed to the spread of breast-milk substitutes through their distribution of the product as relief assistance in developing countries with the purpose of fighting hunger (Palmer 2000: 190, 224).

At about the same time that condensed milk appeared, Henri Nestlé developed powdered milk in Switzerland, partly as a philanthropic deed, and began selling the product in 1868. Sales increased in only five years to 500,000 cans annually, and powdered milk was also distributed internationally. Like the American manufacturers of condensed milk, Nestlé recognized the importance of a relationship with the health profession to legitimize the new product. This proved a winning strategy, and the company became very successful. In the early 1900s, Nestlé merged with the Anglo-Swiss Condensed Milk Company, and in 1920, the first factory was established in a developing country (Brazil). In 1976, Nestlé had 130,000 employees and some 300 factories in 24 countries on five continents, and in 1980, it had become the world's largest alimentary company (Buffle 1986: 16, 24).

Negative Effects of Artificial Feeding Being Recognized

Reports on problems with artificial feeding had already appeared by the end of the nineteenth and early twentieth centuries, but the reasons for these problems were not clear at the time. However, researchers and doctors maintained their belief in science and continued to advocate use of these products rather than a return to breast-feeding (Buffle 1986). It was not until individual health professionals began working in the field in developing countries that these issues were raised once again and, with the joining of NGOs, that criticism of the companies producing the products appeared.[5]

During the 1940s, infant malnutrition grew as a concern within the UN system. In 1955 an ad hoc coalition, the UN Protein Advisory Group (PAG), was established, consisting of representatives of UN agencies, developing country governments, academic institutions and industry, mainly paediatricians and clinicians. From the start, the focus of their work was mainly on scientific aspects and resource availability, but with time this focus shifted to the influence of institutions (e.g., industry) on breast-feeding practices. In 1972, the group issued the 'PAG Statement 23', with recommendations to governments, physicians and industry with regard

---

5   Among these were the British paediatrician Cicely Williams, who experienced first-hand the problems with breast-milk substitutes in developing countries. In the early 1930s, she published her findings on protein deficiency in infants, and in 1939 she gave an often cited speech under the provocative title 'Milk and Murder' to the Singapore Rotary Club. Williams was later employed in the newly established WHO for a short period. In late 1960s, Dr Derrick Jelliffe, a UN consultant who previously had collaborated with Cicely Williams, raised the issue of the relationship between declining breast-feeding, infant mortality and industry advertising in seminars and scientific articles, defining this as 'commerciogenic malnutrition' (Craddock 1983, Buffle 1986, IOCU 1986, Sethi 1994).

to breast-milk substitutes. The industry was asked to emphasize (not discourage) breast-feeding, not to direct advertising at new mothers, and to revise instructions, labelling and literature for infant formula preparations in order to ensure safe use of the product (Sethi 1994: 50). This represented a change of attitude from that of the early twentieth century, when trust in product development had taken precedence. Allegations followed that the group had become politicized in now considering the social aspects of infant-feeding as opposed to only the technical aspects relevant to product safety.

Interest among Non-governmental Organizations and Response from the Industry

Up until the 1970s, the issue of breast-milk substitutes had been dealt with by individual experts, IGOs, individual governments and industry, but not by civil society organizations. This was to change in the 1970s. The International Organization of Consumers Unions (IOCU) was one of the first NGOs to become engaged in the issue.[6] In 1972, the organization submitted a memorandum on a 'Draft Code of Practice for Advertising of Infant Foods' to the Food and Agricultural Organization/World Health Organization Codex Alimentarious Commission (responsible for issues concerning international quality and labelling requirements for products for human consumption). The issue was, however, seen as being outside of the group's area of competence and was not dealt with further at the time. Instead, it was an article and a call for action in the *New Internationalist* in 1973, in which nutrition experts criticized the industry for contributing to malnutrition in the 'Third World', and in particular a report in 1974 by the UK-based NGO War on Want with the spectacular title *The Baby Killer*, that brought the issue international attention (IOCU 1986, Chetley 1986: 5, 42).

The Baby Killer criticized the infant food industry in general (and Nestlé in particular) for its marketing practices in the Third World – such as salesgirls dressed as nurses, encouragement of bottle-feeding, sales-related payment to nurses, mass media consumer advertising and labels that associated the product with healthy (often European) babies, free samples to mothers, free gifts and samples to doctors, and distribution of educational literature in hospitals. The report recommended a ban on consumer advertising and promotion to the medical profession, that companies should refrain from activities that discouraged breast-feeding and cooperate with international organizations on nutrition issues, and that measures should be taken by developing countries. The allegations in the report were, however, rejected by the industry at the time (Sethi 1994).

The spark that really ignited the controversy was the partly reedited and translated version (translations were made into several languages) of the report

---

6   Other organizations involved in the issue of breast-milk substitutes in the late 1970s included breast-feeding groups in Malaysia, Kenya and Papua New Guinea and the Consumers Association of Penang, Malaysia (Chetley 1979: 175).

by a small Swiss NGO, which also gave it a new title, *Nestlé Toetet* [sic] *Babys* (Nestlé Kills Babies). Nestlé immediately sued for libel, on account of:

- the title;
- the charge that the practices of *Nestlé* and other companies are unethical and immoral (stated in the rewritten introduction and in the report itself);
- the accusation of being responsible for the death or the permanent physical and mental damage of thousands of babies by its sales promotion policy (in the rewritten introduction);
- accusation that in developing countries, the sales representatives for baby food are dressed like nurses to give the sales promotion a scientific appearance (Chetley 1979: 109).

Nestlé later realized that a lawsuit had been the wrong strategy to fend off criticism and offered to settle out of court, but this solution was refused by the Swiss NGO, seizing the opportunity to make use of the public attention given to the trial, which started in Berne in 1975. A small NGO sued by one of the largest TNCs in the world! During the court proceedings, Nestlé dropped three of the charges, pursuing only the first charge, regarding the title of the report. When the proceeding ended the following year, the Swiss NGO was found guilty of libel and fined, but Nestlé was also given a reprimand by the judge for the inappropriateness of its advertising practices and was asked to revise them (Chetley 1986).

A few days before the trial, on Nestlé's initiative, a majority of the companies in the industry formed the International Council of the Infant Food Industries. The aim as stated was to cooperate and respond to critics and to develop self-regulation instruments, and a code of ethics was also issued. Nestlé wanted through this initiative to create a united front against its critics (although not all companies joined) and make the critics perceive the issue as an industry-wide problem rather than one linked to Nestlé alone. However, internal disagreements and the external distrust that confronted the organization made the activities of the International Council of the Infant Food Industries difficult, and it was eventually disbanded in 1983. Another organization by the name of The International Association of Infant Food Manufacturers was to replace it the following year (Sethi 1994: 146).

The trial naturally brought the world's attention to the issue, which gave the NGOs involved in the Nestlé boycott a unique opportunity to unite and mobilize. Among the many activist organizations that participated in a meeting in Berne just before the verdict was the ICCR. The ICCR was to play an important role in initiating the US boycott, a boycott that later spread to other countries, and in the launch of the boycott organization INFACT in 1977. The ICCR was already active in the issue and had submitted shareholder resolutions to US infant formula manufacturers in 1974 and 1975. In 1975, local US churches were also showing a documentary on bottle feeding, in which a reference to the Berne trial and a critique of Nestlé appeared. Nestlé responded by, among other things, hiring public relations firms to counteract the boycott and ameliorate its image, which led to a letter being sent to 300,000 clergy of religious denominations in the US (Buffle 1986: 57). This strategy proved to be less successful.

An important step in the boycott was a deliberate move to get the issue on the public agenda through a massive lobbying campaign directed towards US Senator Edward Kennedy, persuading him to conduct hearings in 1978 on the issue. In these hearings Nestlé allegedly showed:

> an almost total misunderstanding and disregard of the American political process, the nuances of the congressional hearing process, the strategies and tactics of the activists, and above all, the role of news media. Ballerin's [the Nestlé representative] statements questioned the motives of the religious institutions and raised the spectre of the threat to communism … making him and the company the object of public ridicule (Sethi 1994: 80).

This only aggravated the situation for Nestlé. In a later meeting with Kennedy and representatives of the industry it was decided (on the suggestion of Nestlé) to take the issue to the WHO (Sethi 1994). The decision allowed Kennedy to conclude the matter, and Nestlé could bring the issue 'home' (both Nestlé and WHO were headquartered in Switzerland).

An international consultative meeting of WHO and UNICEF was held in 1979 that included representatives of governments, international organizations, industry, health experts, and NGOs. In connection to this meeting, a new organization, the International Baby Food Action Network (IBFAN), was created, consisting of the International Organization of Consumers Union; the Baby Milk Action Coalition, UK; Oxfam, UK; Third World First; and the Geneva Infant Feeding Association. IBFAN was to become an important actor in the campaign.

The WHO negotiations that followed were conducted with multi-stakeholder participation or consultation, but with drafting being done by the WHO secretariat staff. After only two years of negotiations, although at times in turbulent conditions, the WHO in 1981 adopted the Code of Marketing for Breast-milk Substitutes, regulating the sale and marketing of infant formula. In 1984, Nestlé and the NGOs involved in the boycott signed a joint agreement in which Nestlé expressed a commitment to the WHO Code in return for the NGOs calling off the boycott.

Implications of the Early Phase of Norm Emergence

The three cases discussed above in Chapter 3 and in this chapter aptly demonstrate the transformation of the international system, where new actors, issues and activities have increasingly come to influence the international agenda and international relations in general. A distinction can be made particularly between the group of dominating actors, motives and social processes involved in the case of the UN Code and in the two other cases, i.e., anti-apartheid and the Nestlé boycott. There is an apparent difference in the process, where prominent participation by governments and IGOs (with only some consultation by business and a few established trade unions and NGOs), as well as the Western and male bias seen in the UN Code case is replaced by a more mixed process in the two other cases. Not only does the degree of involvement by NGOs per se differ between the cases, but the particular NGOs that participate, the aims and activities, and issues involved are also clearly different. Also the concerns in the UN Code case differ from that of the other two cases.

In *the UN Code case*, the Chilean government and the ECOSOC were the main initiators – the expected actors and setting for an international affair. However, this event took place in a time of change. Apart from the obvious effect of world events, such as the ITT affair, the breakdown of the Bretton Woods system, and the activities of other IGOs (in particular the ILO and the OECD), the national and international trade union movements only partly contributed to the developments in the UN Code case. One should bear in mind that this case occurred within a Cold War context, with the 'politicization' of IGOs and trade unions.

Individual automobile industry workers in developed countries, concerned over the loss of jobs to low-wage developing countries, had called on their respective trade unions to act. The national trade unions, and later the international trade secretariats of the industry sectors involved, recognized the problem at an early stage and attempted unsuccessfully to establish the so-called world company councils. This failure was partly due to the free trade and 'containment' policies to which the non-socialist trade unions had given their support, as well as to internal differences within the trade union movement. Other NGOs had not made such a commitment and were 'free' to act in any way they saw fit.

Other factors also contributed to constrain the trade unions. A belief in industrialization and its positive effect on development (including views on poverty as an individual issue), a mainstream view up until the 1970s, made criticism of TNCs difficult. The growing membership of developing-country trade unions in the ICFTU had to be considered. There was, consequently, a need to keep the organization unified by balancing many different interests (developed and developing countries, industry and political concerns). Not being directly part of the actual negotiations also made the ICFTU's task difficult. Although the ICFTU was in a better position than the World Federation of Trade Unions or the International Metalworkers' Federation to advocate for international labour standards (ICFTU having consultative status at the ECOSOC), the ICFTU had other priorities. The anti-apartheid movement was thus seen as a cause of greater interest to and with greater potential for the trade union.

What the negotiations on the UN Code did was to bring underlying unresolved issues of a more political nature (related to the Cold War and decolonialization) to the forefront, manifested as disagreement on the treatment of TNCs rather than the seemingly uncontroversial technical issues (economic or jurisdictional) stated in the UN Code. Surprisingly enough, from today's perspective, labour and human rights were only minor issues in the negotiations on the UN Code. A parallel to the situation of underlying unresolved issues in international politics is seen in the need to develop two human rights treaties instead of one, with the differences in the focus made by the great powers on either political and civil rights (US and its allies) or on economic, social and cultural rights (socialist countries).

Unlike the previous case of the UN Code, in the case of the anti-apartheid movement, targeting the TNCs was mainly drawn from civil society and involved a more heterogeneous and uncoordinated group of participants. Yet *the anti-apartheid issue* was a unifying cause, where each participating organization could find its own reasons for involvement and choose its own methods of action.

Civil rights organizations were able to link their cause to support of the South African anti-apartheid activists. Church organizations, with a history of anti-slavery opposition, were already involved in the US civil rights movement and had an interest in developing countries through their long history of relief assistance and missionary activities. In addition, the church organizations were sometimes themselves institutional investors needing to address their own responsibility. University students and student organizations were other important groups. Due to an increase in the number of university students, a large number of young people were gathered on campuses and exposed to the influences of the various movements of the time. As mentioned earlier, the trade unions had their own reasons for involvement: the ICFTU and World Federation of Trade Unions were 'competing' to gain the trade unions in South Africa as their allies. In summary, the different church, civil rights, student organizations and trade unions could complement each other's activities, even though each had different motives for involvement.

Among the new strategies developed and employed were shareholder activism, calling for either disinvestment or divestiture, and the Sullivan Principles. They represented two different approaches, where one pointed to the moral responsibilities of shareholders (to divest or use their power to act on annual company meetings), and the other, the Sullivan Principles, pointed to concrete actions for changing the situation of those affected in cooperation with business. This created some controversy within the movement, i.e., whether or not to include companies in the campaign against apartheid. In the case of shareholder activism, the focus was now on the role of the institutional investor. Among institutional investors, the obvious targets for the student movement were the universities and their pension fund holdings (for faculty and administration, whose organizations were also involved). Both of these strategies contributed to initiatives that are present in today's CSR landscape in the form of socially responsible investments, corporate codes of conduct and multi-stakeholder approaches. Other strategies were also employed, such as boycotts and sit-ins, with civil obedience and arrests as a way of deliberately acting inappropriately so as to draw attention to the issue. A combination of these activities introduced new issues into environments (board rooms, annual shareholders meetings, etc.) where they had not been a part of the normal agenda and partly contributed to changing the attitudes and behaviours of TNCs.

In *the Nestlé boycott* case, we can see a combined effect of the activities of the WHO and of NGOs in establishing the WHO Code. Although the WHO and health professionals in the field originally called attention to the problem of malnutrition among artificially fed infants, the developments in the 1970s were very much driven by NGOs. I see this as an effect of the changing views on poverty mentioned previously, where the focus is shifted from seeing the problem as that of individuals being poor to seeing poverty as an issue of collective responsibility. This means replacing policies of industrialization as a strategy to address poverty among developing countries with policies of development. The changing perception of poverty, in combination with increased knowledge of the effects of artificial feeding (through the personal experience of development workers and interest by scholars) questioned the infallibility in science and technology as well as their perceived apolitical nature.

That the initial NGO involvement came from an international consumer's organization shows a connection between the issue of artificial feeding and the questioning of the effects of consumption in the Western world at the time. Consumer protection was also evident in the negotiations on the UN Code, where the issues of false and misleading publicity (the traditional concern of consumer organizations, apart from product safety) and consumption patterns were raised.

Mothers who were unable to breast-feed their infants (working mothers) or who would not breast-feed them were also a part of the process driving product development (apart from factors such as technological innovations and milk surpluses). This is also the industry's argument, i.e., their product was serving a need. From the NGOs, references to the different breast-feeding practices in developing countries compared with those in developed countries were used as an argument against the TNCs. This points to a view of mothers in developing countries as natural and 'traditional' in comparison to those in industrialized and alienated developed countries. The reasons given for mothers in developing countries unwillingly giving up breast-feeding are the forces of industrialization and aggressive marketing by the industry; although one can argue that there are also mothers in developing countries who view substitutes as a convenient solution (like mothers in developed countries) to breast-feeding.

Science and expertise also played an important role, both in the development of the new product (satisfying a need among working mothers and finding outlets for surplus milk) and in the initial warning signals (field observations of health conditions among developing country populations). Expertise was also employed on both sides of the controversy in supporting and legitimizing the different arguments during negotiations on the WHO Code. Apart from the views on poverty changing, from industrialization to development policies, there was also a shift in the role of science and expertise involving a gendered aspect with the movement from a mechanistic, progress-oriented world-view to one that also involves social reproductive considerations.

Like the issue of apartheid, the Nestlé boycott was a unifying cause, bringing together various NGOs. A difference can be seen, however, in that the anti-apartheid movement in the West paralleled the continuous struggle of the South Africans themselves, whereas in the Nestlé boycott the struggle against breast-milk substitutes was waged mainly by 'self appointed' representatives of the women in developed countries who were being affected. An additional aspect of the Nestlé boycott is that the issue took on an emotional nature, supposedly partly due to the physical nature of breast-feeding, the consumers involved (infants) and possibly also the behaviour of the NGOs in contrast to the representatives of business. This situation bears similarities to the views on the politicization of the ILO during the Cold War and decolonialization. It indicates the growing conflict between the prevailing standards of appropriateness in international relations at the time and the challenges to these standards.

In the present chapter, it has been made clear that the Nestlé boycott and the anti-apartheid cases represented manifestations of an initial norm emergence in the area of CSR and in part an expansion of international relations to other sectors (apart from the political), levels and actors (not just governments and IGOs) in the international system. The UN Code case thus represented the traditional workings of the international system, which began to change due to what we today refer to as globalization. In the following chapters we will turn to the development of CSR that followed in the 1980s, when a new wave of organizations and activities began to emerge.

In the next chapter I will show how norm emergence expanded and intensified and eventually shifted into a norm cascade in the middle of the 1990s. The expansion and intensification of CSR norm emergence refers both to the increase in CSR organizations and initiatives and to the involvement of other sectors and levels of the international system. The discussion will also explore the different stages in more detail, particularly with regard to the different actors, motives and social processes involved.

Chapter 5
Development Towards 'Norm Tipping' and Activist Organizations

In the shadow of the three major events of the 1970s, discussed in the previous chapters, new CSR organizations and initiatives slowly mushroomed. The real growth was seen in the mid-1990s, when a 'norm tipping' occurred and the development of CSR shifted into the stage of 'norm cascade'. I define these organizations as norm entrepreneurs.

The initial stage of norm emergence within the CSR norm cycle continued with the appearance of norm entrepreneurs and their activities in the late 1980s and early 1990s, the period immediately prior to the norm cascade stage. The norm emergence stage is characterized by the presence of certain *motives* – ideational commitment, altruism and empathy – and the *social process* of persuasion. I will explore here the background, aims and activities of the CSR organizations that began to appear in increasing numbers during this period. The point of departure is the larger group of selected CSR organizations, to give an overview of the CSR organizations involved: their general characteristics and a brief description of their aims and activities are presented. This will demonstrate the existence of three different categories of CSR organizations, which reveals a dynamic already present among the CSR organizations.

The overview of CSR organizations will be followed by an in-depth discussion of five focus organizations:

- Clean Clothes Campaign;
- International Business Leaders Forum;
- International Labor Rights Fund;
- Global Exchange;
- Fairtrade Labelling Organizations International.

These organizations are all early movers within their category and show how the norm entrepreneurs, mainly motivated by ideational commitment, worked to persuade others of the necessity and advantage of CSR in view of existing standards of appropriateness. It is argued here that their framing and advocacy of CSR, in combination with the activities of the many other CSR organizations, contributed to the norm tipping and norm cascade seen in the mid-1990s.

Characteristics of Norm Entrepreneurs

Two observations emerge immediately from the list of CSR organizations seen in Appendix 1. The first is a pattern regarding the time of establishment of the organizations. The second is the concentration of geographical locations. If one disregards the events of the 1970s discussed in Chapters 3 and 4, the emergence of CSR organizations points to CSR mainly being a phenomenon of the late 1980s and the 1990s.

As can be seen from Figure 5.1, below, most of the CSR organizations studied here (close to 90 per cent) were established after 1980. Of these, the majority were created in the 1990s. Organizations were also active in these issues in the 1970s that no longer exist or have turned to work with other issues.[1] Most of these organizations had a national orientation as far as I have been able to conclude and hence are not of direct interest here, where internationally oriented organizations are the focus. Some of the organizations of the 1970s, however, still remain active, including Baby Milk Action, the International Baby Food Action Network (IBFAN), International Confederation of Free Trade Unions (ICFTU), Interfaith Center on Corporate Responsibility (ICCR) and War on Want. It should also be noted that some of the organizations listed in Appendix 1, although established early, did not address the issue of CSR until fairly recently, such as Amnesty International and Human Rights Watch, or have remained nationally oriented in their activities, as in the case of the German Coalition against BAYER Dangers (CBG) and Business in the Community (focused on the UK). Apart from these organizations, the striking growth in the 1980s of new organizations targeting the negative aspects of TNC activities clearly points to a new or renewed interest in the issue of CSR during this period. As will be seen below, this new interest in CSR is related to the emerging issue of globalization, and particularly its impact on international production and trade. New organizations were seen as necessary to address the effects of these changes.

A clear trend can also be seen in the geographical location of the CSR organizations. The often-alleged domination of NGOs from the North in world politics is also evident in the issue of CSR. Furthermore, these organizations are mainly located in the large cities or capitals of the world. This points to activities around CSR being very much an urban phenomenon and often appearing in NGO-dense environments at centres of power (political or economic). These cities to a large extent become the 'arenas' for norm construction.

As can be noted from Appendix 1, the very large majority (close to 90 per cent) of organizations are located in North America or Europe, and in cities such as Washington, DC, San Francisco, New York, London, and Amsterdam. With a few exceptions, the organizations in North America are almost all found in the US; this is also the country with the largest number of CSR organizations. The organizations with offices in Europe are mainly found in the UK and The

---

1   See lists of organizations in *A Who's Who of Corporate Responsibility Action Groups* (1972) and Oden (1985).

Netherlands, but also in Germany, Switzerland, Belgium and France (in order of frequency). The remaining organizations are found almost exclusively in Asia, with several of them in China. Like the organizations in North America and Europe, they appear in large cities like Hong Kong or Bangkok. Only two of the organizations are found in South America (Ecuador and Chile). I have so far not come across a single organization located in Africa or the Middle East that meets the selection criteria and was established in the period studied.

This geographical pattern should not come as a surprise, since the home countries of TNCs are mainly industrialized countries, and their investment and outsourcing policies are to a large extent directed towards Asia. Asia is also where the negative effects of TNC activities often manifest themselves. However, the uneven distribution of CSR organizations also reflects other factors, such as the political opportunity structures (see Chapter 2 for a discussion) of a country making the creation of such organizations difficult. An additional consideration is the capacity of the individual to engage in CSR advocacy, due to resources constraints or cultural circumstances, or that the individual and organizations see the problem and address the negative effects of TNCs activities differently, i.e., choosing not to focus on TNCs.[2] Other factors, such as bias in media reporting, are also relevant.

Three Different Categories of Corporate Social Responsibility Organizations

Apart from patterns in terms of time of establishment and geographical location of the CSR organizations studied here, a closer look at the organizations themselves reveals other unanticipated, and perhaps more significant, differences. The CSR organizations are not, as one might expect, all the same sorts of social change NGOs engaged in traditional activism targeting TNCs for their alleged human and labour rights abuses. These are organizations that I have defined as Activists Organizations (hereafter Activists). Two other categories of NGOs also appear that address the issue in a different manner than the Activists, and thus contribute in their own way to the development of CSR. They also constitute a form of competition to the Activists and give the process a dynamic. These other categories of CSR organizations I have labelled Business Initiatives Organizations (Business Initiatives) and Multi-stakeholder Organizations (Multi-stakeholders). The categories are based on the membership of the organizations in question, which are:

- Individual activists, or NGOs with individual activist members, in the case of Activists;
- Individual business leaders or companies in the case of Business Initiatives; and
- Mixed membership or participation in the case of Multi-stakeholders.

---

2 An example is Focus on the Global South, an organization based in Bangkok, Thailand, that focuses on multilateral institutions and does not regard the issue of CSR as important (Interview with Bello 2005).

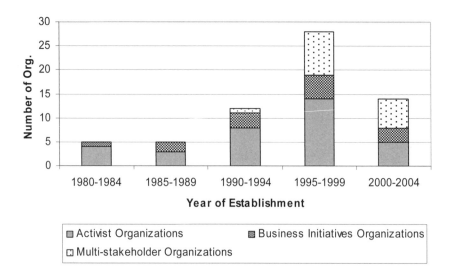

Figure 5.1   Establishment of CSR Organizations 1980–2005

Source: Data collected by the author on selected CSR organizations.

Multi-stakeholders could furthermore be divided into organizations with no government representation and organizations that do have this representation. In the latter case, one may question whether the organizations actually ought to be considered NGOs, or whether they should actually be in a separate category defined as hybrid organizations (neither governmental nor non-governmental). Here, these organizations are included as NGOs.

More than half of the organizations belong to the *Activists* category (see Figure 5.1 above). About one-fifth of the organizations belong to the *Business Initiatives* category that started to emerge mainly in the 1990s, and the remaining organizations belong to the *Multi-stakeholders* category, appearing mainly in the mid-1990s.

The two latter categories point to a novel development regarding CSR: the establishment of new kinds of organizations in the area of CSR. The emergence of Business Initiatives constitutes a particularly interesting phenomenon and illustrates, in my opinion, the necessity and/or an interest on the part of the business community to approach the issue of CSR. The Multi-stakeholders are manifestations of the fact that various actors now collaborate to find solutions to problems, including to define the problem.

In the remainder of this chapter and in the next chapter, I will develop the arguments for the distinctive categories further in a discussion of the aims and activities of the organizations in all three categories. The study of the aims and activities of the organizations points to certain recurring themes in the image that the organizations want to project of themselves and confirms the distinct differences between the three categories of organizations. This is seen especially when comparing the category of Activists to the other two categories, Business Initiatives and Multi-stakeholders.

Activist Organizations

Membership in Activist Organizations consists of individual activists and/or other like-minded organizations. These organizations also include NGOs with no formal membership structures, in which case 'members' refers to supporters in general or to members of governing structures. In a sense, these NGOs are less democratic, although possibly more efficient in not having to devote time and resources to consultation. It is in this category that one finds the majority of the new organizations that began addressing CSR in the 1980s. These organizations represent a new wave of CSR activities, introducing new CSR initiatives in the area, compared to the organizations active in the 1970s.

Overview of the Category

As was mentioned earlier, most of the organizations covered in this study belong to this category. They are what may be considered traditional advocacy organizations engaged in activism and campaigning. In general, these organizations include a more explicitly critical perspective on various CSR issues (including TNCs) in their aims and are also involved in more action-oriented activities than the other two categories.

Aims   The aims of this category of organizations are predominantly focused on changing international labour standards or trade union and workers' rights; i.e., what is defined as the working poor, sweatshops (the term making reference to labour conditions of the nineteenth century garment industry) or poor labour conditions, treatment of workers and abuses in factories, forced labour, demands for a 'living wage' and the like. Other often-recurring aims are to address (global) inequality and injustice, whether economic, political or social, and they sometimes also explicitly refer to unjust or harmful corporate policies. More action-oriented aims also appear, such as empowerment and capacity building, worker solidarity and education. These also include work related to monitoring, control over companies and accountability, at times linked to specific references to human rights and democracy, the rights of communities or peoples, and a preference for the local over the global as an alternative to what is perceived as corporate-led globalization.

When specific economic sectors are mentioned, these are mainly fresh produce supply chains or agricultural products (mainly bananas, coffee and tea), the 'maquiladora' industry, the natural resources and extractive industries, the manufacturing industry for garments, sportswear and toy production, and the export industries in general.

An example of how these aims are expressed can be seen in the aims stated by the International Labor Rights Fund as 'an advocacy organization dedicated to achieving just and humane treatment for workers worldwide', working 'for and with the working poor', and being 'committed to ending child labor, forced labor, workplace violence and exploitation, and other abusive labor practices' (ILRF 2002).

Activities   The organizations often refer to the general wording of 'campaigning', which includes a number of different activities. Generally, these activities concern research and investigation, lobbying specific target groups, promotion and advocacy in general, raising awareness and dissemination of information. However, campaigning activities may also cover what one might call activism, such as 'urgent actions', pressuring various targets (companies, public authorities, etc.), and calls for accountability and legal action. Other activities are work with specific programmes in various developing countries, the exchange of information, experience and resources, and work in coalitions.

Again, the ILRF may serve as an example of activities undertaken by these organizations:

> ILRF works directly to pressure corporations to end abusive labor practices, and expose companies that exploit workers … we have initiated groundbreaking litigation to hold companies … accountable for their labor rights abuses … developed sweatshop monitoring programs … We raise public awareness of labor abuses, and promote labor standards to prevent various forms of worker exploitation (ILRF 2002).

Geographically, the organizations in this category are mainly found in Europe or North America. However, it is in this category that most of the organizations from outside of Europe and North America are found. Most of them are located in Asia (one organization is found in Latin America). Although many of the organizations in this category were the first to address CSR in the 1980s (i.e., as early norm entrepreneurs), most of the organizations were established in the 1990s.

In the next sections, I will discuss three focus organizations selected from this category. They are the International Labor Rights Fund, Global Exchange and the Clean Clothes Campaign. The reason for the focus on these particular organizations (including those in the other two categories) is to explore in-depth their role as norm entrepreneurs. The focus will be on the different key elements of the norm emergence stage of the CSR norm cycle, concerning the actors (norm entrepreneurs), motives and social process (see Chapter 2). The later developments in the latter half of the 1990s will be taken up in Chapters 7 and 8. The discussion here will deal with the reasons behind the creation of these organizations and their aims and activities at the time. The purpose is to understand the role of these organizations as 'early movers' in the work to bring CSR onto the international agenda.

The International Labor Rights Fund

The International Labor Rights Fund (ILRF) developed out of an informal Washington, DC-based group of individuals from various NGOs (see also Appendix 2).[3] This group included several national trade unions, but also human rights, labour, and religious organizations. At the time, there was widespread concern in the US over the transfer of production to developing countries, the narrow protectionist position of US trade unions and the selective support given to independent trade unions in socialist countries by the Reagan administration. In order to address the narrow focus of human rights issues in the US (rather seeing the causes of human rights problems rooted as much in economic as in political and Cold War realities), a central US trade policy, the Generalized System of Preferences (GSP) was found to be a useful instrument. The GSP scheme had been proposed by UNCTAD in 1968 and was first employed in the EU in 1971. It was established in the US in 1974 and gives products from selected countries and territories preferential duty-free entry to the US market. The purpose is to give market access to certain developing countries in order to support their economic development. An amendment to the GSP system could address violations of workers' rights internationally without constituting a violation to GATT (General Agreement on Tariffs and Trade) rules because the GSP already included conditionality (terrorism, expropriation, etc.) (Compa and Vogt 2001: 199, 202, Interview with Harvey 2004).

This was the context within which the initial framing activities of the ILRF developed.

Initial Target: US Trade Policy   The idea initially developed and advocated was to amend the US GSP trade policy with a labour rights clause linking the beneficial status of a country under the GSP to its labour rights situation. The labour rights clause included provisions based on the internationally recognized core labour standards found in the ILO conventions. The clause sought to balance the interests of developing countries in using lower labour costs as a legitimate competitive advantage, but not at the expense of labour rights. In a rather short period of time (involving the usual political negotiations and compromises), the work of the informal group proved successful, when the US Congress in 1984 included such an amendment in the GSP Renewal Act of 1984 (Compa and Vogt 2001: 201).

Thus, what the informal group achieved by the GSP amendment was in fact to indirectly target (and restrain) the foreign operations of TNCs through the home country trade policy, thereby addressing labour conditions in host

---

3   Pharis Harvey, who merged the group together in 1982, was at the time the Director of the North American Coalition for Human Rights in Korea. He is an ordained minister of the United Methodist Church, a former Director of the ICCR, and former Executive Director of the ILRF as well as the author of several books and reports. He has also been awarded for his achievements by US President Bill Clinton (ILRF 2001a).

countries by creating a link between trade policy and labour rights standards. The governments involved were required to address and take responsibility for deficient implementation of labour rights standards in various ways and restrain the negative aspects of TNC activities at the same time.

The effort of this informal group of activists was not the only factor important to this success; other factors were also significant. The political opportunity structure in the US, including the support of individual politicians dedicated to the issue of international labour rights, enabled the use of congressional staff resources in the development of the GSP amendment provision. The political situation in the US Congress at the time was also helpful – a Republican administration, but with the Democrats holding the majority of seats in the US House of Representatives.[4]

The absence of a political opportunity structure in host countries with severe human rights violations (including labour rights violations) such as Guatemala, which was at the time holding GSP status and enjoying the benefits of trade, aid and investments, thus contributed to expressions of solidarity in other countries, such as the US.

Another important result achieved by the informal group was to create a platform for further action. The amendment contained a mechanism for challenging a country's GSP status, i.e., rules for a procedure open to workers and organizations for filing petitions concerning workers rights violations.

As of 2001, some 100 reviews of GSP status had been completed after the GSP amendment was passed in 1984. As a result, some 30 countries have been suspended or placed on a temporary extension (some of the suspended countries regained their status after labour reforms).[5] Although the GSP labour rights clause may be of limited economic impact (a small part of overall trade and a general trend towards the lowering of tariffs over time), there is symbolic value in maintaining or losing GSP status. Losing GSP status may give the impression that trading with a country is bad business, and it may lead to sanctions due to trade-related conditions in other trade policies. The GSP amendment was followed by a number of similar trade-related measures that were adopted as part of US legislation and a broader approach to trade agreements in general (Compa and Vogt 2001: 203).

Focus on Labour Rights After their successful initial achievement, the informal group decided that a more permanent, formalized organization was needed to monitor the implementation of the amended GSP as well as for research (providing an independent source of information) and educational (awareness

---

4 Support for the ILRF in general was also given by retired officials from the US Department of Labor (Compa and Vogt 2001). Ronald Reagan's term of presidency was 1981–1988. Jimmy Carter had served before him and the presidency of George Bush followed that of Reagan.

5 The ILRF and other plaintiffs also filed a lawsuit against President Bush and the US Trade Representative for failure to enforce the social clause amendment to the GSP in 1990 (ILRF 1990).

raising) purposes, and in 1986 the ILRF was established. Among its activities were conferences on related issues organized for the members and staff of the US Congress and the general public, the publication of reports, and the provision of information to the US Congress and the US Trade Representative. Although no permanent, paid staff was hired until 1990, the organization was fairly active, partly due to a large and active Board of Directors. In 1986, the Board of Directors and the International Advisory Council consisted of some 50 persons (Interview with Harvey 2004, ILRF 1986).

The focus on worker rights is seen as vital by the ILRF early on, i.e., to incorporate respect for international labour rights in official US foreign and trade policy and the policies of US TNCs.[6] At the time, US legislation was seen as giving incentives to TNCs to take advantage of 'oppressed workers and labor movements overseas' (ILRF 1986). Denials of these rights were considered especially detrimental for developing countries, as they 'tend[s] to perpetuate poverty, to limit the benefits of economic development and growth to narrow, privileged elites and to sow the seeds of social instability and political rebellion ... The blatant exploitation of unprotected workers undermines the development of self-reliant local economies' (ILRF 1986).

These incentives were also seen to contribute to capital flight and overseas production, whereas labour was immobile, and to undermine the conditions for all workers, including those in the US. Arguments of a more contentious nature were also heard as part of the advocacy, with occasional references to terms such as 'GATTzilla' and 'Maquilamonster' when discussing various aspects of TNCs, US trade policies and the free trade agenda in general (Cavanagh et al. 1988: vii, Brecher and Costello 1991: 9, 11).

The claim of the ILRF was that 'an open trading system can only be sustained if workers are given as much of a stake in it as consumers and financiers', and this called for an effort parallel to that of organizations like Amnesty International and Human Rights Watch – i.e., organizations that focused world attention on violations of workers' rights. Trade unions and collective bargaining are seen as essential to this struggle. The ILRF also proposes a number of strategic activities in this pursuit. These include transnational networking and movement coalitions, upward harmonization, coordination of activities, democratization, and also a multi-level system of regulation with different forms of 'ownership' apart from the nation state, similar to the multi-stakeholder initiatives appearing in the second half of the 1990s (Cavanagh et al. 1988: vi, xiv, Brecher and Costello 1991: 34, ILRF 1986).

One can note that the ILRF actually does make use of 'urgent actions' similar to those of Amnesty International to mobilize action in pressing situations around the world and has participated in multi-stakeholder initiatives such as the Fair Labor Association.

---

6   The US has, as of June 2009, ratified only two of the eight core labour rights conventions of the ILO; namely, the Convention on the Abolition of Forced Labour (105), ratified in 1991, and the Convention on the Worst Forms of Child Labour (182), ratified in 1999.

The NAFTA Negotiations   Towards the end of the 1980s, one major focus of the ILRF was the trade negotiations for the North American Free Trade Agreement (NAFTA). This time, the ILRF formed a coalition (Alliance for Responsible Trade) with counterparts in Canada and Mexico to develop a common strategy, which would consider the social conditions in all three countries. There had been growing resistance on the part of developing countries to attempts to link labour rights clauses to trade agreements. The aim of the coalition was to achieve recognition of the importance of good labour and environmental conditions as well as investment rules protective of national interest in trade relations (Interview with Harvey 2004, ILRF 1986).

However, the work of the coalition on NAFTA was not as successful as in the case of the GSP, as there was no direct link between labour rights and NAFTA itself. Instead, a separate, side agreement, entitled the North American Agreement on Labor Cooperation (NAALC), came into force in 1994.[7] However, once again, the NGOs were able to create a platform for further action, since a complaint mechanism was included similar to that in the GSP. Immediately, in 1994, when both NAFTA and NAALC came into force, the ILRF and other organizations filed the first complaint, concerning the Sony Corporation.[8] However, due to the construction of the side agreement, the complaint mechanism was not as efficient.

The filing of complaints in general (both GSP and NAFTA) also required close cooperation with local NGOs in GSP-favoured countries and Mexico, both to provide information and as co-petitioners. An example of this is the delegation to Guatemala, led by the ILRF, in connection with the filing of a petition. Over the years, the ILRF has established an extensive network of contacts and relies heavily for its activities on its partners worldwide, which may include local NGOs, academics, trade unions, and others (ILRF 1992, Interview with Athreya 2003).

The Child Labour Issue   Apart from the work on NAFTA, the ILRF also became involved and took leadership in other coalitions, such as the Child Labor

---

7   The NAALC is the first international agreement on labour issues that is linked to a free trade agreement. The Commission for Labour Cooperation (established for the cooperation between member countries on labour issues and ensurance of effective enforcement of domestic labour laws) is the first international body on labour rights since the founding of ILO.

8   Sony was alleged to have unduly interfered in the rights of association of its workers in Mexico, and the complaint claimed that the Mexican government had conspired in that suppression and therefore failed to enforce applicable labour law. The ILRF was highly critical of the proposed measures to remedy the situation – meetings of Mexican authorities to inform the workers, discussions with local authorities, and appointing a panel of independent experts for investigations. In 1996, the Commission for Labor Cooperation claimed that significant developments were taking place in Mexico in the areas of labour-related legislation, labour-management relations and labour organization and no further steps were taken. The critics considered this a defeat for the NAALC institution as a whole (ILRF 1995a, 1995b, Commission for Labor Cooperation 1996).

Coalition (Interview with Athreya 2003). The issue of child labour has been an important part of the work of the ILRF since the early 1990s. This interest had specific results: the creation of a labelling system for hand-knotted carpets called RUGMARK in 1994, the Foul Ball Campaign in 1996, the Sanders Amendment in 1997 and the participation in the Global March Against Child Labor launched in 1998. The Sanders Amendment involved campaigning for a provision banning the importation of products made with forced or indentured child labour (though not child labour in general). The ILRF immediately put the amendment to the test by filing a complaint the year the amendment was adopted, targeting the South Asian carpet industry.

Global Exchange

At about the same time (1988), the US organization Global Exchange was created (see also Appendix 2). Global Exchange was founded by a group of individuals working together on issues concerning development, social justice, right and access to food at the San Francisco-based think tank Institute for Food and Policy.[9] Some of the members of this group had previously been involved in the anti-apartheid movement and the movement expressing US solidarity with Central America.

There were two main reasons for the establishment of Global Exchange. First, there was the wish to take progressive issues and values to a more mainstream audience by using a way of communicating that was more accessible to the average population than the 'echo-chamber of the Left'. Second, the need was felt to educate Americans about the situation in other countries and present alternative information to what was being provided by mainstream media in the US. Global Exchange describes the organization as a 'player in the progressive movement to transform US foreign policy and support grassroots development' (Interview with Mark 2004, quote from Global Change 1994: 2).

Visions of Internationalism   The central principle or foundational ideology for the organization (i.e., internationalism) was highlighted in its very first newsletter, with a reference to the labour internationalism of the nineteenth century but refashioned to fit a globalized era. This internationalism is meant to bridge the gap between 'us' and 'them' as well as expose the false dichotomy between the domestic and the foreign in order to bring various grassroots initiatives together and strengthen the internationalist movement as a whole. The purpose is to 'mold them [grassroots' initiatives] into an integral whole that will not only provide sustenance to our allies overseas but will also strengthen a similar movement for change here at home' (Global Exchange 1989b: 2, see also Benjamin and Freedman 1989). These principles take the form of both commandments and a political manifesto, and list a number of what can be defined as moral principles for individuals, such as

9   They are Medea Benjamin, Kevin Danaher, Kirsten Moller and Kathie Klarreich (Global Exchange 1994: 1–2).

'develop a sense of compassion', or 'We try to live simply', as well as more issue-related principles that include references to specific rights (economic rights, rights of workers or women), international issues (debt cancellation) or groups (poor farmers and landless peasants) (Global Exchange 1991: 8–9). The position on international trade and TNCs is explicitly expressed in two separate statements:

> International trade should be based on mutual benefit, not the exploitation of the poor by the rich. The negotiation of international trade agreements should include significant input by workers and the poor.

And:

> We believe that businesses – especially transnational corporations – should be responsible to their workers and to the communities where they do business (Global Exchange 1991: 8–9).

This laid the groundwork for the issues that Global Exchange were to address, including views that visits in other countries should be made with a purpose, the importance of partnership with people and organizations, aid as solidarity not philanthropy, human rights, Fairtrade, and similar items. This partly resembles a political programme to build a completely new political and economic system.

This internationalism has distinct leftist sympathies (including a rather biased support for Cuba), although the ideology of socialism is not fully embraced. Top-down and statist socialism, including the 'rigid, ideological aversion to entrepreneurialism and the use of market mechanisms', is criticized, and grassroots civil society is recognized as having shortcomings (bureaucracy, dependency and corruption). However, these failures by developing countries and grassroots movements are explained by blaming the external forces trying to undermine them, including the foreign policies of the US (Global Exchange 1991: 7).

Educating the US Public   The creation of Global Exchange involved the merger of already existing but uncoordinated initiatives on exchanges between the US and other countries, such as Africa Exchange, Caribbean Exchange and Central America Exchange (Interview with Mark 2004, Global Exchange 1989a: 1). The organization thus began its work with established activities surrounding exchange programmes, including a number of staff, which in combination with the ideas laid out on internationalism, enabled the organization to get up and running in a short time.

The organization from the start saw its role as a facilitator in communication and cooperation between various groups in the US and different regions of the world – hence its name, Global Exchange. The activities in the beginning go in three directions: mobilizing the internationalist movement and organizing facilitating mechanisms for this mobilization, working on raising awareness and support, and practical solidarity work (Global Exchange 1989c: 3).

A central idea was the development of so-called Reality Tours, a new kind of tourism, where Americans were able to travel and discover the realities of people's lives in other countries. Upon returning home, the travellers are supported by resources provided by Global Exchange, inspiring them to maintain contact with the grassroots organization and support continued activism. In the initial years, the tours often targeted issues and areas that either were controversial (problem of the landless, or US military bases abroad) or less known to the general public (underdeveloped areas in the US). The first Global Exchange Reality Tour, in Appalachia, US, drew attention from the media and others, with both negative and positive responses to the claim that underdeveloped areas existed in the US (Global Exchange 1990a: 1).

These Reality Tours have another purpose in the work of Global Exchange, representing a kind of 'citizen's diplomacy' as a balance to the foreign diplomacy of the US government. Not only are the Reality Tours an important strategy in the work of the organization, they also make up around 50 per cent (as of 2004) of the total revenue of Global Exchange and contribute to its existence (Interview with Mark 2004).

Another way of making the work of other grassroots organizations known is through publications or 'speaking tours' in the US by representatives of these organizations (for example, a Honduran peasant leader or labour organizer), giving those living in the US the opportunity to learn first-hand of their experiences. Other educational and awareness-raising activities include the publication of books and articles, distribution of audio tapes with recorded speeches (by, e.g., Noam Chomsky and Ralph Nader), videos and the creation of a Speaker's Bureau of experts in the various areas of concern of Global Exchange.

Exchange and link-building activities also included more practical aspects, manifested as direct material assistance (monetary relief and support, and equipment supply), support for human rights activists, partnership programmes and development of alternative trade. Alternative trade not only served the practical purpose of building links between producers in poor countries and consumers in wealthy countries, but also functioned to educate the US public about inequalities in trade and development. Activities organized in the so-called Bay Area of San Francisco, in the form of screening films, mounting exhibitions, and presenting seminars, were other important mobilization and awareness-raising activities (Global Exchange 1990b, 1990c, 1992: 5).

Multilateral Institutions   Although the statements and writings issued by Global Exchange related to TNCs, TNCs were not an explicit target for the organization's initial campaign activities. Rather, TNCs appear as part of other matters of concern to the organization — for example, as themes for Reality Tours, or in discussions of their connection to the policies of the IMF or the World Bank. However, the Global Exchange position on TNCs is quite clear. They are seen mainly as powerful and sometimes even 'omnipotent' actors interfering in the politics of foreign countries (examples are Guatemala, Iran and Chile), sourcing raw materials and cheap labour from the Third World 'While foreign corporations can provide much-needed jobs, the trade-offs are often severe – low wages and benefits, no job security, and environmental destruction' (Benjamin and Freedman 1989: 141). It is not until the mid-1990s that TNCs become part of an explicit campaign combined with activities directed towards the IMF and the World Bank. This includes the campaign on Nike beginning in the mid-1990s, discussed in Chapter 7.

Clean Clothes Campaign

The Clean Clothes Campaign (CCC) originated in The Netherlands in 1990, in direct response to a labour conflict at an Asian subcontractor of the largest Dutch clothing retailer, C&A (Ascoly and Zeldenrust 1999, see also Appendix 2). This gave rise to sustained direct street actions targeting C&A and the later decision to form an organization for continued action. Within a few years, the areas of interest expanded to include other issues and companies, and also extended to other European countries. An important issue during these initial years was the development of the CCC Model Code or the Fair Trade Charter for Garments, as it was called at the time (this will be discussed in Chapter 8).

Initial Years of the CCC   The immediate reason for the creation of the CCC was the news in The Netherlands that a subsidiary of a large British clothing manufacturer in the Free Trade Zone of Bataan, the Philippines, had closed down its plant and fired the workforce for demanding legal minimum wages (minimum wages had just been raised by the Philippine government). The fired women workers organized picket lines in front of the plant that lasted for a year and called for boycotts in Britain of the British contractor. The news of these actions by the workers in the Philippines spread from their local trade unions to The Netherlands through various national organizations in The Netherlands with contacts in the Philippines (CCC 1993b: 5, Ascoly and Zeldenrust 1999).

As the Dutch-based retailer C&A procured part of its clothing from the British contractor, C&A was targeted by various Dutch NGOs, including consumer, development and solidarity organizations. The Dutch Center for Research on Multinational Corporations (SOMO) had coincidentally begun research on the C&A subcontracting chain only a few years earlier (CCC 1995a: 1). The findings from this research became an important resource for the CCC and the campaign against C&A was launched partly on the basis of the data that had been collected. This contributed to there being credible information in support of actions against C&A right from the start.

Direct action was organized in the form of picket lines in front of C&A shops in Amsterdam. The picket line action also included 'inappropriate' behaviour, such as loud noise (drum bands) and the burning of clothes. This led to violent confrontations between the demonstrators and the police, including arrests. These partly violent actions as well as the case in itself (new to the Dutch public) succeeded in attracting a lot of attention, not least from the media. These actions spread to other cities in The Netherlands and also to Belgium and the UK. This particular action was in part successful when the Philippine workers received some of the salary due to them, although they were not able to regain their employment. However, after some further research on C&A, similar cases of labour rights abuses were discovered that could be linked to C&A. It was decided to continue the action by formalizing the collaboration between the organizations. Initially, the work was maintained only by volunteers from the participating organizations (CCC 1993a: 2, 4, 1993b: 5, Ascoly and Zeldenrust 1999, Interview with Eyskoot 2004).

The choice of the name of the organization, Clean Clothes Campaign, also contributed to frame the issue, referring to the situation in the garment industry perceived by the organizations as follows 'The "Clean Clothes Campaign" … aims to focus attention on *the dirty labour conditions* and … circumstances in the worldwide garment industry, and to press for changes' (CCC 1993a: 2).[10] The companies associated with these dirty labour conditions were of course implicitly seen as 'dirty' companies involved in 'dirty activities'. In the organization's awareness-raising activities explaining these conditions and the link to a European context, an example of a framing attempt expressed in one of the first printed materials in English reads:

> The clothes we wear are usually produced by women, under miserable working conditions and for extremely low wages. Women work for a mere trifle long hours in for example garment factories in the so-called third world, in – illegal – sweatshops or at home in Europe. The big retail stores subcontract the production of the clothes they sell. Very often, the subcontracting chain is long, stretching all over the world, for example from the retail store, via intermediary traders to the factory owner who in turn subcontracts to an illegal sweatshop and to homeworkers. In the final analysis, it is the retailers who place the orders. They are firmly in command of the production. They, in fact, determine what is produced where, for what wages and under what conditions (CCC 1993a: 2).

In this way, large retail companies (seen as irresponsible actors) and consumers (portrayed as potential activists and critical consumers) are linked to both far away and also more local exploited women workers. It is important to note that the CCC also refers to sweatshop conditions in Europe, contradicting the claim by some critics that Northern NGOs always point to appalling conditions in the South but forget what is happening in their own backyards.

In these initial years, the CCC focused its activities on one company only, C&A. However, after some time, the strategy of direct action in the street and targeting C&A was partly abandoned, at least as the only strategy (see also the chapter on Nike). The CCC's actions were not yielding the desired results. The general public was also given the idea that C&A was the only company where these labour conditions were present (CCC 1993a: 3, 1995a: 2).

---

10   Italics added by the author.

Expanding the Work   When the direct actions taken against C&A in the initial years began to lose their attraction, the organization decided to expand its activities. It chose to include garment retailers in general in the campaign and also to broaden the campaign. A more general approach to consumers was also developed, with the strategy being to appeal to consumers to be more conscious and to provide them with alternatives. This was done by providing them with information on the garment industry, by giving talks and participating in discussions, and by lending support to the sale of clothes through third world shops and other alternatives (CCC 1993a: 2).

An important activity was to persuade politicians to influence decisions in support of the workers in the garment industry, both nationally and internationally. It is estimated that there were some 8,000 illegal sweatshop workers in The Netherlands at the time. The CCC also began campaigning for sweatshop employees and home workers, advocating for residence and employment permits and improved legislation for these groups. Furthermore, more direct and practical solidarity measures were taken, in the form of financial assistance and a strike fund (CCC 1993a: 5, 8, 1993b: 3).

An overall strategy for this work was collaboration with existing organizations as platforms for the activities of the CCC 'They already have an office, staff, contacts and experience. That way we can reach far more people than when we try to do everything ourselves' (CCC 1995a: 1). It was also seen as more efficient for the organizations that already worked with related issues to just add a 'CCC component'. In addition to continued mobilization of the general public's attention, other NGOs were targeted (not least key NGOs), and conferences were held for exchange of information and experiences. The organization later sought to expand its activities, especially to gain contacts with garment workers (CCC 1993b: 3, 9).[11]

Spread of the Initiative   When expanding the work of the CCC, the goals were to develop new links and exchange information with like-minded organizations in Europe, and also to develop an international network. A European project was established, with funding from the EU, where CCC was presented as a model for other groups. The strategy was to engage NGOs in other countries, through person-to-person contacts in meetings and the dissemination of information, and by visits of Asian organizers and activists.

One strategy was to launch a newsletter in English. The objective was to maintain and expand networking among groups in different countries as well as to function as a medium for exchange and learning among the participants in the network. The newsletter included discussions of different strategies on how to approach the work and problems associated with these issues. Protectionism was one issue where the organization made its position clear 'Just stopping the import of goods on which children have worked will worsen the problem for workers

---

11   Labour conditions in East Europe was at the time a new issue (CCC 1996a).

in the poor countries and will work in a protectionist way for the industrialized countries' (CCC 1993b: 13). The newsletter also included news from other, similar events and the activities of other organizations, including personal statements from workers (as witnesses). The CCC thus were aware of other initiatives and organizations internationally, e.g., the Maquiladora Standards of Conduct, the SEWA (Self Employed Women's Association), etc.

As a result of these activities, other national CCC coalitions were created in Belgium (1995), France (1995), the UK (1996), Germany (1996), Austria (1997), Sweden (1997), Spain (1997), and Switzerland (1999). The creation of national CCC coalitions was often preceded by uncoordinated activities by the participating NGOs, similar to those in The Netherlands. The composition of these coalitions varied, but they generally consisted of a mixture of small and large NGOs involved in women's issues, solidarity work, the youth movement, Fairtrade, church-oriented activities and trade unions (as of 2009 some 200 NGOs are part of the different national CCC coalitions) (CCC 1993b: 8, 2004).

Work on the CCC Model Code of Conduct   Apart from the activities discussed above, the key activity was to press for the responsibility of retailers. This work focused mainly on the development of the CCC Model Code of Conduct.[12]

The main aim of the Model Code was to improve working conditions in the garment industry, and the content was based on the core labour rights of the ILO conventions. This work began in The Netherlands, in cooperation with the national trade union and Dutch Oxfam, and in cooperation with Asian labour networks and organizations. A proposal came into being in 1993, although it was not presented to the Dutch retailers at the time. Initially, the preliminary text was used as a petition for support from other NGOs and potential signatories before being presented to the retailers. The initial idea of the CCC Model Code was that it was to be linked to an independent institution for monitoring, reporting by retailers, handling of complaints and sanctions. Retailers adhering to the Model Code would receive the right to use a trademark as clean clothes sellers (CCC 1993a, 1993b: 3, 2000b).

When the Model Code eventually was presented to the Dutch Federation of Retailers in the Textiles in late 1994, the Federation stated that they agreed in principle but had some reservations. The individual retail companies responded by developing their own codes of conduct, which were much weaker (CCC 2000b). The Federation eventually rejected the idea of a Model Code, but two smaller trade associations eventually decided to join the initiative (CCC 1995a: 2, CCC 1995b, CCC 1996a). The development of a European-wide Model Code continued until an agreement among the participating organizations was reached in 1997.

Although this initiative was successful in calling attention to the issue and reaching agreement on a Model Code, not all of the initial goals of the initiative have been achieved. There is, for example, no trademark linked to the Model Code and no independent institution. There are, however, a number of national

---

12   On the Fair Trade Charter, see CCC 1993b: 3.

pilot projects on independent monitoring. The Fair Wear Foundation in The Netherlands (established in 1999) is the most established of the pilot projects, with a multi-stakeholder organization involved in auditing member companies' recommendations to consumers and advocating for a European verification initiative (Fair Wear Foundation 2003).

We have seen here how organizations in the late 1980s and, in particular, the 1990s, began addressing the negative aspects of TNC activity, i.e., framing the issue and engaging in activities as norm entrepreneurs of CSR. As was shown in the discussion of the focus organizations above, the Activists were at the forefront of this development. However, other organizations were soon to become involved. In the next chapter we will take a close look at the two other categories of CSR organizations, Business Initiatives and Multi-stakeholders, and their respective focus organizations, as well as conclude with a discussion of the implications of this development.

Chapter 6
Involvement by Business Initiative and Multi-stakeholder Organizations

The previous chapter dealt with norm entrepreneurs in the form of Activist Organizations, the kind of organization that you would expect to engage in social change activities. However, in the case of the development of CSR, there are two additional categories of organizations that have become involved in the process: Business Initiatives Organizations and Multi-stakeholder Organizations. To some extent, the organizations in these categories developed as a reaction to the activities of the Activists, when new actors who did not belong to Activist Organizations or identify themselves as activists became involved in the process. A closer look at these two categories of norm entrepreneurs will illustrate the distinction between the categories and the effects from this development. Within each of these categories, focus organizations will also be discussed in-depth; they include the International Business Leaders Forum (Business Initiatives category) and the Fairtrade Labelling Organisations International (Multi-stakeholders category).

Business Initiative Organizations

The Business Initiatives category consists of organizations whose members are basically companies or individual business leaders (see Appendix 1). Approximately one-fifth of the CSR organizations selected for this study belong to this category, a majority of which emerged in the 1990s. Like the Activists, most of these organizations are located in Europe or North America, with the exception of Empresa, which is located in South America. The appearance of this group of organizations is to a large extent a response to the influence of the activities of the Activists. The group represents novel approaches to CSR from the business community.

Overview of the Category

If one disregards The Global Sullivan Principles (mainly active in the anti-apartheid struggle), and the mainly UK-oriented Business in the Community, one can see that the first Business Initiatives were established in the late 1980s with the creation of the Caux Round Table in 1986 and Social Venture Network in 1987.

These early initiatives had very different motives for engagement, in comparison both with the Activists and with each other. In the case of the Caux Round Table, trade tension in the 1980s between the US/Europe and Japan was the motive for a series of dialogues between business leaders from these countries, conducted in Caux, Switzerland, that eventually led to the creation of the organization. Although the future of free trade was the organization's immediate concern, the organization was also influenced by the Minnesota Project on Corporate Responsibility (established in 1978) and the launch of 'The Minnesota Principles: Towards An Ethical Basis for Global Business' in 1992. The Minnesota Principles played an important part in the creation of the Caux Round Table Principles for Business, launched in 1994, in which the initial concerns about free trade merged with the increasing attention being paid to CSR in the 1990s. Today, the organization consists of a small, low profile network of international business leaders aiming to reduce the 'social and economic threats to world peace and stability' and promote 'moral capitalism' (CEBC 2005a, 2005b, quotes from CRT 2002).

The members of the second organization, Social Venture Network (SVN), had from the outset chosen to combine business activities with a social mission as their business strategy (member companies include the US-based Ben and Jerry's Ice Cream and a socially responsible mutual fund, the Calvert Group). Defining themselves as social entrepreneurs (SVN 2002), the members of the SVN merge characteristics of a traditional industry or trade association with those of a CSR advocacy organization. An example of this advocacy is seen in their contribution to the establishment of yet another Business Initiative, Business for Social Responsibility, in 1992, and to standards for CSR launched in 1999.

Although they were early norm entrepreneurs in the field of Business Initiatives, neither the Caux Round Table nor Social Venture Network are as well known as some of the organizations that emerged from 1990 on. This is when the majority of the organizations in this category emerged. They include the International Business Leaders Forum, Business for Social Responsibility (BSR), CSR Europe and the World Business Council on Sustainable Development (WBCSD). Lately, organizations have also been created that combine CSR and industry specific concerns or that focus on a particular issue (not included in this study). Among these are the Ethical Tea Partnership, the International Council on Mining and Metals, and the World Cocoa Foundation.

Aims   A closer look at the aims of these organizations reveals that they often refer to responsible business practices, moral or value-based leadership, and promoting a positive impact on society. An oft-recurring concept is sustainable development, or similarly, sustainable world or sustainable growth. Other concepts cited are business ethics, triple bottom line, moral or principled capitalism, and free, fair, transparent market economy. Less reference is made to arguments used by the Activists – terms such as economic and social justice and human rights or explicit references to the negative aspects of TNC activity rarely appear, apart from the occasional reference to disadvantaged groups. Here, the approach is rather to focus on the positive aspects of and the 'business case' for CSR; i.e., to portray aspects of CSR that benefit the companies or enhance business operations in general. This can be interpreted as translating criticism into what ought to be done, instead of emphasizing what the problem is – i.e., 'a language' that the business community can relate to and accept. It may also be seen as the manifestation of a genuine attempt to address the issue from a business perspective, finding an approach to the issue on the companies' own terms. This does not set aside instrumental motives as reasons for involvement in CSR, i.e., by showing willingness to adjust, even if only through lip service, one hopes to avoid further criticism or the development towards binding regulation. It is clear that the 'carrot approach' is the preferred strategy, in contrast to the combined stick and carrot approach adopted by Activists.

Activities   When it comes to the activities of the Business Initiatives, some occur more frequently than others. These activities include creating tools, models, and principles for business and providing these tools, as well as other services, to companies. Activities also include networking, forum building, dialogue among companies and stakeholders, and the dissemination of good practices, both internally and externally. There is also a focus on activities directed towards aligning the interests of leaders and stakeholders, partnerships and sharing responsibility. The activities of the organizations both assist member companies in addressing and/or managing CSR (internal activities) and in taking part in the development of CSR in general (external activities). In this way, the organizations also become involved in a process of 'norm construction'. Some of these activities could be defined as persuasion (activities such as sponsoring dialogues, networking, and forum building). However, one can also see evidence of social processes relating to demonstration and socialization (discussed further in Chapters 7 and 8) in the creation of tools and models and the sharing of best practices. We will now take a closer look at one of the organizations in this category: the International Business Leaders Forum.

International Business Leaders Forum

The International Business Leaders Forum (IBLF) is an organization that aims to promote 'responsible business leadership', partnerships and 'solutions' for sustainable development, with a focus on recently established and emerging market economies (IBLF 2000: 1, see also Appendix 2). Initially focusing on Eastern Europe, IBLF activities now involve countries in all regions of the world and cover issues involving tourism, health, enterprise development, transparency and corruption, the Millennium Development Goals, promotion of economic stability and the social impact of globalization. Activities include advocacy of CSR and partnership, brokerage of partners, capacity-building (training) and dissemination of ideas and good practices.

Background and Initial Focus of Activities   The IBLF (initially called the Prince of Wales Business Leaders Forum) developed out of two initiatives with the active participation of HRH The Prince of Wales (of the UK), commonly referred to as Prince Charles (hereafter the Prince of Wales). The first initiative concerned the activities of the organization Business in the Community, a British organization of 850 member companies (as of 2009) that operates through a network of local business-led partnerships working to make businesses increase their positive impact on society. Business in the Community was established in 1982, as a result of concern at the time over high youth unemployment rates and inner-city riots in the UK. The Prince of Wales has taken an active part in the activities of Business in the Community and has been its President since 1985 (IBLF 2000: 2, see also www. bitc.org.uk). Both organizations, the IBLF and Business in the Community, are part of what is called the Prince's Charities, a group of organizations that address issues on education, health, responsible business, environment, and the arts.

The IBLF was the result of the meeting in 1990 (initiated personally by the Prince of Wales) that assembled international business leaders in Charleston, South Carolina, US. The meeting was attended by some 100 people from 13 countries (The Prince of Wales 2000). In addition to the Prince of Wales' interest in environmental issues, his concern for the effects of globalization on society and the transition from communism to a market economy, including the role of business in these transformations, were other motives for this initiative. The Prince of Wales was instrumental in the creation of the IBLF, and since then has taken an active part in the work of the organization, in addition to acting as its President.

The idea of the meeting in Charleston was to address the question of what role business could play in the challenges perceived at the time:

> environmental degradation, population increase and unbridled urban growth … the sudden emergence of free market economies following the collapse of Communism … risks to social stability, ethics and a sense of community. Capitalism had to show a more human face (IBLF 2005).

As a consequence of these challenges, one of the objectives expressed at the time was to create a forum for education, the spread of good practices and the development of partnership (The Prince of Wales 1992). Note should be taken that the interpretation of globalization expressed here is different than that expressed by the Activists, discussed in the previous chapter.

The arguments given to business for engaging in sustainable development were that business had the 'means to make things happen', a 'poor workforce and an uncertain market' undermined success, the business case (markets for new products or/and sustainable growth), and mere survival. This was expressed in the speech the Prince of Wales made at the 1992 Davos meeting of the World Economic Forum:

> business is the core of modern society. But with that privileged position goes a special responsibility. I do not believe it is scare-mongering to say that if business does not take that responsibility seriously, someone else will. You may find yourselves operating in a much more collectively-minded, government-dominated, anti-business environment (The Prince of Wales 1992).

As can be seen, there is also fear that criticisms of globalization will lead to changes in society that could undermine the liberal market economy at the time. Initially, the work of the IBLF was focused mainly on the transition economies of Eastern Europe and on the environment, which have continued to be important areas of work. This work involved meetings, launching various initiatives (e.g., management and other training programmes), the establishment of national Business Leaders Forums in Hungary (1992), the Czech Republic (1993), and Poland (1993) and contributing to the creation of sister organizations.

Projects such as reforestation, the reduction of emissions relating to mining operations in Brazil and Canada, providing energy in Africa and India from sustainable sources, and the production of recyclable vehicles are examples of the initial work of the IBLF. The launching of the International Hotels Environment Initiative in 1992 (presently the Tourism Partnership) is also one of the activities initiated in this period (The Prince of Wales 1992).

Expansion and Engaging with International Organizations   In spite of the focus on the transition economies of Eastern Europe and the environment, activities also took place in other parts of the world fairly early. One example is the establishment of the so-called INSIGHT programmes in Brazil and India in 1992 and 1993, respectively (other countries involved in later INSIGHT programmes are Bangladesh, Russia, UK, USA, and South Africa). The INSIGHT programme is an initiative of the Prince of Wales that brings together people from various parts of society to exchange views and share experiences. The programme aims to be cross-sectoral and cross-cultural and operates at the local, regional or international level (IBLF 2000). The programme bears a strong resemblance to the Reality Tours of Global Exchange. Although the issues, countries of interest and the general approach are quite different, the purpose and outcome share the idea of mobilizing individuals for action through their own personal experience.

Activities also involved various meetings with key actors, the formation of partnerships with business organizations and businesses, the creation of programmes and projects in various areas (such as youth, hotels and the environment, civil society and sustainable development). The information disseminated through publication of fairly extensive reports covered issues of community involvement, surveys on the opinions of young future business leaders, partnerships and sustainable development. Here there is a resemblance to the Activists; only the target groups are different. It is not the general public that the IBLF targets with their mobilizing strategies, but current business and community leaders as well as future leaders.[1]

---

1   Reports issued by the IBLF in the initial years include titles such as: *Corporate Community Involvement in Europe: A Report on Changing Trends and New Developments in Corporate Giving and Good Corporate Citizenship in Five Western European Countries*, (1992); *Corporate Reputation in Tomorrow's Marketplace: A Survey of the Opinions and*

In 1992, the IBLF began extending its activities and network of contacts to include work with various international organizations, both inter-governmental and non-governmental. This initially involved contacts with the UN Environment Programme (UNEP), the UN Development Programme (UNDP), and the World Bank. Two years later, in 1994, the IBLF approached the EU for collaboration and funding from the EU PHARE programme, which at the time was assisting the transition of Poland and Hungary after the fall of the Soviet Union (PHARE now provides assistance to new EU member states). EU funding has been provided, for example, for the INSIGHT programme mentioned above (IBLF 2000, 2004, Interview with Moberg 2003, 2005).

This cooperation led to a series of policy meetings with the World Bank, organized around the role of business in development and relating to issues such as micro-enterprise development and information technology. This contributed to other projects, such as a joint mission to Colombia in 1995 to study the oil-extracting sector. In 1996, a four-year programme was funded by the World Bank and UNDP called 'Business as Partner in Development'. This close involvement with IGOs sets the IBLF apart from other focus organizations and most other CSR organizations (see also below for a further discussion on the issue of partnership).

This involvement also included attending the World Economic Forum meeting in Davos, Switzerland in 1992, where the Prince of Wales addressed the issue of global responsibility of business (IBLF 2000, 2004, speech in Davos quoted above) – several years before the appearance of the UN Secretary General, Kofi Annan, at the World Economic Forum in Davos in 1999. It is worth noting that this call for involvement by the Prince of Wales did not receive the same attention as Kofi Annan's appearance seven years later, which led to the creation of the UN Global Compact. This lends support to the argument that in 1992, 'norm tipping' in CSR had not as yet occurred.

In the following section the third category of norm entrepreneurs will be discussed: Multi-stakeholder Organizations. These organizations began to emerge somewhat later than the Business Initiatives and take on partially different characteristics.

Multi-stakeholder Organizations

The third category identified in my research is made up of CSR organizations and initiatives that I define as Multi-stakeholder Organizations (hereafter Multi-stakeholders, see Appendix 1). These represent private, voluntary regulatory frameworks that may involve government or IGO representation. In this case, the

---

Expectations of the Young Business Leaders of Today and Tomorrow, (1993); and *Partnerships for Sustainable Development: The Role of Business and Industry*, (April 1994).

concept of hybrid organizations is sometimes applicable, but Multi-stakeholders are generally seen as non-governmental efforts.[2]

The Multi-stakeholders of interest here involve 'like-minded' as well as 'non-like-minded' individuals and organizations. Groups of like-minded organizations only I refer to as coalitions. The participating stakeholders often have diverging views and interests, and may consist of companies, NGOs, IGOs, government representatives and others, but they all engage with each other to address a specific concern. They could be said to be found in a grey area involving business, policy making and social values.

The concept of stakeholders derives from modern stakeholder theory within management research, which is actually a collection of several theories with contributions from many disciplines. In general, stakeholder theory explains business activity as mainly consisting of value creation and trade. Stakeholder theory is thus different from what has been called the standard story of business activity, shareholder or even cowboy capitalism, with regard to views on business attitudes towards individuals, groups in society and relations to the state. Stakeholder theory may be defined as 'a managerial conception of organizational strategy and ethics', where the success of a company depends on its relations with certain groups in society and on balancing and maximizing their interests over time. The primary stakeholder groups that companies face, according to the stakeholder theory, are customers, employees, suppliers, communities, and investors (Freeman 1984, Freeman and Phillips 2002: 333).

In Multi-stakeholder Organizations there is, however, no company that manages other stakeholders. Rather, the multi-stakeholder approach is ideally seen as collectively managed governance structures devoted to a specific issue of CSR, where a company involved is but one of the participating stakeholders. All participating stakeholders are equals.

Most of the organizations in the Multi-stakeholders category represent developments of the norm cascade stage, i.e., they developed in the mid- to the late 1990s. However, among these organizations one can also find early movers. One of these, the Fairtrade Labelling Organizations International, will be discussed later in this section.

Overview of the Category

The organizations included in this category started to develop towards the end of the 1980s and particularly in the 1990s. Thus, they appeared after the emergence of the Activist Organizations and somewhat after the emergence of the Business Initiatives Organizations. The development of CSR can therefore be described as beginning with Activists consisting of NGOs critical of TNC behaviour, followed

---

2 The multi-stakeholder organizations here should not be confused with another kind of hybrid organization, the so-called quasi-government organizations or quasi NGO (QUANGO) that perform close to government functions in a private form.

by a response from the business community (the creation of Business Initiatives) and later by the development of Multi-stakeholder Organizations. In the Multi-stakeholder case, organizations from the other two categories join forces for dialogue, negotiations and cooperation.

Aims   This group of organizations mainly focuses on work relating to reporting, accountability, standards and codes of conduct, certification, monitoring and inspection – i.e., on concrete schemes and mechanisms (tools) related to CSR. In this work with schemes and mechanisms, there is some reference made to international labour standards, working conditions, child labour, Fairtrade, and sustainable development. However, these are not the dominant features of Multi-stakeholders. The schemes or mechanisms developed to achieve the aims set forth by these organizations are as important as the aims themselves, and it actually becomes difficult to distinguish between aims and activities. An example of this is found in the overall aim of the Fairtrade Labelling Organization International (FLO), which is 'to improve the position of the poor and disadvantaged producers in the developing world, by setting the Fairtrade standards and by creating the framework that enables trade to take place at conditions favourable to them' (FLO 2003:17).

Activities   The fusion of aims and activities is also apparent in the activities of these organizations, which are typically the development of specific systems for voluntary regulation. Furthermore, the activities centre on dialogue and consensus building, connecting and convening different stakeholders, and consultation. These activities differ from the activities of organizations in the Activists category. While some advocacy is apparent (regarding specific initiatives or issues that the organizations are promoting), it is downplayed or presented in a neutral manner. As an example, the activities of the Fairtrade Labelling Organization International are: '(1) defining international Fairtrade Standards, (2) certifying and auditing producer organizations and traders involved in labelled Fairtrade and (3) providing support to producer organizations that need external support' (FLO 2003).

The first organization that emerged within this category was concerned with the social labelling of Fairtrade products, initially coffee. This first social labelling initiative was followed by others, and also by initiatives focused on developing schemes for monitoring workplaces and remediation measures. Another stream of initiatives that developed at the same time suggested ways to manage CSR within companies, such as accountability standards, implementation of codes of conduct, corporate governance systems, and sustainability reporting. Towards the end of the 1990s, these were complemented with initiatives on socially responsible investments and on information technology.

Almost all of the organizations in this category have their main offices in North America or in Europe, many of them in the US. Although the category of Multi-stakeholders as a whole mainly represents a manifestation of the 'norm cascade' of the mid-1990s, some of the organizations and initiatives included represent 'norm emergence' activities, in that they were early initiatives emerging ahead of norm tipping and as such have influenced the development CSR. The first of the social labelling initiatives to develop within the category of Multi-stakeholders was the Fairtrade coffee initiative, developed by the Dutch organization Max Havelaar Foundation, created in 1988 (origins of the FLO). In the following section, I will first provide a background for the emergence of Fairtrade in general, and then turn to the development of Max Havelaar/FLO.

Brief Introduction to Social Labelling and Fairtrade

Generally speaking, labelling in business is a way of creating a product for which higher prices can be obtained by dividing the market into niches; it is particularly common in the clothing sector, as illustrated by the different designer labels. The basis for this labelling is the idea of the economics of information, which allows for determining quality that might not even be visible. In the case of social labelling, we find NGOs applying these traditional economic measures as tools for social change. A definition of social labels from this perspective is that they:

> are words and symbols associated with products or organizations which seek to influence the economic decisions of one set of stakeholders by describing the impact of a business process on another group of stakeholders (Zadek, Lingayah, and Forstater 1998: 19).

Prior to the international labelling scheme discussed below, social labelling schemes have developed nationally. As far back as in 1899, the US National Consumers League introduced the so-called White Label, guaranteeing that stitched cotton underwear had been manufactured under decent working conditions and that no child labour was involved. This was later replaced by trade-union sponsored labels, which were especially widespread on clothing and which continued until imported clothes started to arrive on the market in large volumes. Other social labelling initiatives have been of a more patriotic nature, such as the 'Buy American' labels in the US, or of an environmentally friendly character, such as 'green' labels or 'eco-labels' (Hilowitz 1997: 216).

Table 6.1 (see below) shows examples of labelling programmes (as of 1998). As can be noted, all of them developed in the mid-1990s, and several of them deal with products that are often associated with child labour.

The idea of fair trade began to develop as part of the activities of some churches in North America and Europe in the 1940s and 1950s, when money from the sales of foreign-made handicrafts was used to support refugees and poor communities around the world. This was a result of the contacts that missionaries made in developing countries and represented direct trade through alternative channels with 'fair' prices. Among such alternative trade organizations still active today

Table 6.1   Overview of International Social Labelling Programmes

Programme (year started)	Product	Primary countries of operation		Leaders
		Producers	**Buyers**	
Care & Fair (1994)	Hand-knotted carpets	India, Nepal, Pakistan	Germany, UK, Netherlands, Luxembourg	E
RUGMARK (1994)	Hand-knotted carpets	India, Nepal, Pakistan	Germany, USA, other West European countries, Canada	NGO
Kaleen (1995)	Hand-knotted carpets	India	Germany, Nordic countries	E, G
STEP (1995)	Hand-knotted carpets	India, Nepal, Pakistan, Morocco, Egypt	Switzerland	E, NGO
Double Income Project (1995)	Textiles, handicrafts, jewellery	Kenya, India, Latin America (esp. Peru)	Switzerland	E
Abrinq (1995)	Footwear and other	Brazil	Brazil, other Latin America	E, NGO
Forest Stewardship Council (FSC) (1996)	Forestry products, incl. timber	Brazil, Mexico, Malaysia, Poland, South Africa, Sri Lanka, Sweden, UK, USA	Australia, Japan, West Europe, North America	W, E, NGO
Reebok (1996)	Soccer balls	Pakistan	USA, Europe, Latin America	E
Baden (1997)	Sporting balls	China	Primarily North America and West Europe, some in Latin America, Pacific Rim	E
Fairtrade Labelling Organizations International (1997)[a]	Agricultural products	Africa, Latin America and Asia	West Europe, USA, Canada, Japan	NGO
Flower Label Program (1997)	Cut flowers	Ecuador, Israel, Kenya, Zambia, Zimbabwe	Germany, Austria, Sweden, Switzerland	W, NGO

Note: W: Workers' organizations, E: Enterprise or entrepreneurs, G: Governments, NGO: Non-governmental Organization. a) Originated in 1988 with the Max Havelaar social labelling initiative.

Source: Adapted table from ILO (1998, Appendix: Tables).

in the US are Ten Thousand Villages, established in 1946,[3] and SERRV (Sales Exchange for Refugee Rehabilitation Vocation), established in 1949. The first Fairtrade shop in the US opened in 1958. In 1986, the first US-based organization to import coffee directly from small farmer cooperatives was created under the name Equal Exchange. Equal Exchange is the market leader in Fairtrade coffee in the US today and was the first US organization to adopt the FLO standards in 1991 (Ten Thousand Villages 2004, SERRV 2004, Kocken 2003, Equal Exchange 2004a, 2004b).

In Europe, Oxfam UK, a Dutch organization called Fair Trade Organisatie, and Dutch third world groups were the first to sell foreign-made handicrafts in the 1960s through 'Third World Shops' (later the World Shops; the first one opened in 1969). Fairtrade coffee was first imported in 1973 by Fair Trade Organisatie in The Netherlands. There is also the term 'sustainable coffee', which includes the three main categories of coffee, i.e., organic, Fairtrade, and eco-friendly coffee; this is also partly a corporate-driven definition that appears as an alternative to Fairtrade. The expansion of European Fairtrade sales to food products is partly attributed to an act of solidarity – the sale of Nicaraguan coffee and bananas, which were under US blockade after the overthrow of the government by the Sandinista guerrillas in 1979 (Kocken 2003, Raynolds 2002).

Fairtrade Labelling Organizations International

Fairtrade Labelling Organizations International (FLO) is an international organization for setting Fairtrade standards, including certification of producers of mainly agricultural products, and registering trading companies for authorization to trade FLO products (see also Appendix 2). The FLO products include coffee, tea, rice, fresh fruit, juices, cocoa, sugar, honey, sports balls, wine, and flowers. In 2002, FLO for the first time included non-food products, when it started to certify footballs. The target group to benefit from the FLO Label is disadvantaged producers, mainly small farmers and also plantation workers. The FLO was established in 1997 but originated with the creation of the Max Havelaar Foundation in Amsterdam, The Netherlands in 1988 (FLO 2005b).

The Origins of Fairtrade Labelled Coffee   It was thus yet another Dutch organization by the name of Max Havelaar that initiated the social labelling of coffee in the 1980s.[4] This event is regarded as the beginning of the second major

---

3   Today Ten Thousand Villages is a program of the Mennonite Central Committee (a religious service, relief and development agency), and was initiated by one of its workers, Edna Ruth Byler.

4   The name Max Havelaar originates from the title of a novel by the Dutch author Eduard Douwes Dekker, by the title *Max Havelaar: Or the Coffee Auctions of the Dutch Trading Company*, published in 1859. The novel is built on the author's personal experiences as a Deputy Commissioner in Java, where he documented the corrupt practices

phase of organized Fairtrade labelling, when this activity moves out of the realm of the churches.[5]

Max Havelaar developed from the initiative of two men: a Dutch priest living in a village at the centre of the Union de Comunidades Indigenas de la Región de Istmo (UCIRI) in Mexico, and an employee of a Dutch ecumenical organization for Latin America called Solidaridad. UCIRI is a regional organization of coffee producers consisting of indigenous communities, mainly small coffee producers. The Dutch priest had been involved in the creation of UCIRI in 1983, with the purpose of ameliorating the situation for the farmers in the area (among other things, to circumvent the intermediary coffee dealers and release the farmers from their debts). The two men first made contact at a meeting in Mexico in 1985, where the need to increase the volume of coffee exports from these farmers became apparent. At that time, coffee from UCIRI was only distributed through alternative trade channels like the 'world shops' and church sales described above (Roozen and van der Hoff 2002, Renard 1999).

Solidaridad began approaching coffee roaster companies and supermarket chains in The Netherlands with the idea of making the coffee from UCIRI available for sale in supermarkets. Among the executives approached was the Executive Director of the coffee roaster company Simon Lévelt, who was a pioneer in the ecological area. Although the coffee roaster companies were sceptical about the idea, their trade association, mindful of a boycott in the 1970s of coffee imported from the Portuguese colony Angola, agreed to meet with representatives of the UCIRI. However, the largest coffee roaster company, Douwes Egbert, with 70 per cent of the market share, showed no interest. Instead, Douwes Egbert announced that the new initiative would be allowed to reach a maximum of 4 per cent of the market,[6] and if it passed that level, the company would either drive the new label out of the market; if it did not succeed in doing so, it would then join the scheme (Roozen and van der Hoff 2002: 110). The largest Dutch supermarket (Albert Heijns), however, became interested and involved in developing the initiative further. However, Albert Heijns suddenly withdrew from the project, which was subsequently explained by contact at the highest level between Douwes Egbert and Albert Heijns. The withdrawal of Albert Heijns almost jeopardized the entire project, but the other large retailers and some of the smaller coffee roaster companies finally agreed to distribute the coffee. Douwes Egbert tried to interfere in the Max Havelaar project by simultaneously launching a separate, competing initiative. This initiative also was to make direct purchases from the

---

of the colonial regime and submitted formal charges based on these practices (for which he lost his job). The book received a lot of attention in The Netherlands, Germany and the UK at the time (King 1972).

5   As Fairtrade entered the general market is seen to approach a third phase, needing 'new marketing approaches and new forms of cooperation' (Giovannucci 2003: 39).

6   Studies made at the time stipulated an approximate future market share of 7–15 per cent of this new label.

small producers, but without the price guarantee that the Max Havelaar initiative included. Some years later, Albert Heijns decided to participate fully in the project (as of 2009, Douwes Egbert is still not participating). In November 1988, the first package of Max Havelaar labelled coffee was finally delivered to the King of The Netherlands by the Nobel Prize laureate in Economics, Jan Tinbergen, as a formal launch of the initiative (Roozen and van der Hoff 2002: 113, Interview with Harmsen 2004).[7]

Coordinating the Different National Initiatives   Other national labelling initiatives modelled after Max Havelaar soon developed, as did other social labelling initiatives for coffee. The spread of the Max Havelaar initiative to other countries was spontaneous and not due to deliberate campaigning by Max Havelaar. Assistance was given, however, through the sharing of information, material and experiences. The launch of Max Havelaar involved the mobilization of not only the NGO community, but also other parts of Dutch society (politicians and others), and received quite a lot of media attention, which contributed to the spread of news about the initiative in other countries (Harmsen 2004).

Although the development of the Fairtrade label in The Netherlands was successful and the label spread rapidly to other countries, the process was not without conflict. Differences were apparent both during the initial development of Max Havelaar in The Netherlands and between the labelling initiatives that later emerged in the other countries.

Initially, when the Max Havelaar initiative was beginning to take shape in The Netherlands, there was resistance not only from the business community but also from within the Fairtrade movement. There were two reasons for this. First, there was a general reluctance to cooperate with TNCs, an attitude that has significantly changed over time. Second, there was fear of what the sale of Fairtrade products on the regular market would mean to the Fairtrade movement as a whole. There were concerns that consumers would no longer be interested in making purchases in the World Shops, that these shops would lose 'market share' and close down. This would have undermined the whole movement in the long run. As it turned out, the result was the opposite, and launch on the regular market increased sales in the World Shops and strengthened the movement as a whole (Interview with Harmsen 2004).

We see here that what was once seen as idealistic acts of goodhearted churchgoing women has moved out of the religious framework and now become mainstream. In recent times Fairtrade has received increased attention and Fairtrade labelled products have experienced spectacular growth in sales. Coordination of

---

7   Although Albert Heijns withdrew from the project, it later tried to obtain the Max Havelaar coffee as the launch approached and public opinion grew in favour of the initiative. However, as all the coffee was taken, Albert Heijns were not given any deliveries from Max Havelaar directly and had to approach a competitor who had agreed to participate and lodged advance orders.

the different national labelling initiatives within the FLO will be discussed further in Chapter 8.

Implications of Norm Emergence

A closer examination of the norm entrepreneurs engaged in CSR advocacy that was seen in Chapter 5 and in this chapter shows a more complex setting than one might at first expect to find in a study of NGOs engaged in this issue. The conventional view of social change NGOs – i.e., as progressive or at times radical activists – is only partly confirmed. Such organizations would correspond to the organizations in this study that fall into the category of Activist Organizations. They do exist and were particularly influential in the early wave of CSR organizations that began questioning the role of TNCs in international trade and outsourcing in the 1970s and 1980s, which here is considered the stage of norm emergence of CSR. However, the Activists not only differ among themselves in terms of aims, activities and strategies of persuasion. In the late 1980s and in particular from the 1990s on, they were joined by other categories of NGOs making claims about CSR. These CSR organizations fall into the categories Business Initiatives and Multi-stakeholder Organizations, introduced in this study.

The claims made by Business Initiatives and Multi-stakeholder Organizations have contributed to the engagement of new groups in the process and thereby extended the reach of the debate on CSR into other parts of society. At the same time, the involvement of new groups has changed the debate itself; the debate is no longer the sole domain of the initial norm entrepreneurs (the Activists). The existence of a business case for CSR and its relationship to ideas of 'principled capitalism', as well as the conversion of often vague different perspectives on CSR into concrete tools, as evidenced by social labelling, have affected both the process and the participating actors. Different perspectives and purposes are sometimes at odds, and at times certain tradeoffs are needed to reach out to a broader spectrum of society. The situation with different approaches to CSR need not be seen strictly as a conflict between fixed alternatives in a zero-sum game but can be understood as a new process in the development of CSR. Although these new categories of CSR organizations may still be driven by similar motives of ideational commitment, interpretations of that commitment differ among the participants in these organizations. This development also points to the shift in the social process that was to come later, i.e., when dominance by other motives appear as the norm cascade occurs in the mid-1990s, at which time a more mixed group of actors become involved.

Another notable aspect of the CSR organizations studied here is the dominance of organizations from Europe and North America. This of course has consequences for the development of CSR with regard to the framing of the issue, representation in the process ('the negotiations' being undertaken in various forums), and in the overall sense of ownership of the issue and the process. However, one can also detect a form of international 'division of labour' taking place among NGOs, in which each of them makes use of their competitive advantages. CSR organizations in locations where the negative effects of TNC activity are manifested focus on activities appropriate for their local context, such as direct support to workers, local activism, etc., and collect and report on evidence of various abuses. This information is passed on to CSR organizations located in countries with TNC headquarters, offices of IGOs, international media and consumers. The latter CSR organizations thus engage in activities appropriate to their environment in the hope of affecting the situation in the countries where the human or labour rights violations occur (the boomerang effect). In this way, small NGOs with limited resources can make efficient use of their potential and compensate for their relative lack of material resources (in comparison with other more resourceful actors, such as TNCs, IGOs and individual governments).

Problems of participation or representation and ownership of the process are still apparent and real. No matter how well intended the CSR organizations or other organizations in Europe and North America might be, they cannot fully appreciate the situation in far-off countries. This fact has to, and will, affect the framing of an issue. The framing of the issue in turn will affect the understanding of the problem and the measures undertaken to address various identified shortcomings. At the same time, the CSR organizations in Europe and North America have the necessary understanding of the workings of the context in which they are active, and thus can contribute this knowledge to the process. In fact, the process that is taking place is done so in a more 'multi-stakeholder' manner, and with attempts at making the workers more visible through such initiatives as the Reality Tours. Yet the image of workers in 'Third World' countries as victims of human rights abuses and NGOs in developed countries as the sole activists mobilizing for action and presenting solutions to the problems somehow persists.

In spite of the dynamics both within and between the various organizations in the three categories of CSR organizations, there are aspects of commonality. Linking organizations from the different categories is the awareness of the challenge of globalization and the role of TNCs, although the challenge is identified in different ways, and the solutions presented also differ. For Global Exchange and the ILRF, the multilateral institutions, the US government and US companies are seen as part of the problem, and grassroots internationalism and the (legal) strengthening of workers' rights are seen as the solutions. The role of government is less prominent in the case of the work of the CCC and FLO, where instead changes in international production and the unequal terms of trade in general (including the position of certain vulnerable groups) are the main concerns, and the development of alternative standards for TNCs to rectify the situation is the suggested solution. The IBLF's more diplomatic stance admits to imperfections in the existing political and economic systems and recognizes the need for reform while still valuing the resources and leadership of companies. TNCs are seen as offering solutions (rather than problems) with shared responsibility and partnership with the rest of society.

The general perception of NGOs discussed in Chapter 2 is that they are lacking in political (military) and economic power but are stronger in moral authority. Strategies for achieving social change and the introduction of new norms, therefore, need to make use of strategies of persuasion rather than more explicitly coercive forms of power. The discussion above lends support to arguments for the use of various strategies of persuasion in the initial stages of norm advocacy and norm emergence. These strategies include accessing and mobilizing resources outside the organization, persuasion directed internally within the social movement itself, the development and sharing of good practices or education, partnerships and coalitions, training, expansion through sister or partner organizations, facilitation of initiatives carried out by others, awareness raising, street action and creation of new standards and related institutions.

Among these strategies, there is one that particularly stands out: the activities of the ILRF in using the coercive capacity of the state as leverage (legislation and lawsuits). This strategy has a valuable side effect in creating a platform for further action when working with the reform of US policy and legislation. The strategy can hardly be considered persuasion, apart from initial persuasive action to obtain support for amending existing policy or legislation. Subsequent actions are coercive, although the coercion is undertaken by a third party. This strategy represents a form of outsourcing coercion or a joint venture, where one actor is making use of another actor's resources.

In the next chapter, I will address the development of CSR from the second half of the 1990s onwards. This is the period when the second stage in the norm cycle, 'norm cascade' began. The momentum for this change, norm tipping, as well as change in the interplay between the different CSR organizations and the other actors joining the process are important features in the discussion.

Chapter 7

Norm Cascade of the 1990s: Mushrooming of Initiatives and the Targeting of Nike

Previous chapters described how norm entrepreneurs began working to build awareness of the negative effects of globalization, in particular with regard to the operations of TNCs. These norm entrepreneurs consisted of different kinds of organizations (Activist, Business Initiatives and Multi-stakeholder Organizations) with diverse approaches to CSR, both in terms of their aims and their activities. In spite of these differences, each one managed in its own way to 'persuade' other actors that CSR was an important issue.

As a result of this persuasion, there was a shift in the development of CSR in the 1990s, and the number of new organizations established and initiatives promoting CSR increased. The initial norm entrepreneurs were no longer the only ones addressing the negative aspects of TNC activities. Not only were new CSR organizations established, but many of the organizations created in the 1990s fall into the Business Initiatives and Multi-stakeholders categories, advocating CSR from different perspectives than did the Activists. In addition, states, IGOs, and the TNCs themselves become involved on a broader scale during this period. These developments, taken together, have consequently contributed to norm cascading in the mid-1990s in the area of CSR.

I argue here that as a result of the above developments, there is a change in the norm cycle process regarding CSR. From a situation where norm entrepreneurs have been solitary advocates involved in persuading others to adopt the idea of CSR, there is a shift to a situation where a large number of actors of different persuasions now 'rush in', and where CSR also becomes the subject of dialogue and negotiation. Momentum is achieved in the mid-1990s; when the CSR organizations and initiatives involved attain a certain scale and scope, combined with the involvement of certain key actors in the process, norm tipping occurs. These key actors include influential state actors, such as the US and UK governments, high profile NGOs including Amnesty International and Human Rights Watch, and individual TNCs such as Nike (discussed below). Prominent individuals holding offices or representing institutions of symbolic value or stature in the international system, such as UN Secretary General, Kofi Annan and the Prince of Wales, also emerge as conspicuous actors in the development of CSR.

In this and the following chapter I will discuss specific cases as evidence of the workings of norm cascading, including the targeting of Nike by Activists, the development of voluntary standards for implementation and monitoring, attempts at achieving accountability through law, and efforts in advancing good practices and partnership. First, however, the CSR norm cascade and what it consisted of is introduced.

Mushrooming of Corporate Social Responsibility Initiatives

The CSR organizations and initiatives that appeared in great numbers in the 1990s, I argue, represent a norm cascade and a new stage in the development of CSR. A list of some of the more important initiatives is included in Appendix 3 (see also Table 6.1 above). This norm cascade emanated from various parts of society, i.e., it now also involved actors apart from the NGOs who earlier had acted as norm entrepreneurs (discussed in previous chapters). Motives other than ideational commitment and a social process different than the process dominated by persuasion that had characterized the previous stage of norm emergence now appeared. The motive now is legitimacy and the social process is dominated by socialization.

An inventory by the OECD reveals the existence of almost 250 different codes of conduct towards the end of the 1990s, a large majority of which have been issued by *individual companies and industry or trade associations* (OECD 2001). Not only did companies undertake measures on their own or through their traditional industry and trade associations, they also joined forces with other companies to create new organizations in the form of Business Initiatives to specifically address CSR in the different ways seen in Chapter 6. This development continued into the 1990s with the creation of additional Business Initiatives. Furthermore, companies became involved in various Multi-stakeholder Organizations, engaging in activities such as dialogues, partnerships, monitoring and labelling schemes, sometimes together with their critics, to create CSR tools.

Among the first government initiatives addressing CSR in the 1990s was the Fair Labor Association (formerly the Apparel Industry Partnership), established in 1996 in the US by the Clinton administration as a multi-stakeholder approach for addressing poor working conditions among subcontractor producers for TNCs. In 1998, the UK government initiated the Ethical Trading Initiative (also a multi-stakeholder approach); in 2000 it appointed a Minister for CSR, and in 2002 it mandated that pension funds by law disclose ethical, environmental and social considerations in connection with their investments. Other European governments have also taken similar legislative measures: Finland in 2000, France and Germany in 2001, and Belgium in 2002. Many of the initiatives by the European governments started to develop in the late 1990s, prompted by the priority given to the matter by the European Council at its Lisbon European meeting in 2000 and the European Commission's 'Green Paper' on CSR in 2001. The initiatives include legislation with requirements such as mandatory statements on environmental and ethical considerations of investments in annual business plans; reporting of social and environmental consequences of corporate activities; disclosure of social and ethical criteria for investments and social and environmental considerations in public procurement; and the issuing of a social label by the Belgian state (see also European Commission undated a). An overview of the measures undertaken by EU member states can be seen in Table 7.1.

The table illustrates the dissemination of CSR policies that has taken place among EU member states and also shows that some countries are ahead of others (norm leaders): Austria, Denmark, Germany, and the UK. Even the list of initiatives itself can be seen as a way of furthering the adoption of CSR policies – i.e., a demonstration of good practices for others to follow. Compared to an inventory in 2003, countries now (as of 2007) report the adoption of CSR policies in an additional 50 policy areas or more (European Commission undated a,

Table 7.1   Overview of CSR Policies Adopted by EU Member Countries (as of 2007)

	AU	B	DK	FI	FR	DE	EL	IE	IT	LU	PT	ES	SE	NL	UK
Promoting CSR															
Awareness raising	●	●	●	●	●	●	●	●	●	●	●	●	●	●	●
Research	●		●	●		●	●		●				●	●	
Public-private partnerships			●	●	●	●	●	●	●	●	●	●	●	●	●
Business incentives	●	●	●	●		●	●	●	●	●	●	●	●	●	●
Management tools	●	●	●					●	●			●	●	●	●
Ensuring transparency															
Codes	●			●	●	●				●		●		●	●
Reporting	●	●	●		●					●	●	●	●	●	●
Labels	●	●	●	●	●	●		●	●	●	●	●	●	●	●
SRI	●	●		●									●	●	●
Advertising				●											
Other															
Developing CSR-supportive policies															
Sustainable development	●	●	●	●	●	●		●					●	●	
Social policies			●	●			●	●			●	●			
Environmental policies		●			●		●	●					●		●
Public procurement		●	●		●			●	●			●		●	●
Trade & export policies	●	●	●	●	●	●							●	●	
Other	●	●			●	●		●	●				●	●	●

Note: Countries covered: AU (Austria), B (Belgium), DK (Denmark), FI (Finland), FR (France), DE (Germany), EL (Greece), IE (Ireland), IT (Italy), LU (Luxemburg), PT (Portugal), ES (Espagna/Spain), SE (Sweden), NL (The Netherlands), UK (United Kingdom). Only countries that were members of the EU before 2005 are included.

Source: Adapted from European Commission (undated b).

undated b). However, it does not say anything about the content or 'quality' of the CSR policies adopted.[1]

Intergovernmental organizations (IGOs) have also taken the initiative or adjusted their policies in this area. The OECD Guidelines for Multinational Enterprises, adopted in the 1970s, were revised and strengthened (including references to human rights) in 2000, after an open consultation process with civil society and non-OECD countries. The consultation process with civil society was a novelty. Since the late 1990s, the EU has issued reports, held conferences and adopted policies on CSR (also in an open consultation processes). This has, in turn, set in motion a range of activities among its member states, referred to above. Also, the World Bank has in recent years adopted policies to advice (and support) developing country governments on CSR, as well as on other related topics. In 2003 the UN Sub-Commission on the Protection and Promotion of Human Rights introduced a proposal for human rights norms for business (discussed in Chapter 9).

One can also see evidence of pressure from trade unions in the MERCOSUR countries, resulting in the tripartite MERCOSUR Working Group on Labor Relations, Employment and Social Security, set up in 1992 as an early example of the development of CSR policies outside of North America and Europe. This was later followed by an Economic and Social and Consultative Forum and a Joint Parliamentary Commission. However, since the latter two are only able to make recommendations and give advice, and the governments and employers in the Working Group block proposals concerning progressive labour policies, no significant changes have occurred. A similar problem is seen within the ILO (ILRF 2001b).

The North American Free Trade Agreement (NAFTA) adopted in 1994 has also a side agreement, the North American Agreement on Labor Cooperation (NAALC). This is the first agreement explicitly related to a regional trade agreement that includes sanctions, although these apply only to a limited number of rights and no remedy is included if private employers are involved. Only a few complaints have been filed (see the discussion of the activities of the ILRF in Chapter 5). One can thus conclude that the NAALC proved a disappointment in view of its initial purpose (ILRF 2001b).

Mention should also to be made of the well-known call on business to take action in this area made in 1999 at the World Economic Forum by the UN Secretary General, Kofi Annan. This initiative later became the UN Global Compact (discussed further in Chapter 9). Another important international initiative, undertaken by the International Standardization Organization (ISO), was to develop standards for social responsibility (ISO26000) applying not only to companies but to all organizations. Both of these initiatives confirm that increasing attention was given to CSR internationally, with both the UN and an among the business community well-respected NGO (the ISO) placing the

---

1   Note should be taken that in 10 cases, countries no longer report activities in a certain policy-area. The reason for this has not been established here.

issue on their agendas. The fact that these organizations became involved also contributed to the legitimacy of CSR as an issue.

As a consequence of this mushrooming of initiatives, the activities of the focus organizations studied here changed. After being centred initially on creating awareness, they began developing more precise definitions of CSR. There was also a closer interaction with other actors, including the TNCs. Among the activities of the focus organizations in the 1990s, the targeting of specific companies, often high profile TNCs that are sector leaders as in the case of Nike (discussed below), is prominent. Another activity in which many organizations engaged is the development of standards and monitoring mechanisms, either individually or in multi-stakeholder forums, to transform demands for responsibility into more concrete expectations. One of the focus organizations, the International Business Leaders Forum (IBLF), takes a somewhat different track. It puts emphasis on the importance of good practices and partnerships in parallel with the standards and monitoring activities and the multi-stakeholder cooperation mentioned above. These activities will be discussed in both this and the following chapter, beginning with the case of Nike.

Targeting Nike

As was seen in the case of the CCC in Chapter 5, the initial strategy of the organization was to target specific companies in consumer (home) countries to raise awareness of labour conditions at subcontractors in distant producer (host) countries. However, as the issue of CSR spread, the activities of other CSR organizations became known and targeting at times converged on specific companies. The US-based sportswear company, Nike, was one of them. This was not due to a centrally coordinated campaign, but grew more or less spontaneously out of the spread of information and contacts between the different organizations. The fact that Nike was a very successful and high profile company that initially did not take its critics seriously contributed to it being targeted. All but one of the focus organizations (FLO) became involved directly or indirectly in the campaign against Nike. The development of the campaign shows how, step by step, Nike is socialized into adopting CSR policies, although this does not necessarily mean that Nike has fully complied with its own policies or managed to redress the problems in full, as continued campaigning shows.

Background and Build Up of the Campaign

In the late 1980s, labour conditions in Asian factories producing goods for export, including footwear, were already of interest to the International Labor Rights Forum (ILRF), as evidenced in its filing of GSP (General System of Preferences) complaints, and to USAID (the aid agency of the US) through studies performed. The ILRF began filing GSP petitions on Indonesia, where Nike's products were manufactured, in the late 1980s, but these petitions were not successful. After the Indonesian government undertook measures – albeit limited ones – to counter the criticisms and US business expressed concern for the possible removal of Indonesia's GSP status, the review was discontinued (Compa and Vogt 2001).

The initial motivation for targeting Nike was an article by Jeff Ballinger published in Harper's Magazine in 1992 on the labour conditions at specific Nike subcontractors in Indonesia. Jeff Ballinger had investigated labour practices in subcontracting factories in Turkey and Asia, and he made brief notes on the back of a pay stub on a female worker. These pay stubs, with Ballinger's notes, were published in what was then a well-known periodical, thus making visible both the worker and the entire system of outsourcing of which she was a part (Shaw 1999).

The article drew attention to Nike and to the industry in general, and Nike responded to the pressure that was beginning to build up by adopting a code of conduct in the same year that the article appeared. Although a certain amount of media attention continued, few substantial changes were made in the labour practices employed by Nike's subcontractors. Jeff Ballinger formed an organization to gather information on Nike's abusive labour practices and to raise awareness of the company's behaviour. The organization ran advertisements using Nike slogans, such as 'Just Do It', and combined them with images of workers (instead of the usual successful athletes) as well as information on labour conditions. The revised slogan suggested that Nike should address these labour issues without delay (Shaw 1999: 25).

One needs to take into account that at the time Nike was (and still is) a very successful company from a strictly business perspective. Apart from its substantial profits and revenues, the company epitomized the American dream of building a successful global company from 'nothing' through the hard work of its two founders, Philip Knight and Bill Bowerman. The image that Nike had created around its products by associating them with famous athletes and with the idea of overcoming challenges simply by using the product is described as mythical (Goldman and Papson 1998). This image was built partly on the so-called 'swoosh' logo and the 'Just Do It' slogan.

In spite of the media attention that followed the initial article in 1992, including a longer article by the US scholar Cynthia Enloe (1995), the issue did not reach the US mainstream media until 1996, when an article was featured in *The New York Times*. This article, combined with other events, is seen as a key development in the Nike campaign. The article states that:

> the exposure of Nike's wrongdoing in the *New York Times* and other mainstream national media, the public and political fallout over talk-show host Kathie Lee Gifford's connection to Honduran sweatshops, the entry into the anti-Nike campaign of key groups such as the faith-based investment community and Medea Benjamin and the labor and human rights group Global Exchange, and public exposure of Nike's misdeeds in Vietnam. Associated with all of these factors was the anti-Nike campaign's ability both to capitalize on media opportunities

and to create events that enabled a now-interested media to continually cover the issue (Shaw 1999: 28).[2]

The New York Times article thus had the effect of 'suddenly' making criticism of the abusive labour practices among Nike subcontractors seem 'appropriate' and the behaviour of Nike seem 'inappropriate'. Other mainstream media picked up the story and 'the news' became widespread. However, the media was not responsible for discovering this news story, as will be seen below. The story surfaced as the result of activities by NGOs that turned increasing awareness of international production into news stories about sweatshops – particularly deliberate framing activities carried out by focus organizations like Global Exchange and the CCC.

Activities of Focus Organizations and Nike's Response

Although the articles by Jeff Ballinger and *The New York Times* can be said to have been pivotal in the process, these two articles alone would not have been sufficient to start a campaign against Nike. When *The New York Times* article appeared, the time was simply ripe for the arguments it presented. The preparations had been made by NGOs in their persistent critique of the negative effects of the changing ways that TNCs were conducting their businesses as part of the overall globalization process. What were the activities of the NGOs that led to this and how was the targeting of Nike conducted? A closer look at the activities of the focus organizations involved in the Nike campaign (the CCC, the ILRF and Global Exchange) provides insights. Neither the FLO (for obvious reasons) nor the IBLF participated directly in the campaign, although the IBLF addressed the issue from another perspective, through its involvement in the Vietnamese Business Link Initiative and the good practices advice given on the issue of 'brand-jacking', discussed later.

Activities of Focus Organizations   The campaign against Nike was conducted mainly through the sharing of information by a loosely coordinated coalition that included NGOs in the US, Europe and Asia. Among other things, the information included research findings by different organizations that presented constantly updated information on the working conditions at various Nike subcontractors. The European campaign against the sports shoe industry, focusing on Nike and its operations in Indonesia, started in The Netherlands in 1995 with the participation of the Dutch CCC under the slogan 'Nike: Fair Play?' (CCC 1995c: 4). The campaign was built on information about the activities of NGOs in the US, such as the Campaign for Labor Rights (CLR) and the United States Association for Students (USAS), which was shared with other national CCC initiatives. The CCC

---

2   Kathie Lee Gifford had, apart from being a talk-show host in the US, also developed an individual line of garments under the label 'Gifford' that was produced abroad. Medea Benjamin is a co-founder of Global Exchange (see Chapter 5).

also carried out its own research in cooperation with the Dutch Center for Research on Multinational Corporations (SOMO). (CCC 1996b, 1996c, 2001).

The way in which the campaign was conducted implied a pooling of resources by small organizations otherwise lacking in resources. The participating NGOs in this loose coalition were free to organize their activities as they saw fit and according to their own perspectives. There was no need to devote resources to agreeing on aims, strategies and activities. The effect of this loosely coordinated network was that Nike was constantly attacked by various organizations from different parts of society and in a range of ways, which had the effect that:

> The company [Nike] never knows from where the next criticism will come. Because information is shared the company might have to deal in Australia with the results of a meeting in Europe. More and more organisations and consumers question Nike's working conditions, refuse funding from Nike, for example for sporting departments in schools, or do action on the company. In this way Nike is kept under pressure to clean up their act (CCC 1997a: 14).

The cumulative effect was that because Nike was targeted by a number of organizations, consumers, media, etc., all with different motives, arguments and actions, Nike could not direct its response to one single adversary. This uncoordinated campaign method thus became an advantage and serves as an example of a new way of organizing within social movements, compared with the more hierarchically organized trade unions and other more established NGOs (see also the discussion on social movements and NGOs in Chapter 2).

The campaign methods involved a wide variety of different strategies, ranging from traditional strategies to build awareness to strategies of a more drastic or confrontational nature. The strategies included voicing concerns through letters or phone calls directly to the Nike CEO, Philip Knight, mobilization of consumers and local store employees, seminars, petitions, and persuading city councils to pass anti-sweatshop resolutions.

Examples of action in the European campaign included protesting at the official opening of a Nike playground for children in Amsterdam (covered with the Nike logo) by handing out information and displaying banners reading 'Nike do it. Pay fair wages in Asia'. The activists were allegedly forced brutally away, much to the amazement of the Dutch public attending the opening. This led to extensive press coverage and provided the Nike critics with a further opportunity to spread their message and gain sympathy – the event is described in an article entitled *Nike: Fair Play?* (CCC 1997a: 13). A mass mailing of postcards to Nike was also organized in Europe, where Nike received an estimated 45,000 cards (about 900 cards a day for the postcard campaign period), as confirmed by Nike (CCC 1997b).

In contrast to the activities of the other focus organizations, Global Exchange conducted a focused and vigorous campaign explicitly targeting Nike, which included the active participation of the founder and then Executive Director of Global Exchange, Medea Benjamin. This campaign involved various activities, including production of an educational audio tape with a seminar talk by Medea Benjamin and sale of the book *Nike, Reebok and the Global Sweatshop* (Global Exchange 1997a). Global Exchange produced campaign T-shirts that paraphrased the Nike slogan, 'Just Do It' (as did the advertisements by Jeff Ballinger), as a way to frame the issue. The T-shirts carried the following message: 'JUMP into foreign countries, RUN away from responsibility, STOMP on worker's rights, JUST DON'T DO IT, NIKE'. Other campaign activities included returning Nike shoes to the company and calls for a boycott. As a result of the intense Global Exchange campaign, Nike at one point publicly referred to Global Exchange as extremists (Global Exchange 1997b, 1997c: 2, 1998: 4, Shaw 1999: 64).

On one occasion, Medea Benjamin attempted to enter into a conversation with the Nike CEO, Philip Knight, as documented in a photo in the organization's newsletter that shows her chasing him, with the following text: 'At Nike's annual shareholders' meeting GX Director Medea Benjamin asked NIKE CEO Phillip Knight why his company can't treat its Asian workers better – but Phil ran away'. The image given of the Nike CEO running away from an activist is very well staged to parallel the criticism of Nike as literally running away from responsibility (Global Exchange 1997d: 3).

Other activities pressured Nike to engage in direct dialogue with its critics. A report on China issued in 1997, compiled in cooperation with organizations in Hong Kong, reveals that Global Exchange had requested Nike to meet with representatives of these organizations, to which Nike agreed. A first meeting with a representative of Nike and Global Exchange took place in connection with an International Nike Day of Protest organized in the US and 12 other countries, with extensive press coverage. Other concessions made by Nike during this time were to pay minimum wages in Indonesia and Vietnam. (Global Exchange 1998: 4)

The campaign on Nike reached such proportions that in a public speech in 1998 the CEO, Philip Knight, felt the need to try to make a joke about the negative image of Nike: 'So, I figured that I'd just come out and let you journalists have a look at the great Satan, up close and personal'. However, Nike not only made jokes, the company also felt the necessity to present six commitments regarding its operations on issues such as factory safety, raising the minimum age to 18, involvement of NGOs in monitoring and disclosure of monitoring reports, educational programmes, micro-enterprise loan programmes, and funding university research. This did not satisfy the critics, and in 2001 Global Exchange released yet another report on Nike, *Still Waiting For Nike To Do It*, referring to the very same commitments. The report concluded that Nike had failed to honour most of the commitments, with the exception that progress had been made on factory safety (Connor 2001, quote from Shaw 1999: 93 referring to a speech made at the National Press Club in 1999). Every time Nike made a concession, the critics promptly followed up on whatever measures were taken by the company. This gradually 'socialized' Nike on the issue of CSR. Moving from interaction at a distance in the early 1990s, Nike and its critics began to approach each other for dialogue by the end of the decade. This movement represents a change in Nike's attitude.

Apart from the GSP petitions, the ILRF also highlighted the footwear industry, including Nike and other high profile companies, in connection with research on child labour in India and in the Foul Ball Campaign[3] in 1996 (Harvey and Riggin 1994, ILRF 1999). The ILRF furthermore entered into public dialogue with Nike in the *Financial Times* in 1999. The article exposed correspondence from a Nike executive to a member of a Vietnamese business organization, in which the Nike executive tried to brush aside criticism by putting Nike's critics in a bad light, claiming that they were not friends of Vietnam. This article led to a letter to the editor by the ILRF and a letter sent directly to Nike, signed by the ILRF and three other members of the Fair Labour Association, of which Nike was a founder (Harvey 1999). Nike was thus exposed to have, on one hand, agreed to participate in the Fair Labor Association, together with its critics, for a multi-stakeholder dialogue and to assume responsibility, and on the other hand, to write off its critics in contacts with business representatives.

The content of the code of conduct adopted by Nike was also criticized for more general reasons, such as for not covering issues of freedom of association and a living wage, and for not allowing compliance to be monitored by an independent body. On the issue of monitoring, a former ambassador to the UN and former member of the US Congress, Andrew Young (working on an assignment at Nike – see also below) was criticized for not having conducted the monitoring of Nike subcontractors properly. He had therefore not been able to obtain the information required to substantiate his favourable statements on Nike's compliance with its code of conduct (CCC 1997a: 12, 1997b: 9).

What is seen here is the development of continued pressure to make Nike adopt more and more CSR policies. The codes of conduct initially adopted by Nike are targeted, first for their weak content and then for the absence of independent monitoring. When monitoring is performed by Nike, it is criticized for not being conducted accurately. The company is thus not able to get away with satisfying its critics simply by 'lip service' or public relations, which is often alleged to be the case when companies adopt CSR policies. Pressure from the organizations is not diminished by the response of the TNCs, but shifts to another level.

Legitimation of the Campaign   Support for the campaign against Nike in the US was eventually received from established organizations such as the United States Student Association, women's organizations (the Feminist Majority, the Black Women's Agenda and others), and the Asian Pacific American Labor Alliance (Global Exchange 1997e: 7). The entry of the Interfaith Center for Corporate Responsibility (ICCR) and the United Methodist Church into the campaign was also important. These organizations were well-respected US organizations whose

---

3   The Foul Ball Campaign focused on the issue of child labour in the soccer ball industry in Sialkot, Pakistan, and timed to 'coincide' with the European Cup. It received broad attention as well as the involvement of the International Federation of Football Association (FIFA).

support for the Nike campaign gave it legitimacy. These activists could not be discredited by calling them 'extremists'.

During the course of the campaign, a learning process was also involved for the Activists themselves. As companies began to respond to the campaign and address the problems that the NGOs exposed, the NGOs had to revise their own activities. For example, at one point, the European Nike campaign decided to broaden its focus from sports shoes and child labour to sportswear in general, as this:

> prevents campaigns from falling into a too one-sided approach by concentrating on a single topic. Reebok for example is speeding up its doing-good image by publicising its progress in abolishing child labour in the soccer ball production in Pakistan. Child labour is an important issue, but you run the risk of spending all your energy on a single issue such as child labour, … Big brands and retailers are all the more keen on trying to get all media and public focused on child labour and keep the other topics behind the curtain (CCC 1997b: 9).

Although child labour was an easy issue to use to mobilize support, when companies dealt with that particular issue, they could be seen to have solved the problem of CSR, even if many other issues were still outstanding. Consequently, the Activists had to revise their strategies (in response to the activities of the companies) and reflect on the motives behind various choices. Thus, a socializing of the Activists also occurred.

Exploring Legal Actions   An important event in the European campaign against Nike was the International Forum on Clean Clothes, organized in 1998 together with the Permanent Peoples Tribunal (CCC 1998a: 5). The event was organized as a traditional courtroom hearing, with a jury that listened to witnesses who testified on the working conditions at seven garment and sportswear companies, including Nike. All companies were invited to attend, but only the Swedish clothing retail chain H&M heard the call. Nike, however, sent a written statement and reports on labour conditions at its subcontractors, including the much criticized report by Andrew Young that was favourable to the situation at the subcontractors in general. The aim of the event was primarily to provide a forum for people who focused on workers' rights and to strengthen the networks for the participating witnesses, workers, NGOs and trade unions. The event also represented a possible arena for continued negotiation by presenting both sides of the argument, although the companies apparently did not see this benefit, as most of them decided not to participate. The 'verdict' of the jury was that voluntary codes of conduct needed to be transformed into formal agreements with trade unions and other NGOs, and that companies needed to institute independent monitoring of these codes of conduct. The jury also commented on the different ways that legal means could be employed in the future – among other things, through the development of national and international legal standards that also included consumer rights (the right to information about a product) and initiatives in the form of social labelling (CCC 1998b: 4).

Although it was a staged event, this tribunal had the effect of once again bringing up unfavourable information regarding Nike's activities. Nike's failure to show up and face its critics gave a bad impression of the company's behaviour.

Australian activists also participated in the campaign against Nike trying, among other things, to pressure Nike to sign the Australian joint industry-union initiative, the Homeworkers' Code of Practice, using the slogan 'Just Sign It'. This Code of Practice would allow independent monitoring of the working conditions of home workers employed by Nike's subcontractors. At about the same time, Nike was tried and convicted of a breach of Australian labour law and obliged to pay a penalty, which meant a victory for the Activists involved in the campaign.

In the US, another lawsuit, the so-called Kasky vs. Nike case, was filed against Nike. This suit was filed in San Francisco on the grounds that Nike had misrepresented working conditions in its public relations material. The controversy was over whether companies had the right to freedom of speech or whether such statements had to reflect reality (in that case comparable to 'commercial speech'). The case was eventually settled out of court in 2003, and there were fears at the time that companies would not dare address CSR issues publicly in the future. Nike was not the only company that risked lawsuits. A lawsuit was also filed against a competitor of Nike, adidas, by a former Chinese prisoner, for having been forced to stitch adidas' footballs while in prison (see also discussion in Chapter 8 for other lawsuits) (Joseph 2004).

These legal actions represent the more coercive aspects of the socialization of Nike's behaviour, that is, making use of legislation as leverage with regard to CSR. In combination with the negative campaigning discussed earlier, Nike felt the need to begin to actively restore its legitimacy.

Responses of Nike   After the initial response by Nike of adopting codes of conduct in 1992, continued criticism led the company to additional responses to the activities of the NGOs. These responses included several measures to counteract the negative publicity, including the establishment of a labour relations department to deal with the many issues that Nike confronted. Following Nike's annual stockholder meeting in 1996, when a shareholder resolution supported by the Interfaith Center for Corporate Responsibility (ICCR) was presented requesting independent monitoring of the company's code of conduct, Nike also began addressing the issue of monitoring. Nike decided to engage a well-known accounting firm as well as former UN Ambassador Andrew Young (mentioned earlier) to begin monitoring factories and investigate Nike's compliance with its code of conduct. Nike also participated in the establishment of the Fair Labor Association as a founding member (Global Exchange 1997b).[4]

---

4   The Fair Labor Association was established in 1996 by an initiative of the US Clinton administration. Nike is a founding member of the Fair Labor Association (FLA) and of the Business for Social Responsibility, another Business Initiative. Global Exchange has been critical of the organization, saying that this initiative lets the participating companies get off

As mentioned earlier, Nike was pressured to engage in direct dialogue with its critics or to engage in solving labour-related problems at subcontractors. Dialogue took place in 1996 with Global Exchange as well as with other representatives of Activists, including European campaign representatives. At the meeting with the European Nike Public Relations employees, Nike was presented with a petition signed by 5,000 individuals and organizations. According to CCC, the Nike representatives were not well informed about how Nike was working with CSR issues at the time (CCC 1997a: 13). This supports the argument that the code of conduct initially adopted in 1992 was not well implemented within the Nike corporation.

Other concessions made during this time occurred in connection with a labour conflict in a Nike factory in Mexico, reported in 2001, where Nike yielded to pressure and began mediating between factory management and a worker. Since Nike had denied taking responsibility in similar situations in the past, this represented a new strategy (Global Exchange 1998: 4, 2001: 6).

A more recent and quite radical measure by Nike was the decision in 2005 to openly identify the company's subcontractors. This kind of information is usually kept confidential by garment producers, who regard it as strategic information. Making the information public means that anyone can investigate the labour conditions at these factories, providing that access is given by the local factory owner. Workers can of course always be contacted outside of the factories, and knowing the location of the factories facilitated research by Activists.

The campaign against Nike thus contributed to CSR becoming a priority for Nike, diverting company resources and staff to attend to CSR matters through the creation of a specific department as well as engaging external resources for this purpose. The accounting firm in question (and probably other accounting firms) received new tasks, and a new line of accounting services would be developed. Nike also became yet another company to join a Business Initiative (Business for Social Responsibility) and contributed to the foundation of a Multi-stakeholder Organisation, the Fair Labor Association. Although there might not have been genuine interest in the issue at the time, through these activities Nike also contributed to the process of increasing attention to CSR.

Business Perspective on the Campaign on Nike   Although the IBLF did not take part in the Nike campaign, it became indirectly involved in the sportswear industry through its engagement in the Vietnam Business Links Initiative and in the publication of a brief report on the issue of 'brand-jacking', i.e., the situation in which the logo and goodwill of a brand is tarnished by the campaigning of Activists (brand-jacking will be discussed further in Chapter 8).

---

the hook too easily. On the occasion of the publication of an FLA report, Global Exchange publicized its comment on an advance copy. Medea Benjamin also testified before the FLA in 1997 on the issue of monitoring (Global Exchange 1997f: 1, 1997e: 3, CCC 1997a: 13, Shaw 1999).

The Vietnamese Business Links Initiative was established in 1999, following a UK government report (commissioned by the UK sportswear and garment corporation Pentland) on the use of chemicals in the footwear industry in Vietnam. The findings in the report led to consultation by the IBLF with various stakeholders, including the Vietnam Chamber of Commerce and Industry, representatives of the Vietnamese and UK governments, industry (Nike was one of the companies), NGOs and others. This consultation eventually led to the formation of the initiative (IBLF 2000: 17). In addition to its support for the Vietnam Business Links Initiative, as of 2004 Nike is also involved in the IBLF Partnering Initiative as a Programme Partner.

The Vietnamese Business Link Initiative focuses on safety and health, not labour conditions in general. In 2005, the initiative was expanded to cover the garment industry as a whole. The focus on safety and health is due to the issues raised in the 'Pentland report', mentioned earlier, which had been commissioned to investigate the use of chemicals. Thus, there is a contrast between the campaigns of the Activists, which addressed a range of labour rights issues, and the focus on health and safety by businesses, trade associations, governments and others involved in the initiative. However, without further insight into the development of the initiative, it is difficult to determine the motives behind this focus. Vietnam, like China, is a communist-ruled country that has adopted liberalization policies with a mix of state-owned and private enterprises. It is a country in transition, particularly after the fall of the Soviet Union. When the political opportunity structure of Vietnam is considered, it is comparable to that of China, with no free trade unions. Health and safety in the workplace may be perceived as a non-controversial arena in which to indirectly attend to other labour conditions. At the same time, this initiative provides businesses with legitimacy, showing that they are actively working on the issue without having to address more sensitive issues.

To conclude, the discussion of the Nike campaign demonstrates the process by which various activities targeting Nike for labour conditions at its subcontractors gradually compels the company to assume responsibility in new areas. Initially, this change was made reluctantly and without really serious interest, based on a belief that the mere adoption of a code of conduct would satisfy the critics, the general public and consumers. As the pressure became more intense, involving actors other than (allegedly radical) activists, Nike begins to make concessions in order to protect its reputation and maintain the image on which the company is built. As a consequence, it has now become in Nike's best interests to work with CSR, not only because of criticism from some US activists, but also because of a more international widespread expectation that no longer targets Nike alone. In the next chapter, we will see how the norm cascade plays out in specific issue-areas, further illustrating the actors, motives and social processes involved.

Chapter 8

Continued Norm Cascade: Voluntary Standards, Accountability Through Law, and Good Practice and Partnership

Another area of activity within the norm cascading stage of CSR in the 1990s is the development of and debate over standards and accountability. I will discuss here two types of standards: private voluntary standards (sometimes referred to as soft law) and standards that are formal in character (hard law). Standards are both an important means for CSR advocates to frame an issue and also serve as tools for advocacy, apart from the obvious purpose of attempting to regulate the behaviour of TNCs. The process by which standards are developed, launched and adopted is also a means of socialization: the participating actors interact in various ways, as adversaries, negotiators, and partners. The same can be said of legal accountability, the difference being that here existing 'standards' (i.e., legislation that also entail formal sanctions) are involved. Other examples of norm cascading, such as good practice and partnerships, are discussed later in this chapter.

As seen in Chapter 3, the regulation of TNCs was an important issue on the international agenda in the 1970s, when international organizations developed codes of conduct, guidelines or principles for TNCs. The involvement of IGOs in this issue diminished in the 1980s, to be replaced by involvement of NGOs and TNCs (Kolk and van Tulder 2006: 151). The voluntary codes of conduct we see from the 1980s have been developed in the garment and sportswear, hand-knotted carpets and agricultural industries (agribusiness), the retail sector in general, tourism and electronics. These sectors represent consumer products where awareness and mobilization of support is easier to achieve than in other sectors.

The development of standards has in fact been an important activity for the focus organizations. Unlike the CCC and FLO, not all of the organizations have developed standards of their own, but they have in that case participated in or supported the development by others of codes of conduct. The findings in this study regarding of the activities of the CSR organizations thus support the arguments that a norm cascade occurred in the mid-1990s. I will begin here with a discussion of the social labelling initiative of the FLO, the CCC Model Code, and the involvement of the IBLF in the development of the Voluntary Principles for Human Rights and the UN Global Compact Principles.[1]

---

1 Global Exchange has not developed standards of their own, nor have they specifically advocated for any particular standards. Support is, however, given to advocacy

Fairtrade Labelling Standards

The Fairtrade labelling initiative that began with the work of Max Havelaar in The Netherlands (discussed in Chapter 6) involved a difficult negotiation on the tradeoffs between alternative trade and involvement with market economy that included representatives of the large coffee companies. Although the development of the Fairtrade label in The Netherlands was successful, and the label spread rapidly to other countries, the process was not without conflict.

Competition between the National Initiatives

When the social labelling scheme had reached enough countries, there was a push to develop an international label. This push meant that the various national social labelling initiatives had to agree on a common standard for this label, and there was a certain amount of competition between the nationally developed labelling initiatives. The competition between the German initiative and the other national labelling initiatives became especially contentious. Aside from internal differences within the movement, what became apparent was that social labelling involves a difficult tradeoff, i.e., the exclusion of small growers who do not meet the standards or attain the quality required to get their coffee to market. In order to satisfy consumer demand for a certain quality, some coffee farmers had to be left out.

According to the founders of the Dutch labelling initiative (Roozen and van der Hoff 2002), the main obstacle was the German national initiative TransFair, established in 1993 by Gepa (a German alternative trade organization established in 1975). There were at the time differences within Gepa on whether the proper strategy for the organization was to cooperate with business or not. The path chosen was to develop a German version of Max Havelaar, keeping control over the distribution of Fairtrade labelled products within the alternative trade organization and not cooperating with commercial coffee companies, distributors and retailers. There was also an interest in taking the lead in launching a European-wide label and a European organization. Gepa consequently actively advocated for their version of Fairtrade labelling in Italy, Canada, the US, Japan and Austria. Gepa thus wanted to develop a labelling initiative within the system of the traditional alternative trade organizations, whereas Max Havelaar represented a new approach that included working with the coffee companies and using commercial distribution channels. Other disagreements concerned the issue of inclusion of plantation workers and the degree to which the new organization of Fairtrade would be centralized (Eshuis and Harmsen 2003).

---

for governmental procurement resolutions and for the regulation in general of TNCs and of the global market as a whole, although not through the proposal of specific model standards.

These differences were eventually overcome, and the different national labelling initiatives were able to agree on a common international label and organization, resulting in the establishment of the FLO in 1997. The motivation behind the creation of FLO was, however, not simply pragmatism, i.e., to allow producers and consumer countries to avoid having to deal with each and every national labelling scheme separately, thereby facilitating contact. There were also more strategic reasons for the participating national initiatives, in that a common organization would give the labelling scheme a stronger profile and better image, which, in turn, would be of assistance in, e.g., obtaining funding from other NGOs, IGOs and others (Harmsen 2004). As of 2002, there is a common Fairtrade label for all participating national initiatives. Consequently, the development of Fairtrade was a process of change not only for the participating companies but also for the Fairtrade movement itself.

In conclusion, the creation of FLO may be seen as an important event in the second phase of the development of Fairtrade, the general professionalization of Fairtrade. Together with the presence of other Fairtrade organizations mentioned above and their coordination in FINE, one also may find support for the argument of a third phase in Fairtrade, i.e., when issues of marketing, cooperation, quality, etc., become important. The third phase will be discussed further below.

Institutionalization of Roles and Functions

FLO and its members (the national labelling organizations) play different roles in carrying out the aims and activities of the organization. *The national labelling organizations* work to encourage both industry and consumers to support the Fairtrade system and contract for the use of the FLO Fairtrade label with the FLO licensee companies in each country. This involves a careful compromise, as the industry should join the labelling system but at the same time be made aware of the working conditions of the small farmers and plantations where the coffee is produced. The main tasks of FLO are: (1) acting as a guarantor of the standards; (2) facilitating business for the producer; and (3) supporting the organization and production of producers (FLO 2004a). In brief, the organization simultaneously plays an activist or advocacy role as well as a technical and monitoring role, which involves maintaining a delicate balance between protecting interests and positive campaigning.[2]

The standards are guaranteed through *certification*, which includes control of compliance, the use of benefits, making sure that the Fairtrade price is paid, and the use of the label. This control is accomplished using independent inspectors, whereas traders and retailers are controlled using a trade auditing system. There are different standards for small farmers (cooperatives), organized workers on plantations and in

---

2   Unless otherwise indicated, the data presented in this section is based on information from various Internet websites of FLO, see Bibliography.

factories (concerning wages, trade unions, etc.) and specific products.[3] The standards contain 'minimum requirements', a requisite for certification, and 'progress requirements' to encourage improvements beyond the minimum requirements. For traders, participation involves the following requirements:

- Price that covers costs of sustainable production and living;
- Premiums for investments in development;
- Partial advance payment on demand;
- Contracts that allow for long-term planning and sustainable production practices.

The requirements for traders are at the core of the Fairtrade idea in general, i.e., they represent standards that reveal terms of trade in which producers are equal partners with importers and traders – a levelling of the playing field. A brief look at the actors in the FLO Fairtrade supply chain may explain the need for the Fairtrade label as leverage for improving the situation of small farmers and plantation workers; among the many actors involved in the supply chain are producers (small farmers), processors (of the product in the country of origin), exporters, importers (paying the FLO Fairtrade price/premium to the country of origin), manufacturers (in the consuming country), subcontractors (providing processing or distribution service to a trader), and agents (facilitating buying or selling for a commission).

As of 2007, well over 600 certified producer organizations representing over 1.5 million farmers and workers in 60 countries are involved in FLO. Apart from the certified producers, there are also a number of registered traders, licensees and authorized users of the Fairtrade label for final sale to the consumers. This represents quite a development from the Fairtrade movement's beginning just two decades ago with the establishment of Max Havelaar (FLO 2007).

The producer organization as a whole is formally subject to the standards in the ILO conventions; only the Fairtrade part of the trader organization's activities is subject to the FLO Fairtrade requirements, not the organization as a whole. However, there are also so-called maintenance criteria for traders, and FLO has the right to exclude traders who bring FLO Fairtrade into disrepute with actions not directly related to Fairtrade, such as serious and repeated contraventions of the core ILO conventions. This last issue became a matter of dispute when Nestlé recently received Fairtrade approval for one of its coffee products (Derbyshire 2005, see also Chapter 4 on Nestlé).

A complex organizational structure manages the coordination of these activities and the fulfilment of the stated aims and tasks. The structure is designed so as to, on the one hand, consider stakeholder representation, and on the other,

---

3   In the case of the standards for small farmers, these are especially based on the ILO conventions, as well as export ability (including quality), and gradually acquiring export process responsibility (FLO 2003c).

accommodate the need for independent standard-setting and certification. The more important bodies of FLO are responsible for the governance structure and the standards and certification activities. These activities are carried out in compliance with ISO Standards for Certification Bodies and the ISEAL (International Social and Environmental Accreditation and Labelling)[4] Code of Practice on Standards Setting, i.e., the standard setters themselves are submitted to standards. The requirements for certification and that trade auditing activities be carried out in compliance with the ISO Standards reduces the risk of financial liability. Financial stability is further improved by diversifying income; all stakeholders contribute to financing.[5]

At first glance, FLO might be regarded as focusing only on creating an alternative to current trade to benefit a certain group of producers, namely, small farmers, and thus be perceived as a more inward-looking organization. However, FLO also indirectly aspires to achieve a transformation of international trade as a whole into trade based on more equitable terms of trade. This is where the role of the national labelling organizations is important and complements the more 'technical side' of FLO's activities. The national labelling organizations are in charge of promoting the initiative, both to business and consumers, whereas FLO works with the functioning of the Fairtrade labelling system.[6]

The activities and governance structure of FLO are to some extent far removed from that of the traditional NGO and suggest a combination of a company, an NGO and an IGO. The organization is partly concerned with profit making (for the producers and the commercial actors), but not with profit maximization. At the same time, there is a social-change purpose, with a focus on empowering the producers but with the need to be attentive to market mechanisms (supply and demand, marketing, including the market actors) and to take into consideration national initiatives, producer organizations, and others, while still providing independent and transparent decision procedures – a complicated task, to say the least. To achieve this, a very structured and one might say bureaucratized organization has been constructed, bureaucratized in the sense that specific roles and functions are created to maintain the working of the system as well as its credibility (see also Chapter 9 on agents of internalization).

---

4   ISEAL is an organization of the prominent international standard-setting, certification and accreditation organizations within the areas of social and environmental issues (see also Chapter 9).

5   This includes the national initiatives (the largest share) through licensees for the use of the Fairtrade label, a part of which is passed on to the FLO. The producers contribute a smaller share through the fees paid for certification and the volume sold under Fairtrade conditions. The registered traders pay fees based on their total annual turnover, and finally, the consumers pay through a higher price.

6   As TransFair USA explains, its second purpose is to use Fairtrade as leverage for change in general in the area of CSR. The US experienced growth of 90 per cent between 2002 and 2003 of Fairtrade coffee (Interview with Funkhouser 2004).

Clean Clothes Campaign's Model Code

The CCC's success in drawing the attention of the general public and of companies to problems in the production of garments by subcontractors in foreign countries (seen in Chapter 5) was soon followed by the expectation that CCC would also be able to tell the public and the companies what should be done to fix the problems. However, CCC had no specific answers to offer and so began exploring ways to address this issue.

Answering to the Expectations

CCC had to respond to the reactions to the pressure it had exerted on companies and the general public and to go through a learning process to expand its first specific concern into more generalized aims and solutions. This led to the need to bring into the process other actors with knowledge about labour matters, such as trade unions.

Various solutions to the subcontractor problem were contemplated, such as union labels, alternative trade, international law, and social clauses in trade agreements. In 1992, the Fair Wear Charter working group, based in The Netherlands, was established to continue this work. A first draft of what was to become the CCC Model Code (then called the Fair Wear Charter) was issued in 1993 and shared with other organizations, including organizations in Asia that the CCC had contact with or knew about. At this time, the general points raised related to specific standards regarding wages, hours of work, and health and safety, as references to ILO core conventions alone were not seen as sufficient to guarantee adequate working conditions in the garment industry. This implied that specific standards should be stated in the CCC Model Codes, not left up to negotiations between employers and employees or national legislation. A later draft was also shared with the retailers' association in The Netherlands, who at the time found the demands unrealistic and did not enter into serious dialogue with the CCC but simply referred the responsibility to the government. This reluctance on the part of the retailers and garment producers was to change later (CCC 1995d, Ascoly and Zeldentrust 1999).

After this initial work on the CCC Model Code, it was decided to expand the effort beyond The Netherlands and involve other national CCC initiatives and other organizations in Europe. This need coincided with another, broader need among NGOs in general, and the CCC Model Code provided an impetus for mobilization and unification (a form of socialization). According to the perception of the CCC themselves, this related to the following:

> For most of these organisations the Clean Clothes meetings were the first time they were together in one room. The potential for building this type of coalition was a real incentive for many organisations to become active at their national level. Unions as well as development NGOs, and those with a background in

the solidarity movement, felt a real decline in membership, mobilizing power, and public attention. This had been going on for years, but had gotten to a stage where it was so serious that people were willing to try new things, and form new alliances. The rifts caused by the social clause debates had closed many doors, preventing collaboration even in areas where it was politically possible. Providing a way out of this impasse was welcome (Ascoly and Zeldentrust 1999).

The activities of the CCC and the development of the CCC Model Code had a unifying effect similar to that seen in the anti-apartheid campaign and the Nestlé Boycott discussed in Chapter 4. It marked a new development in campaigning that seemed to energize the movement as a whole.

Simultaneously, companies started adopting individual codes of conduct as a response to the growing concerns being voiced by Activists. It was therefore seen as important that the CCC construct a joint model code, to set high standards for companies (perceived as developing too-lax regulations for themselves) and for European and Asian organizations to speak with one voice. During the course of the process, it was also deemed practical that the NGOs in Europe be given the task of addressing the retailers and companies in the North due to their easier access, being in the same location (Ascoly and Zeldentrust 1999). Asian NGOs carried out their activities on site at the local subcontractors. A division of labour was thereby created among the participating organizations, which would contribute to the relative invisibility of Asian NGOs in CSR advocacy.

The CCC Model Code not only clarified the demands of the CCC in a fairly extensive document (as opposed to brief and general guidelines), it also filled another purpose 'we saw the use of codes as a way to enter into a political debate, forcing companies to talk about the notion of a living wage and of job security, and forcing authorities to react to violations of the right to organize' (Ascoly and Zeldentrust 1999).

The CCC Model Code became a tool for framing that could be launched in various contexts to serve different purposes. Whereas a picket line in front of retailers would attract attention for a moment, an elaborate statement in a document used in a strategic way would last longer. The more stringent CCC Model Code was also seen as a 'reality check', i.e., it served as a check on whether companies complied with their own codes of conduct and challenged weaker company codes of conduct (Ascoly and Zeldentrust 1999, CCC 2000c: 19).

The final CCC Model Code was launched in 1998 and signed by international trade unions, Asian organizations and the approximately 250 NGOs and trade unions that had participated in the current national CCC initiatives (CCC 2002: 23). Some companies also signed the CCC Model Code and participated in multi-stakeholder initiatives on the national level that carried the work on to the next step, i.e., projects discussing implementation, monitoring, verification and 'road-testing' of the CCC Model Code.

One interesting development that has followed is a garment industry initiative in 2003, when a joint code of conduct was established within the Business Social

Compliance Initiative (BSCI). The Business Social Compliance Initiative was developed by the Foreign Trade Association, which consists mainly of retailers in Europe. According to CCC, however, the BSCI code of conduct and monitoring system has several flaws: it is weak on issues of freedom of association, not all companies are monitored, workers cannot submit complaints and there is a lack of transparency and stakeholder involvement in general (CCC 2005).

We can see here a continuation of the interaction between the CCC and the garment industry. However, the debate has shifted, from initial rejection by the clothing industry and the retailers of the idea of a code of conduct to other aspects of the issue. Instead of debating whether companies have responsibility or not, the discussion now involves what that responsibility might possibly include as well as more practical matters, i.e., how to monitor compliance in an accurate and credible manner. This represents, in my opinion, an example of socialization, where the initial norm entrepreneurs have actually managed to achieve a change in the perception of the clothing industry and retailers, who now actually engage in CSR.

Although the CCC can be said to have been successful in forcing garment companies to address the issue of labour conditions with their subcontractors, even if the companies do not fully comply with the CCC Model Code, aspects of self-criticism also appear. CCC's self-evaluation not only covers what strategies were most effective, but also more general issues, such as the risk of legitimation when non-complying companies are involved with CCC, enhancement of voluntary standards at the cost of formal regulation, and contribution to a process that is leading to an undermining of the state (CCC 2002: 23).

Influencing others in order to change existing structures ultimately involves a change to the norm entrepreneur as well. Managing to draw attention to the issue of labour conditions in the garment industry meant that the norm entrepreneurs, like CCC, now had expectations to live up to. The process involved is one of mutual constitution, where engaging in social practices means affecting others and being affected oneself.

Standards by Business Initiatives

Business Initiatives also promote specific standards of their own, such as the Global Sullivan Principles, the Caux Round Table Principles for Business, and the SVN Standards. These specific standards vary in form and content. *The Global Sullivan Principles* include eight brief principles that refer to universal human rights, equal opportunity, freedom of association, compensation, safety and health, the environment and sustainable development, fair competition, community involvement, promotion and transparency of application of the principles. They were influenced by previous civil rights struggles and are fairly similar to the UN Global Compact Principles. The former UN Secretary General, Kofi Annan, participated in the launch of the Global Sullivan Standards in 1999, just as the UN Global Compact was initiated (Leon H. Sullivan Foundation

2005a, 2005b, see also Chapter 4). *The Caux Principles* (adopted in 1994) are also fairly brief, with a section clarifying the general principles of human dignity and 'kyosei' (referring to the stakeholder perspective and the importance of contributing to economic and social development), and another section dealing specifically with stakeholders. Among the general principles are references to avoiding trade friction by respecting international and domestic rules as well as to supporting multilateral trade systems and their institutions. Both the Global Sullivan Principles and the Caux Principles focus on principles rather than specifics, i.e., they are more brief and general in form and therefore also more vague and difficult to implement as well as to check for compliance.

In contrast, the *SVN Standards* represent an elaborate formulation of a CSR standard (SVN 1999). The SVN Standards are the result of the contributions of some 220 individuals involved in CSR, drawing from many sources (e.g., other NGOs, local government, international instruments, IGOs, etc.). These standards could be said to represent a more multi-stakeholder-approach-influenced document with a higher degree of specificity without explicit detailed standards (reference is made to various other standards).

The SVN Standards takes CSR further than brief guidelines that focus on content, as they are more specific and easy to measure against actual performance in the areas that they cover. One can thus check for compliance or 'reality', and the argument could be made that these more specific standards are evidence of a step towards internalization of CSR within the business community. Whereas the vagueness of briefly stated general principles makes for more easy mobilization of support, vague general principles are difficult to implement or check for compliance.

Although not all organizations in the Business Initiative category present standards of their own, support the standards of others or openly declare their affiliation to a certain definition of CSR, they may of course contribute to CSR advocacy in other ways. Some Business Initiatives take part in joint efforts, as in the case of the IBLF, mentioned above, or the World Business Council on Sustainable Development, in their support for the Global Reporting Initiative. In addition, the development of independent monitoring schemes, 'dialogues' or multi-stakeholder forums also constitute arenas for framing, even if more implicitly or unintentionally (and sometimes in a less transparent way). The framing of CSR may thus take other forms than the development of specific standards, i.e., but be less obvious or transparent.

The IBLF has not developed its own standards, such development clearly not being within the scope of the organization. However, it has participated in the development of standards by others and has also given support to similar initiatives. In the case of the Voluntary Principles on Security and Human Rights, launched in 2000, the IBLF and Business for Social Responsibility (another Business Initiative) jointly provided its secretary with a secretariat (as of 2004). In other cases, the IBLF has acted as a founding partner of initiatives (IBLF 2001a). The Voluntary Principles is a multi-stakeholder initiative with guidelines for companies to develop appropriate safety policies to protect their operations without jeopardizing respect for human rights. The initiative involves governments in The Netherlands, Norway, UK and the US; companies, mainly in the extractive industry; and NGOs. The initiative is built on dialogue and reviews reported by an internal working group. Thus, no independent monitoring scheme is involved.

The IBLF has also provided input to the development of the UN Draft Norms (an initiative of the former UN Sub-Commission on Human Rights to develop standards for business) and on other occasions issued statements in support of these norms. The IBLF has stated that the UN Draft Norms:

> go further than any of the existing codes and guidelines defining human rights responsibilities of the private sector. The Draft Principles are the most authoritative and comprehensive set of guidelines to date which make the UDHR applicable to companies. … The Draft principles are complementary to the UN Global Compact and could very usefully build upon the human rights components of that initiative … providing a unique common reference point for companies and bringing much needed clarity to a difficult area (IBLF 2002, 2003a).

The IBLF goes even further in advocating their views on future application of the suggested UN Draft Norms, putting emphasis on the importance of strong implementation and verification to strengthen the framework of CSR as guidance for companies. In response to criticism that the UN Draft Norms are not flexible, the IBLF claims that the norms present guidelines in the area of human rights, in contrast to various other initiatives. This sets the IBLF apart from one of its partners, the International Chamber of Commerce (ICC), as well as from other trade and business associations in general, such as the International Organization of Employers (IOE) and the United States Council in Business (USCIB) that, in contrast to the IBLF, are strongly opposed to the UN Draft Norms (see also Chapter 9).

Accountability Through Law

Attempts to make TNCs assume responsibility for the negative aspects of their operations have in the past mainly comprised voluntary initiatives. Yet there are also attempts at developing formal accountability, involving such initiatives as lawsuits in national courts, national legislative measures, a European Parliament resolution (the so-called Howitt Resolution), and the UN Draft Norms, which will be discussed in the next chapter. One effort that has drawn considerable attention are the US Alien Tort Claims Act (ATCA) lawsuits that the ILRF has participated in launching.

Legal action and litigation became an important part of the work of the ILRF during the second half of the 1990s (ILRF 1993). This trend had already started with the GSP complaints (see Chapter 5) in the late 1980s and continued with the work on NAFTA in the early 1990s, but a new phase of legal-action activities began with the cases brought under the ATCA. These cases represented an innovative use of legislation dating back to the eighteenth century that allowed a foreign national to sue US citizens for violations of international law. The crimes under ATCA are limited to serious human rights violations, including genocide, war crimes, slavery, extra judicial killings, torture, unlawful detention and crimes against humanity. A network of lawyers, law students and law teachers called the ILR Advocates had been created some years earlier as a resource for this work (as well as for the GSP and NAFTA complaints). The purpose of the ILR Advocates was to provide assistance in legal analysis and advocacy for the ILRF and other groups promoting worker and trade union rights for those engaged in or affected by international trade. In spite of limited resources, the organization was able in this way to access professional staff resources without having to find funding.

In 1996, ILRF filed the first case under the ATCA on behalf of a group of Burmese refugees. The case concerned Unocal Corporation (a US-based oil and gas company) that was accused of using forced labour to construct a gas pipeline in Burma and seeking competitive advantage by cooperating with the Burmese military government (the case was settled out of court in December 2004). Examples of additional lawsuits under the ATCA concerning serious human rights violations are (ILRF 2002, Collingsworth 2003):

- *Exxon Mobile Corporation* (2001) – alleged cooperation with Indonesian security forces that committed human rights violations;
- *Del Monte Corporation* (2001) – alleged torture and unlawful detention of trade union leaders in Guatemala;
- *DynCorp* (2001) – alleged responsibility for wrongful death, crimes against humanity and other property crimes as a consequence of spraying fumigants on coca plants in Colombia on contract for the US government;
- *Coca-Cola and Pan American Beverages, Inc.* (2001) – alleged cooperation with death squads in Colombia;
- *Drummond Company* (2002) – alleged cooperation with paramilitaries in Colombia;
- *Occidental Petroleum* (2003) – alleged role in the murder of innocent civilians in Colombia;
- *Daimler Chrysler* (2004) – alleged to provide names of union leaders, suspected 'subversives', to the former Argentinean military government.

These lawsuits represent an expansion of the focus on labour rights in the work of the ILRF to include the issue of TNCs and their implications in human rights violations in general and, in particular, serious human rights violations. Holding companies legally accountable for violations of human rights, including labour rights, thus became an important part of ILRF activities in the 1990s.

The challenge to TNCs in the ATCA lawsuits has not gone unnoticed and has spurred the business community to fight back. In a statement to the US Supreme

Court, nine US and international business and trade associations, including the ICC, raised concerns over the development of the lawsuits.[7] The overall concern was that these cases 'strain relations between the United States and the foreign governments' and that they 'discourage foreign investments'. The statement also pointed out that the lawsuits target 'companies with deep pockets' and that the plaintiffs, lawyers and organizations are using the lawsuits to 'embarrass foreign governments and pressure business to abandon operations in targeted nations'. Concerns over the lawsuits were also voiced in *The Wall Street Journal* and by the Institute for International Economics in Washington, DC, terming them 'judicial imperialism', and were accompanied by calls to the US Congress to take action (Bork 2003, Hufbauer and Mitrokostas 2003, Magnusson 2002). These lawsuits have brought matters to a head, very similar to what can be seen in the case of the UN Draft Norms discussed in Chapter 9, and provoked a strong reaction from the business community and others. This situation no longer could be characterized as troublesome criticism from Activists but rather as the possibility of coercive legal measures by the state.

The CCC has also considered legal measures, and it established a working group in 2001 to explore possibilities in this area. An example is the advocacy of so-called Clean Clothes Communities where local government and authorities such as cities, schools, etc. adopt resolutions that support the purchase of ethically produced garments in different ways (CCC 2000a) (compare with Fairtrade Zones advocated by Global Exchange). Litigation similar to that in the UK and the US and formal legislation are also means that were explored in forums such as the International Forum and other seminars (CCC 2003). Thus, some of the focus organization explored a whole range of activities, including binding regulation, whereas other organizations remained limited to mainly private voluntary measures as will be seen below.

Good Practice and Partnerships

Whereas certain focus organizations addressed specific negative aspects of trade or TNC activities, the IBLF chose to focus on the positive aspects of trade and TNCs, and explore how these could be turned into a force for good. Recurring themes are the development of what is labelled 'good practice' and advocating partnership.

---

7   Brief for the National Foreign Trade Council, USA*Engage, The Chamber of Commerce of the United States of America, The United States Council for International Business, The International Chamber of Commerce, The Organization for International Investment, The Business Roundtable, the American Petroleum Institute, and the US-ASEAN Business Council as amici curiae in support of petitioner, No. 03–339, In the Supreme Court of the United States, Sosa v. Alvarez-Machain, et al., On Writ of Certiorari to the United States Court of Appeals for the Ninth Circuit. 23 January 2004.

Framing Good Practice

The promotion of 'values-based leadership amongst the business community to improve responsible business practice in all aspects of a company's operations' is an important goal of the IBLF (IBLF undated a). This promotion is accomplished by providing practical assistance to companies, including tools such as 'good practice' advice. Good practice can be regarded as a form of standards or codes of conduct formulated more as incentives than as constraints focusing on compliance and deviance. Good practice is something that is shared among companies. The company that has experience working with CSR also has good practice advice to share with others and is given a leadership role in demonstrating the possibilities and benefits of such behaviour. The motives given to businesses for adopting responsible business practices and engaging in development are:

> By championing the pursuit of good business standards and development objectives through company operations, business leaders can address the downsides of globalisation, set standards to encourage other business leaders to engage in societal issues and enhance long-term shareholder value. Business leaders can define the boundaries of business involvement in development and encourage leaders of civil society to recognise the positive role of the private sector in development challenges and embracing diversity (IBLF undated a).

Here business leaders are given a role in creating a win-win situation by adopting responsible business practices and engaging in their definition. Business leaders are thus given an opportunity to address the negative aspects of globalization, which TNCs are part of, to convince the representatives of civil society of the values of business, and to participate actively in setting limits on responsibility, which otherwise is left to other actors. Those who do so are portrayed as taking a 'leadership' role or exercising stewardship, which should seem attractive to business leaders used to 'being in charge'. In this way, they can be a role model for others. In the long run, this approach is also portrayed as producing economic returns in terms of increasing shareholder value, i.e., the bottom line, and the business case is satisfied.

It is worth noting that the IBLF in a subtle way is suggesting that the TNCs, as actors in the international system in general and CSR in particular, have a stake in the development of CSR. As key actors in this issue area, they should have a say in what CSR is all about. Furthermore, introducing the perspective of the business case hopefully serves to remind the other actors that economic transactions and business is still very much a central aspect of any discussion of CSR.

The IBLF have in various ways attempted to persuade companies of the benefits of good practices. An early report from 1994, *Partnership and Sustainable Development*, discusses the role of business in partnerships in various areas, such as in the workplace and the marketplace, research and training, host communities and in public policy. In the case of the workplace and the marketplace, it is suggested that the company can:

> co-operate more closely with its employees (including trade unions), its customers, suppliers, financiers, and even its competitors and environmental activists, to develop cleaner processes and products, to establish voluntary standards and policies, to market sustainably managed resources and to share experiences and burdens (IBLF and UNEP 1994: 10).

Similarly, certain activities are suggested as appropriate for partnerships, such as developing new technologies, products and management styles; contributing to the quality of life through social investments; and participating in work on incentives and regulatory frameworks. A number of model cases of different successful partnerships are presented as real examples to demonstrate to companies that such partnerships actually work in real life and to inspire them to do likewise.

In 1995, the Partners in Development programme, which dealt with good practice with the purpose of 'encouraging replication and wider implementation' was launched in cooperation with the World Bank and the United Nations Environment Programme (UNEP). The contributions of companies through this good practice are in particular related to:

> the profitable, responsible and innovative performance of its core business activities, through its social investment and strategic philanthropy programmes, and through the advocacy and advisory role that the private sector can play in the public policy debate (Nelson 1996: 6).

The IBLF raises the good practice argument in several other areas, such as in regard to the issue of HIV/AIDS and the discussion of the role of business, including examples of actions taken by well-known companies (Rio Tinto plc., Chevron Corporation, Levi Strauss and Co.). These companies become showcases for good practices. Again, we can see an argument for business leaders to combine business activities, although perhaps not business as usual, with responsible conduct and engagement with society. This also points to business taking an active part in the development of CSR, participating in defining what CSR is to constitute.

The good practice argument also receives attention from a more theoretical or a tool-oriented perspective in the development of a more elaborate framework, as seen in the launch of the so-called societal shareholder value-added framework. Building on the experiences of the Partners in Development programme, this framework identifies and discusses the content of five pillars of corporate performance that simultaneously add value for both shareholders and society. Whereas the previously mentioned strategies of persuasion simply argued for responsible business practices and presented concrete examples of such practices, this framework enhances the argument when referring to lessons learned from concrete projects, company experiences, and research.

Later advocacy by the IBLF of good practices involves more explicit 'stick and carrot' arguments. One example of an explicit incentive is the World Business Award in support of the Millenium Development Goals, which is an award given by the IBLF together with the ICC and the UNDP for business contributions made to development. The Award has been given in 2004, 2006 and 2008, and among the recipients are some of the better-known TNCs, including De Beers, Proctor and Gamble, GlaxoSmithKline, and Tetra Pak (IBLF 2006).

However, the risks ('sticks') involved by not addressing these issues are also highlighted. The IBLF had already begun to raise the issue of human rights in 1997 with the organization of dialogues. In 2000 and 2002, two joint publications with Amnesty International followed, entitled *Human Rights: Is it Any of Your Business?* (Frankental and House 2000) and *Business and Human Rights: The Corporate Geography of Risks* (Amnesty International and IBLF 2002). These publications linked the operation of particular TNCs with specific human rights violations in the country of operation. The reports cover various risks and dilemmas involved in TNC operations in countries with records of human right violations, showcase TNCs that took measures in support of human rights and list various guidelines for good practice. The TNCs are not explicitly accused of human rights abuses, but the argument is that these companies run a high risk by not taking measures to assure that there is no link to such abuses. In a sense, the business and human rights issue is inadvertently framed by exposing the TNCs through what could be called 'guilt by association', indirectly providing a road map for activists to target TNCs. The presence of Amnesty International in this effort lends important legitimacy and credibility to the issues as well as to the IBLF.

Another example that illustrates a somewhat similar approach is the discussion of the phenomenon of 'brand-jacking', i.e., the situation in which activists target a company by using the logo or similar unique brand characteristic of a high profile company in their campaigns; in the Nike case, for example, their slogan, 'Just Do It' (see Chapter 7). Brand-jacking is a situation where:

> a third party hitches a ride on a brand's fame, positioning and slogan and uses them for its communications' own purposes – whilst undermining the brand's reputation in the process. Cynical! Perhaps. Effective? Usually. Here to stay? Definitely! (Enterprise IG and IBLF 2004).

Other sections of the publication refer to this phenomenon using stronger words, such as 'exploitation' by the third party and acting 'like a parasite'. The purpose of highlighting this threat is to turn it into a challenge to which a company has to rise. Also implied is a transformation of the traditional role of business to a role that addresses the needs and opinions of stakeholders and the behaviour of the company as a whole, and where CSR is at the centre of successful business practices. As the cases of Nike and Nestlé show, this is a reality for some TNCs. Here, the IBLF and other companies frame the issues as issues of appropriate behaviour, and companies trying to avoid or improve a bad reputation and in search of legitimacy are given guidance on what to do.

Importance of Partnerships

As was seen in the previous chapter, the IBLF began working with international organizations, particularly IGOs, early, and the idea of partnerships was and still is an important part of the IBLF work. It is, in fact, one of its stated aims to:

> develop cross-sector partnerships between governments and NGOs to stimulate collective action on social, economic and environmental issues (IBLF undated a).

Partnerships is also one of the dominant themes of the more than 60 reports and briefs that the IBLF has issued since it started in 1990.[8] These reports deal both with specific partnerships, what they consist of and what they have achieved, and with the idea of partnerships in general and how to create them. The partnership strategy is both a way to address pressing issues like development and, for the IBLF, as a relatively small organization, to engage others in its activities. Partnerships are also integral to the view of the IBLF that there is a need for shared responsibility to meet the challenges of globalization. Companies have a responsibility to contribute to the solution but cannot do so alone. Other actors have to do their part.

Apart from advocating the benefits of partnership, another feature that distinguishes the work of the IBLF from the other focus organizations is the organization's early involvement with IGOs – i.e., its own participation in partnerships. Although the IBLF does not hold consultative status at the UN, a few years after its establishment the IBLF had already initiated cooperation with some of the more prominent international organizations, including the World Bank, the United Nations Development Programme (UNDP) and the UNEP (IBLF 2003b).[9]

This cooperation with IGOs manifests the organization's different status compared to other NGOs, having a representative of a well-known royal family as its President and being from a country that still holds a position as an important centre for world finance. Having large TNCs among its members has also contributed to the organization's special status. These particular features provide the IBLF with unique opportunities for access not available to other NGOs, which therefore do not have the same potential for engagement and influence. A discussion of the

---

8   About one-third of the publications of the IBLF from 1992 onwards make explicit references to partnership.

9   In the case of CCC, the organization does not give priority to work with IGOs. The contacts mainly concern events that the CCC has been invited to or provided information for. The CCC, however, targets both the EU and member countries on certain issues and receives funding from the EU (Interview with Eyskoot 2004).

work of the IBLF with the various IGOs shows that the IBLF tends to work 'from inside', as opposed to other NGOs, which work on the outside.

The cooperation with the World Bank, UNEP and UNDP resulted in the above mentioned programme, Partners in Development, launched in 1995. This programme referred not only to economic contributions to society but also to activities outside the traditional sphere of business activities, regarding businesses as important contributors to:

> widening economic opportunity and participation, investing in human capital, promoting environmental sustainability and social cohesion. It [the Partners in Development programme] promotes the positive multiplier effect that business can have through the profitable, responsible and innovative performance of its core business activities, through its social investment and strategic philanthropy programmes, and through the advocacy and advisory role that the private sector can play in the public policy debate (Nelson 1996: 6).

Cooperation with the World Bank also included activities such as a joint mission to the Colombian oilfields in 1995 to examine the effect of business activities on society, and various meetings and seminars, including a World Bank Corporate Citizenship Day in 1996 to discuss good practice and private-public partnerships (IBLF 2003b, Nelson 1996).

This cooperation has been maintained, even though the Partners in Development programme has ended, the former President of the World Bank, James Wolfensohn is (as of 2009) a member of IBLF international advisory board. Since the termination of the Partners in Development programme, the issue of development has mainly been dealt with in cooperation with the UNDP and in relation to the Millennium Development Goals. The IBLF and the UNDP have jointly published supplements to the *Financial Times* on the issue of business and development in 2004 and 2005 (in 2003 and 2006, supplements on HIV/AIDS were published in cooperation with the Global Business Coalition).[10] The cooperation with UNDP also includes the Partnering Initiative, which is conducted in cooperation with Cambridge University and provides courses, research and publication, tools for practice, and the like concerning partnerships (IBLF undated b).

The IBLF has also been closely involved in other UN activities, such as in the development of the UN Global Compact. This involvement included contributing to the development of the UN Global Compact principles, their website, and support to the UK Global Compact network by providing a secretariat to the initiative in its initial years (IBLF 2001b). The IBLF has furthermore contributed to advocacy of the work of the UN Global Compact by issuing a guide to companies for implementation of the UN Global Compact Principles at the local level.

---

10   In 1997, a report was issued in cooperation with UNAIDS with the title *The Business Response to HIV/AIDS: Innovation and Partnership* (IBLF and UNAIDS 1997).

Unlike most other businesses and business associations, the IBLF also lends its support to the UN Draft Norms. In addition to providing support to the UN Draft Norms in the public statements mentioned above, the IBLF has also assisted the UN Special Representative on Business and Human Rights, John Ruggie, in a survey on the policies and practices of the Fortune 500 companies (Ruggie 2006). Here, the IBLF parts company with large parts of the business community such as the ICC, an organization with which the IBLF has cooperated in the past and continues to cooperate in other CSR-related matters.[11] The IBLF thus lends its supports both to the more legalistic approach taken in the UN Draft Norms and to the voluntary approach of the UN Global Compact; according to the IBLF, the two complement each other, rather than being opposed to each other.

The IBLF's work with the various UN organizations points to various strategies by the IBLF to link business to UN work on development and sustainable development issues. The IBLF has contributed through these activities to ensuring that the issue of the role of companies in crucial international issues is part of the international agenda. However, the partnership strategy also signals something else, i.e., companies cannot take sole responsibility for CSR. The partnership idea assigns responsibility to other actors in society and could be seen as corresponding to the multi-stakeholder approach, only from a different perspective. In the multi-stakeholder approach, stakeholders demand a say in matters of concern to them. In the partnership approach, the perspective is that of shared responsibility and the interests of equal partners.

Implications of Norm Cascading

The important points raised in Chapter 7 and in this chapter are that when the focus organizations succeeded in bringing the issue of CSR to the international agenda, more and different actors joined in the process. As a result, a norm tipping occurred in the mid-1990s, followed by norm cascading with a mushrooming of CSR organizations and initiatives. This mushrooming involved not just the prime targets of the norm entrepreneurs, the TNCs (as in the case of Nike and similar high profile companies), but other NGOs, governments and IGOs also became engaged in CSR. Among these were key actors who were important for providing support and also lending legitimacy to the process – such as the US and UK governments, Amnesty International, and certain UN agencies and programmes. These actors of course had their own reasons for engaging in the development of CSR, but whatever their motives were, they all intentionally or unintentionally contributed to the norm tipping that occurred. They also contributed to give legitimacy to the

---

11   As, e.g., in the World Business Awards in support of the Millennium Development Goals and with the ICC environmental group WICE in the preparation of the 1994 report on *Partnership and Sustainable Development*.

advocacy of CSR and to those engaged in this advocacy. This, in turn, contributed to making involvement in CSR organizations and initiatives even more attractive.

Whereas the focus organizations as norm entrepreneurs had mainly been guided by ideational commitment, the other actors drawn into the process at this stage were guided by a variety of motives. These motives both 'pushed' and 'pulled' actors into an involvement in CSR, i.e., some actors felt constrained to address CSR, and others were attracted to the status of appropriateness that it was beginning to attain. The push and pull motives are captured by the concepts of legitimacy, esteem and reputation in the norm cycle model.

Another result was that after having previously had 'ownership' of the issue, the focus organizations now became engaged in a different kind of interaction and with other actors. The initial awareness-raising of the issues involved in CSR that had taken place during the norm emergence stage shifted to engage the initial norm entrepreneurs in more direct interaction as part of specific struggles or negotiations, as seen in the cases discussed in this chapter. This change meant encountering different kinds of actors, and although all actors had joined with different perspectives, all were now collectively making claims concerning CSR. Instead of persuasion, which was no longer necessary as actors began joining the process in large numbers on their own initiative, the participating actors rather became involved in a process of socialization. The most obvious case of socialization is seen in the interaction between Nike and its critics but is also present in the development of standards or good practice and in the work concerning partnerships.

The changing views on the operations of TNCs, particularly by consumers but also by other actors, led to a situation in which companies felt a necessity to or, at the least, began seeing that it was in their own best interest to address the problems for which they were allegedly responsible. The problems that the companies were associated with, such as the use of child labour by subcontractors in developing countries, were obviously not new phenomena. However, as the attitude in general toward the responsibilities of TNCs began to change, these problems rapidly became issues to which the companies needed to attend. The attention given to CSR from other parts of society consequently reinforced the activities of the norm entrepreneurs. This furthermore 'coincided' with revelations that large and well-known TNCs were involved in human rights abuses (world events), which also contributed to the process.

This norm cascading also involved the development of a number of CSR initiatives that manifested the various claims made on TNCs, or, in other words, the framing of CSR by different actors. These different framings met with varying degrees of resistance or support, depending on the views held by the participants. The next chapter discusses in more detail the clustering that took place around some of these manifestations as part of the shift into norm internalization.

Chapter 9

Incipient Norm Internalization and the Case for Norm Consolidation

This chapter deals with the third stage of the norm cycle – norm internalization. Since norm internalization of CSR is not complete, the discussion of this issue will be more tentative and emphasize norm consolidation (see Chapter 2). The discussion of norm consolidation suggests that at least three different developments resulted in convergence on specific manifestations of CSR: the development of social labelling (in particular, Fairtrade), the attempt within the UN to establish formal standards for TNCs through the so-called UN Draft Norms and the voluntary initiative on the UN Global Compact. These are not the only examples of convergence; there are similar examples in the case of socially responsible investment and the development of various monitoring and verification schemes. However, the three developments covered here are in different ways important examples of the consolidation process that I argue is needed for the shift from norm cascade to norm internalization.

Before discussing norm consolidation, I will recapitulate the main arguments of the norm cycle model that pertain to norm internalization and relate them to indications of the internalization of CSR.

Indications of Norm Internalization

According to the arguments of the norm cycle, it is presumed that when norm internalization has occurred, norms are more or less taken for granted and become the prevailing standards of appropriateness, i.e., they are to a certain extent difficult to actually perceive. Internalized norms are ideally no longer controversial and are part of what is regarded as ordinary activity.[1] The actors, the motive and the dominant social process that characterize this stage are agents of internalization (the law, bureaucracy and professions), conformity and institutionalization.

Agents of Internalization

Important agents for internalization of norms are the *law, bureaucracy and professions*. Laws and other formal regulations exemplify the institutionalization

---

1 Examples of such norms are seen in like concepts as market exchange, sovereignty and individualism, which however have also been made problematic in recent research.

of norms most explicitly and visibly, whereas bureaucracy contributes to institutionalization more indirectly. Professions, professional training and associations for professionals not only represent a set of knowledge, they also contribute to internalizing certain values and normative perceptions. From this it follows that the *motive* involved in this stage of norm development is that of conformity, both as an obvious consequence of the kinds of agents identified above as well as of the *dominant social process*, institutionalization and habit.[2]

Can these key elements of the third stage, norm internalization, be found in the development of CSR? A discussion of each of these key elements will show that there are indications to support this hypothesis.

Law and Regulation   In the case of the law, examples of both hard and soft laws can be found in the various activities related to CSR. Where international human rights law is concerned, the responsibility for human rights is traditionally assigned to states and state governments, although the Universal Declaration of Human Rights (UDHR) refers in its preamble to the responsibility for human rights as pertaining to 'every individual and every organ of society'. However, the question of human rights and non-state actors is not static. In current research, arguments are made among legal scholars for an expansion in the interpretation of international human rights law. Those arguing in favour of an expanded responsibility for human rights often refer in arguments for making TNCs responsible for human rights to the wording in the UDHR quoted above and to other legal matters, as well as to the transformation of the international system in general (see, e.g., Alston 2005 and Clapham 2006). The arguments on the UN Draft Norms, discussed below, are evidence of this tendency.

Apart from international law, international agreements are also made to regulate certain issues that can be included as (soft) law. The WHO Code, the OECD Guidelines and the ILO Declaration discussed in Chapters 3 and 4 are examples of such agreements, which may also be considered agents of internalization. Lately, organizations have begun actively campaigning for making greater use of the OECD Guidelines and filing complaints through the complaint procedures included in it. Although the complaint procedure is a non-judicial review process, it is formalized through a system of 'national contact points' within government and therefore has somewhat judicial implications.

The proliferation of codes of conduct and similar standards represents another form of soft law. These forms of soft law are used by actors in different ways to further various interests and causes. At the same time, they represent standards of appropriateness, which the different actors involved directly refer to or have to relate to in other ways. They also serve as the basis for the development of monitoring schemes that contribute to internalization by creating routines, roles,

---

2   As was seen in Chapter 2, repeated interaction and cooperation may develop 'habits of trust' that, when internalized, change the behaviour, identity and identification of participating actors and ultimately may contribute to a change of norms.

etc., that contribute to institutionalizing the standards in question as well as creating bureaucracy.

On the national level, amendments to existing legislation (e.g., to the GSP system in the US) and the lawsuits brought under the ATCA in the US were discussed in the previous chapters. What is important here is not just the legal content of the legislation and the extraterritorial effect of these legal means, but also the platform for action created through the complaints procedures. Other national legislative measures include the adoption of 'disclosure regulations' requiring pension funds to state whether the fund managers are applying ethical criteria to their investment decisions. These measures contribute to a continued and constant attention to the issues at stake through the mechanism of filing complaints and disclosure of information.

Bureaucracy   As for bureaucracy, I argue that within the issue of CSR, bureaucracy is found in sociall labelling schemes, in the adoption of codes of conduct and corresponding monitoring schemes, in the screening activities involved in socially responsible investment and in the development of social auditing and reporting. Apart from the development of the content of the standards themselves, standards activities involve designing credible systems for verification and require trained and specialized staff and procedures for carrying out the actual monitoring activities, including reporting and tracking the results.

In this area, several initiatives on local, national and international levels involve various aspects of bureaucracy. Examples include the social labelling of FLO, the Fair Labour Association (FLA) and the FLA Workplace Code of Conduct, the Global Reporting Initiative and the G3 Guidelines for social reporting. In recent years, the International Standardization Organization (ISO) has begun developing a management standard for social responsibility, ISO 26000, that is applicable not only to companies but to all organizations (to be published in 2010). This growth points to the standardization of CSR, where standards, monitoring schemes and standardization organizations are not only created but also need to be organized.

Professions   A side effect of the development of CSR is the involvement of professionals and the creation of new professions, which can be regarded as agents of internalization. The need for trained staff to deal with the different issues involved in CSR has grown as CSR has expanded into more and more areas. There is even talk about the development of a CSR industry, referring to 'mass production' of CSR and with it staff to perform the work.

Evidence of this is seen in companies that employ *CSR managers or officers* and create CSR units to handle new demands or, if they prefer to outsource this function, demand similar expertise and services from *accounting or consulting firms*. These latter firms have recognized a business opportunity in CSR and actively advertise and provide CSR expertise and services to the business sector. In the *socially responsible investment sector*, specialists (such as ethical fund managers) are needed at financial institutions to screen companies for inclusion/ exclusion in ethical funds, among other things.

From this it follows that professionals need professional training and their own associations, to further their interests. There is, consequently, a growth in education focused on TNC and human rights as well as degrees awarded to those wanting to specialize in the area. In 2003, two-thirds of European universities offered some form of CSR education, and around 10 per cent also provided MBAs or master programmes in CSR (Ethical Corporation 2006). In a later survey of top schools offering MBA programmes (Ethical Corporation 2007), an increase from 2005 to 2007 was reported in the number of elective courses per school that feature some or are largely dedicated to social/environmental content by 50 and 20 per cent respectively. In Europe, this development has been enhanced by the presence of the European Academy of Business in Society (EABIS), established in 2002 by representatives of businesses and universities with the support of the European Commission.[3] Organizations are also created to link CSR professionals in specific associations, such as the US-based NetImpact, established in 1993 by MBA students and with (as of 2008) more than 15,000 members. Another example is the US-based organization, the Ethics and Compliance Officer Association (ECOA), founded in 1992, which is functioning more as a traditional professional association, with some 1,300 members (NetImpact undated, ECOA).

These agents of internalization (law, bureaucracy and professions) in combination serve to continuously internalize CSR in various social structures. They also help further the two other key elements, conformity and institutionalization, that are at the centre of norm internationalization.

Conformity and Institutionalization

Conformity to CSR would obviously involve both the adoption of and compliance with legislation (hard law) and support for and adherence to important voluntary regulatory initiatives (soft law). This adherence need not involve the large majority of actors, as those that do comply (key governments, market leaders, established NGOs, individuals holding certain positions) act as catalysts, creating the expectation that others will follow suit. As a threshold or a momentum is reached, with a significant number of (key) actors, CSR organizations and initiatives, and a certain amount of media attention, the process takes a different turn and has partly a dynamic of its own.

In the case of conformity to and institutionalization of CSR into legislation, some governments have already taken steps in this direction. The regulation mentioned previously requiring pension funds to disclose whether they apply certain criteria to investment decisions is one example. Similar legislation can be found in Australia, France, Germany, Sweden, United Kingdom and the EU. In Belgium, there is also a social label law issued by the government to products (not companies) that comply

---

3   The creation of EABIS resulted from the attention being given to CSR by the EU at the time with the launch by the European Commission (2001) of its so-called 'green paper' on CSR and the subsequent 'white paper' by the European Commission (2002).

with certain standards and inspections. This represents a small group of mainly European countries who have adopted such a strategy; whether this will develop further remains to be seen. The EU has so far kept a low profile on CSR, although it stated in 2006 that it wanted to give CSR greater political visibility with the launch of the European Alliance for CSR – a partnership with business to face global competition, sustain growth and create more and better jobs. The EU has been criticized by Activists for its inaction and also for not conducting an inclusive and open process, which has led to the undue influence and favouring of business (e.g., the EU has developed a version of CSR that promotes European products for having been made under better working conditions). An exception is seen in the European Parliament, which is active in discussions and proposals relating to CSR[4] such as the so-called Howitt resolution of 1999 on 'EU standards for European Enterprises operating in developing countries: Towards a European Code of Conduct'.

When voluntary non-binding regulation is considered, the trend is more evident; at the same time it is also debatable whether such regulations have any effect and, if so, what the effect is. Apart from the legislative measures mentioned above, many EU member countries have adopted additional CSR policies (listed in Table 7.1). Not only have CSR policies been widely adopted by the EU member states, a compilation of these CSR policies is posted on the EU website and represents an example of how conformity can be increased (European Commission undated a, undated b). The list displays, for everybody to see, what public policies the different member states have adopted to promote CSR, making it possible for all member states and others (and not least Activists) to compare their performances.

Moreover, as companies and other organizations are joining particular CSR initiatives in large numbers; studies also show a steady increase in social reporting among companies (KPMG International 2005, 2008). This reporting marks a further change from 1999, when reporting moved from covering just the environment to include social aspects. Among the 250 largest companies in the Fortune 500, 80 per cent of the companies issue sustainability reporting (an increase of 54 per cent since 2005, which in turn represents an increase of 45 per cent since 2002). Most of the reports issued by the surveyed companies refer to UN standards (predominantly the UN Global Compact Principles, but also standards issued by the ILO and the UDHR) and to the OECD Guidelines and, to a lesser degree, to management standards such as SA8000, AA1000, and the Global Sullivan Principles. As can be seen, it is the well-established multilateral agreements that have been in existence for some time that are most relevant for companies as opposed to the large number of recent new standards, which would seem rational.

This discussion of agents of internalization, conformity and institutionalization suggests that there are indications to support the argument that norm internalization is incipient. The rest of this chapter will discuss whether one can distinguish support for norm consolidation as a step towards norm internalization.

---

4   For an enumeration of activities within the EU on CSR see European Parliament (2006).

Market Reform Through Social Labelling

In the 20 years that Fairtrade labelling has existed, the growth of the FLO initiative has been continuous and somewhat spectacular. The effects of the initiative can be seen in the changing behaviour of actors other than consumers, i.e., coffee companies and the Fairtrade movement itself.

Growth of the Fairtrade System and Sales

As of 2007 the FLO system involves 19 labelling organizations covering 23 countries in Europe, North America, Japan, Australia, New Zealand and South Africa: a growth of about one organization per year. There are at present 632 certified producer organizations (compared to 224 in 2001), which means that an estimated 1.5 million farmers and workers in some 60 countries worldwide are affected. When dependents are included, this involves a total of an estimated 7.5 million people. If other participants along the supply chain are included, another 469 business entities are part of the system (FLO 2006, 2007).

This means that close to 1,100 organizations and business entities along the supply chain are involved in Fairtrade labelling. Such a supply chain requires a well-organized system. From an organizational point view, the system suggests a bureaucracy and is therefore an indication of norm internalization.

When the growth in sales is considered, the annual increase from 1997 to 2002 was at a steady rate of 10–20 per cent annually. Between 2002 and 2003, there was a significant change in the growth trend, when sales suddenly doubled, and growth since then has been constant, at approximately 40 per cent annually (as of 2008). This marked trend coincides with the launch of the common Fairtrade logo in 2002, which might have provided Fairtrade products with increased attention and a clear profile through the use of one single logo instead of several national variants. Fairtrade products are furthermore sold in some 100,000 sales outlets in the US and Europe. The Fairtrade movement has thus partly benefited from traditional market strategies (FLO 2003, 2004, 2005a, 2005b, 2006, Krier 2005: 9, TransFair USA 2004).

Effects on Other Actors and Market Significance

The growth of Fairtrade, particularly its introduction on the US market and spectacular increase in US market share, has even attracted the attention of important media, such as *The Wall Street Journal*, *The New York Times* and *Time Magazine*.[5] This has led other actors to address the underlying issues, such as when

---

5   See, e.g., Moskin, J. 2004. Helping the third world one banana at a time, in *The New York Times*, 5 May; McLaughlin, K. 2004. Is your grocery list politically correct? Food world's new buzzword is 'sustainable' product: Fair trade certified mangos, in *The Wall Street Journal*, 17 February; and Is your coffee unfair?: Politically correct beans are gaining

the US Congress in 2002 passed a resolution calling upon the US government to address the coffee crisis and cooperate with coffee companies to come up with a sustainable solution to the industry's problems (FLO 2003). The World Bank has also taken an interest in the issue and has supported a study of the sustainability of the coffee sector (Giovannucci 2003).

Individual consumers are not the only ones affecting the development of Fairtrade. Institutions have started to offer or purchase Fairtrade coffee and tea or other Fairtrade products (at times exclusively), including Yale, Harvard and Georgetown universities in the US (TransFair USA 2002), institutions within the EU and two large UK retailers, Sainsbury and Marks & Spencer. Apart from contributing to the considerable increase in the demand that purchases by institutions represent compared to individual consumption, such developments also legitimize Fairtrade as such.

However, in spite of the remarkable increase in the sales of Fairtrade products, their impact on the market when compared to the sale of non-labelled ('unfair') products is still quite small (in the early 2000s, still less than 5 per cent) (Krier 2001: 16, TransFair USA 2005). Although the economic 'threat' of the Fairtrade product is evidently less critical, with increased competition on the global market even small changes in market share can be important. But the symbolic value of the labelling initiative is certainly much greater, both for the Fairtrade movement and for individuals and organizations involved in CSR or issues concerning economic and social justice. Fairtrade labelling is not only a concrete alternative but also a statement and a practical demonstration that alternative methods of trade are, in fact, possible. In my view, the role of institutions and market actors other than those already involved in Fairtrade will be important to the future development of Fairtrade.

Effects on the Fairtrade Movement

An interesting effect of the development of Fairtrade labelling is the labelling of the Fairtrade organizations themselves, with the need to distinguish themselves from other labelling initiatives. As of 2004, the International Fair Trade Association (IFAT) administers a Fair Trade Organization (FTO) mark that identifies Fairtrade organizations and distinguishes them from other commercial organizations involved in Fairtrade (such as Utz Kapeh and C.A.F.E. established by companies). The mark is available only to IFAT members who fulfill the requirements for the FTO mark, a sign that the market mechanism of competition has penetrated the Fairtrade sector (Kocken 2004).

The growth of Fairtrade labelling has led not only to the need for coordination of the national labelling initiative, as seen in the development of the FLO and the FTO mark, but also of the Fairtrade movement as a whole. The different

---

ground in the US. Is this enlightened capitalism – or just meddling in the free market?, in *Time Magazine*, April 2004.

organizations within the Fairtrade movement have also decided to cooperate. Two main organizations support this cooperation, FINE and the International Social and Environmental Accreditation and Labelling Alliance (ISEAL). FINE unites the four major organizations within Fairtrade, i.e., FLO, IFAT, Network of European Worldshops (NEWS!) and European Free Trade Association (EFTA), with the purpose of exchanging information and coordinating activities like lobbying and awareness-raising initiatives. The International Social and Environmental Accreditation and Labelling Alliance (ISEAL) is a collaboration of the leading international standard setting, accreditation and labelling organizations and is not restricted to Fairtrade.[6] This cooperation began in 1999 due to areas of overlap in the individual organizations' focus issues and similarities in the way they were operating. The purpose of the ISEAL is furthermore to enhance the credibility of their standards and programmes, improve the organizations and defend common interests.

The development discussed above can be seen as a further argument for a third phase of Fairtrade, which would involve new approaches to marketing and cooperation, changes in the purchasing patterns of retailers, and issues of demand, price and quality. The Fairtrade movement has thus grown and is no longer an effort by a few church members or other idealists. It now needs to coordinate its actions and can begin contemplating more organized strategies. It is becoming professionalized. Some small coffee farmers' cooperatives have, in fact, been able to invest their Fairtrade premiums in quality improvements and can even be found among the top quality brands. Fairtrade has come a long way from its beginnings as the individual initiative of churches or dedicated activists and could be seen as partly institutionalized.[7]

Towards Binding International Law: The UN Draft Norms

The social labelling discussed above represents a market-oriented initiative to address CSR issues. A quite different initiative of a more regulatory character that has attracted much attention is the proposal by the UN Sub-Commission on the Promotion and Protection of Human Rights (the Sub-Commission) in 2003 of Norms on the Responsibilities of Transnational Corporations and Other Business

---

6   ISEAL includes Conservation Agriculture Network (CAN), Forest Stewardship Council (FSC), International Federation of Organic Agriculture Movements (IFOAM), International Organic Accreditation Service (IOAS), Marine Stewardship Council (MSC), Social Accountability International (SAI), and Fairtrade Labelling Organizations International (FLO).

7   The first phase consisted of existing organizations or the creation of new organizations that initiated trade directly with disadvantaged coffee farmers in developing countries in order to give these farmers a fair price for their products. This took place in the 1950s to the 1970s. The second phase began with the establishment of the Max Havelaar Fairtrade labelling system in 1988. See Giovannucci (2003: 38).

Enterprises with regard to Human Rights (UN Draft Norms) (Sub-Commission resolution 2003).

The UN Draft Norms represent a wide-ranging set of principles that cover the responsibilities of companies in regard to equal opportunity and non-discriminatory treatment, right to security of persons, rights of workers, respect for national sovereignty and human rights, consumer protection, environmental protection when related to human and labour rights. It also includes provisions for implementation that involve reporting and monitoring, as well as the responsibility for states to provide legal and administrative mechanisms for this purpose. The initiative resembles the UNCTC initiative of the 1970s, discussed in Chapter 3, in that it attempts to construct an international instrument at the UN level to regulate TNCs. However, several aspects of both the content and the context differ significantly from the earlier initiative, as will be seen in the discussion below.

Emerging Concerns on Transnational Corporations

The work on the UN Draft Norms was initiated in 1998 when the Sub-Commission established a working group to examine the activities and working methods of TNCs (Sub-Commission resolution 1998). The UN Draft Norms were therefore initiated as part of the norm cascade of the mid-1990s. However, this was not the first time that the Sub-Commission had raised the issue of TNCs. Concern over TNCs had appeared in the work of the Sub-Commission as far back as the late 1980s and early 1990s. The concern related to the effects of privatization and investments, the role of TNCs in society, whether TNCs should be forced to compensate for negative effects or regulated in general, the right to development and self-determination in relation to natural resources and cultural intellectual property rights. The group seen as most exposed to the negative effects of TNC activity was indigenous peoples; this was a group that had already been an important focus for work within the UN in the previous decades.

The issue of indigenous peoples was partly responsible for the Sub-Commission adopting a resolution on various problems in developing countries: economic, social and cultural rights, economic adjustment policies arising from debt, extreme poverty, human rights, environment, the right to development, and adequate housing (Sub-Commission resolution 1994). It was mainly also the indigenous peoples' NGOs, together with certain members of the Sub-Commission, who were bringing these issues to agenda of the Sub-Commission (Sub-Commission 1992, 1993a, 1993b). In the resolution, which covers several issues, such as the role of the international financial institutions (the World Bank, the IMF and the WTO), only the last paragraph deals briefly with the relationship between human rights and TNCs.

In the period between the 1980s and the decision in 1998 to establish a working group, there was a major shift toward a clearer focus on TNCs, but at the same time the issue of indigenous peoples was downplayed. This development was a response to the increasing attention being given to the effects of globalization and, in particular, the role of TNCs. Another reason that the Sub-Commission established a working group and began this work is that the Commission as a whole would not, in spite of an explicit request from the Sub-Commission to do so. In 1996, the Sub-Commission had called for the establishment of a working group by the Commission. However, although the Commission took note of the Sub-Commission's request, including reports and resolutions,[8] it did not act on the Sub-Commission's recommendations. Instead, the Commission adopted a resolution in very general terms on the realization of economic, social and cultural rights and the problems of developing countries, without any reference to the resolution by the Sub-Commission or any specific mention of TNCs (Commission resolution 1997/17, 11 April 1997).

Apparently, the proposal by the Sub-Commission did not sit well with the Commission, which was composed of country representatives with a variety of interests; the Sub-Commission was made up of experts elected as members in their personal capacity. The disinterest of the Commission did not discourage the Sub-Commission which, in 1998, established the above-mentioned working group on its own. The Sub-Commission almost immediately included the drafting of the so-called UN Draft Norms in its work (Sub-Commission resolution 1998/8, 20 August 1998. See also Weissbrodt and Kruger 2005: 322).

Support for and Resistance to the UN Draft Norms

Although the original intention of the working group was to construct a legally binding document, the group came to understand that this was not feasible at the time. Instead, the group decided that the proposal would be constructed to be 'Implemented as soft law, the Norms could be similar to many other UN declarations, principles, guidelines, standards, and resolutions which *interpret existing international law and summarize practice* without reaching the status of a treaty'[9] (Weissbrodt and Kruger 2005: 325).

In spite of this pragmatic stance, however, the UN Draft Norms attempted to achieve something more than the UN instruments mentioned above. It aspired to interpret international human rights law and practice in a way that considered the changing context of globalization. This intent is, in fact, stated in the preamble to the UN Draft Norms 'Noting also that new international human rights issues and concerns are continually emerging and that transnational corporations and other business enterprises often are involved in these issues and concerns, such that further standards-setting and implementation are required at this time and in the future'.

Although the intent was not to create a treaty, the UN Draft Norms does assign explicit obligations to companies, states and the UN. TNCs 'shall

---

8   Commission note 1997. Written support for the Sub-Commission's request is made by the Human Rights Advocate (an NGO with consultative status to the Commission) and by certain members of the Commission (Cuba, Iran, Morocco, and Nigeria), see Commission written support 1997 and Commission draft resolution 1997.

9   Footnotes have been omitted, italics added by the author.

adopt, disseminate and implement internal rules', 'periodically report on and take other measures' and 'apply and incorporate these Norms in their contracts or other arrangements and dealings', and 'be subject to periodic monitoring and verification by United Nations, other international and national mechanisms already in existence or yet to be created'. They are also to 'provide prompt, effective and adequate reparation to those ... adversely affected'. States are expected to 'establish and reinforce the necessary legal and administrative framework' to ensure the implementation of the Norms as well as other relevant laws. Thus, in spite of not attempting to construct a legally binding treaty, the proposal represents a bold attempt by the working group and the Sub-Commission to extend or reinterpret the boundaries of responsibility for human rights.

The conviction that the project was beneficial was not shared by the Commission. In an unanimous decision, the Commission made it clear that although the question of the responsibility of TNCs was an important one, the UN Draft Norms had no legal standing and the Sub-Commission was not to perform any monitoring (Commission resolution 2004/116, 20 April, 2004). This was a clear signal to the Sub-Commission that it had acted on its own in presenting the UN Draft Norms, and that it was not to proceed in this direction. Without the mandate of the Commission, neither the work nor the UN Draft Norms were to gain formal recognition.

The reaction to the UN Draft Norms has been quite strong, creating a division between those in support of the norms (NGOs in general) and those opposing them (such as the large business associations). However, not everyone in the business community shares the views of the latter group. In 2004, the French-based retailer Carrefour expressed public support for the UN Draft Norms, one of the few individual companies to do so (Carrefour 2005a, 2005b). The French retailer is also cooperating with the International Federation of Human Rights (FIDH) to improve the working conditions at Carrefour subcontractors. Business support is also present indirectly through one of the focus organizations, the IBLF that has voiced support for the UN Draft Norms. Another group of companies involved in the Business Leaders Initiative on Human Rights (BLIHR) expressed a cautious statement in favour of the UN Draft Norms.[10] (BLIHR had agreed to 'road-test' the UN Draft Norms and would therefore be expected to be more favourable to the initiative).

Among the more notable critics are the ICC and the IOE. The ICC had previously made somewhat similar criticisms on the occasion of the release of the EU 'Green Paper' on CSR in 2001 (ICC 2001). The criticisms of the ICC included duplication of already existing initiatives, the issue is the responsibility of governments, there are cultural and other differences between countries, and voluntary activities of companies are already being undertaken in this area.

---

10   BLIHR was an initiative of seven companies, chaired by the former UN High Commissioner of Human Rights and President of Ireland, Mary Robinson, that ran between 2003 and 2009.

The UN Draft Norms elicited similar criticisms from the ICC and the IOE as that presented by the ICC on the EU initiative on CSR, although in connection to the UN Draft Norms it is now stated somewhat differently (ICC and IOE 2003) (see also the discussion on the ATCA lawsuits in the previous chapter). Criticism of the UN Draft Norms focused mainly on the question of TNCs being made responsible for the actions of foreign governments (human rights is the responsibility of governments). However, the argument is more conciliatory this time. The argument central to criticisms of the EU initiative is that non-binding and voluntary initiatives developed and implemented by the companies themselves are preferred to the 'legalistic approach to human rights' of the UN Draft Norms. The latter is even accused of being counterproductive and provoking a negative response from business. Voluntary initiatives can bridge 'cultural diversity within companies' and enhance 'awareness of societal values and concerns' through 'persuasion and peer pressure rather than prescription'. The arguments in relation to the UN Draft Norm centre on support for voluntary as opposed to binding regulation, rather than on global as opposed to regional solutions. This should be compared to the criticism of the EU initiative, when global solutions were sought after instead of the regional initiative of the EU. Other business associations, such as the United States Council for International Business (USCIB) and the Confederation of British Industry (CBI), have offered similar arguments in opposition to the UN Draft Norms.

The emphasis is clear: binding regulation is to be avoided. It is not the responsibilities or the boundaries of those responsibilities that are the focus of the criticism; rather, it is concern for whether or not the requirements are voluntary. One interpretation of this position is that almost any responsibility could be acceptable, provided it is voluntary or non-binding, which amounts to a contradiction. The position is, rather, that voluntary and non-binding responsibility in practice is interpreted as equivalent to no responsibility, which is hardly the intention of the UN Global Compact.

Although the UN Draft Norms proposed by the Sub-Commission to the Commission were not adopted, they resulted in a decision by the Commission to study the scope and legal status of existing initiatives and standards. The result of this study was to be the basis for identification of outstanding issues, in order for the Commission to look at options regarding setting standards for companies. Once again, a study was presented to the Commission which dealt with the outstanding issues and a number of existing initiatives (including the UN Draft Norms). The recommendations were that assigning the responsibilities for human rights needed further clarification, but also that the UN Draft Norms were worth evaluating more carefully, as they had been the subject of 'road-testing' by the Business Leaders Initiative on Human Rights (BLIHR) (Commission resolution 2004, Commission report 2005). The report thus expressed subtle support for the UN Draft Norms. As a result of the study, a Special Representative on the Issue of Human Rights and Transnational Corporations and Other Business Enterprises was appointed to try to solve the many thorny issues involved. These included the divide that had emerged between supporters and opponents of the UN Draft Norms (Commission resolution 2005).

The Special Representative has presented several reports dealing with various aspects of the issue, but with a more moderate interpretation of the direct and indirect legal responsibilities that can be inferred from the present international law than the interpretation made by the Sub-Commission. According to the Special Representative, there still remain 'protection gaps' for the human rights of individuals and 'predictability gaps' for companies uncertain of the 'verdicts' of public opinion. It has, however, also been pointed out that states have not fully taken advantage of the potential to legislate nationally in the area of responsibility for the acts of non-state actors in foreign countries. This remark is interesting in view of the discussion in the previous chapter on the ATCA lawsuits in the US and other national legal measures. Here the UN Special Representative actually welcomes the development of extraterritorial national legislation in the area of CSR. There was also discussion of the clarification needed on the concepts of 'sphere of influence' of companies and of 'shared responsibility' between states and companies, concepts that have evolved from grey areas in the soft law initiatives that represent a new development in international law. The Special Representative has recently presented a 'conceptual and policy framework' for business and human rights (endorsed by the Human Rights Council), based on the following principles – the state's duty to protect, the company's responsibility to respect and remedy – and is now working on how to make this framework operational. In the case of companies, this amounts to a 'do no harm' policy implemented through a process of due diligence, i.e., do not simply comply with legislation, but also actively take measures to avoid implications in human rights violations (policies, impact assessments, etc.) and provide non-judicial remedy when harm has been done. This framework rejects the approach of the UN Draft Norm, which is to list specific human rights for which TNCs are responsible, and instead focuses on the responsibilities of companies in relation to all human rights. The policy framework appears to be a compromise between the legalism of the UN Draft Norms and the voluntarism of the UN Global Compact, and is in fact an example of soft law. Although the policy framework mainly rests on established international agreements and principles, it does keep the door open for new ways for TNCs to approach the issue of the responsibility for human rights, e.g., in pointing out that the issue of extraterritoriality remains unregulated but does not prohibit states from passing such laws, and that this is even encouraged in certain international instruments. The content of future operations will provide a structure for the policy framework and answer the question of its potential to actually regulate in this area (Human Rights Council 2007, 2008).

Voluntarism and Private-Public Partnerships: The UN Global Compact

The work of the Sub-Commission on the UN Draft Norms and the UN Global Compact (UNGC) initiative developed partly simultaneously. The UNGC was formally launched in 2000 but had already been announced to the business community by the former Secretary General to the UN, Kofi Annan, in a speech in 1999 to the World Economic Forum meeting in Davos, Switzerland (UNGC 1999). The speech called for business to cooperate with the UN in order to give 'a human face to the global market' and expressed concern about economic globalization that, although it was 'a fact of life', meant that societies and political systems no longer had a say in their development and, even worse, experienced difficulties from its effect. The idea behind the UNGC was that TNCs would support and implement core values based on already established international standards, including the UDHR, those of the ILO, and the standards that came out of the UN Conference in Rio on the environment. It was to provide a platform for TNCs and other actors to engage on the issues and develop action plans.

Content and Gradual Formalization

The former Secretary General to the UN rejected the idea of putting restrictions on trade and investment regimes, while at the same time expressing support for the concerns on which such ideas were based. As such, his statement represents clear support for free trade, a market economy and capitalism, or in other words, the existing economic order. However, to preserve this order (which was not bringing benefits to everyone, contrary to the mainstream argument), there was a need to restore harmony between the 'economic, social and political realms'. Kofi Annan implicitly gives business two choices, presented as a problem for the international community as a whole: (1) to encourage states to develop international policies within multilateral institutions, or (2) to take action themselves in their own corporate sphere. In practice, this meant a choice between binding or voluntary regulation. If business chose the second alternative, voluntary regulation, the UN was there to offer its support. For those inclined to minimal interference in business operations, this of course represented a choice between the least harmful alternatives.

The basic idea consisted of creating a UN-sponsored platform, where the UN would act as a facilitator for dialogue and action. Constructive participation is particularly emphasized in the early years. Future participants are asked to 'recognize that a non-confrontational approach is conducive to arriving at solutions to the social challenges of globalization', thus excluding more critical voices. Within this framework, business, together with a number of UN agencies and representatives of labour and civil society, were given the task of exploring ways that companies could take responsibility (within their spheres of influence) for the development of globalization to benefit all people. The core values of the UNGC were formulated in nine principles relating to human rights, labour rights and the environment (a 10th principle on corruption was added later, referring to the OECD Convention on Corruption) to which companies joining the UNGC had to formally commit themselves in writing. Furthermore, companies were initially requested to post their activities on the UNGC website once a year and to participate in partnerships with UN organizations to advance the principles (UNGC 2002a, 2002b, quotes from 2002b). Participation in the UNGC also permits the company to use the much criticized UNGC logo under certain conditions.

This commitment does not include any systematic monitoring, but as of 2003, the participating companies are requested not only to *share* but to *report* on activities that are relevant to the UNGC principles. This is called Communication on Progress, and the reports provided are accessible through the UNGC website. The status of participants who do not report is changed, first to non-communicating, and then from non-communicating to inactive if they repeatedly continue to fail to report. In other words, the UNGC does not expel any member for not fulfilling the reporting requirements or their commitment in general. However, companies that are 'non-communicating' or 'inactive' are listed publicly on the UNGC website, and their use of the UNGC logo is restricted or not permitted at all. Those that report can, of course, also be found on the UNGC website. Recently an interesting decision was made: as of 1 July 2009, business participants that have not submitted a report for one year will be taken off the website. Certain minimum criteria for reporting have also been introduced (UNGC undated, 2009). Hence, although there is no monitoring of company activities by the UNGC, there is a mild form of sanctioning (through a strategy of transparency and disclosure of information, actually close to 'naming and shaming').

It is worth noting that the UNGC also publicly lists participants who, according to the UNGC, are undertaking measures that can be useful in guiding others – i.e., they represent best practices. These companies become role models for others, demonstrating appropriate standards (see also Chapter 8 on good practice).

Linkage of the UN Global Compact to Other Initiatives

The UNGC encourages companies to use the reporting guidelines of the Global Reporting Initiative (GRI), the so-called G3 Guidelines, which are an elaborate set of criteria on how any organization, not just a company, can adequately report economic, environmental and social performances. This was the result from the strategic alliance that the UNGC entered into with the GRI in 2006 (UNGC and GRI 2007). Here, we can see the joining together of two voluntary initiatives, the UNGC and the GRI, that on their own have been successful in attracting quite a number of participants in a fairly short time. The initiatives strengthen and benefit each other, and also contribute to a formalization of the UNGC. With this link, the initial UNGC general principles are given substance through the GRI.

A connection has also been made to the OECD Guidelines. In a recent report, the GRI has combined and matched elements in the GRI Sustainability Reporting Guidelines with elements in the OECD Guidelines, with the purpose of facilitating the use of the OECD Guidelines and strengthen the complementarity of both. Through this, the GRI 'can be used to help measure and report on performance in relation to some of the recommendations set forth in the OECD Guidelines' (GRI 2004).

The GRI initiative makes the OECD Guidelines operational, which might result in greater attention to and application of the OECD Guidelines, with more cases being brought to a test. Some Activists Organizations, including the CCC, have also begun campaigning for use of the OECD Guidelines in the monitoring of TNCs. This campaigning could also serve to enhance the work of the actors involved in the UNGC.

What therefore began as a loosely coordinated and loosely structured endeavour by former Secretary General Kofi Annan to address the issue of globalization and the role of TNCs at the end of the 1990s has undergone significant development over the years. The initial core values to which Kofi Annan referred in his speech to the World Economic Forum have developed into 10 principles with direct reference to existing international standards. They have developed from 'simply' values and aspirations into more explicit and concrete standards of appropriateness. Their link to specific established international standards enhances this development. There is also a tendency towards 'bureaucratization' of the UNGC initiative, referring here not to a massive increase in the number of employees at the UN Global Compact New York offices, but rather to the development of the content, the procedures and the organization of the initiative itself, due to its growth in scale and scope.

Even though the intent of the UNGC is not to develop a monitoring system for adherence to the UNGC Principles, developments point in the direction of participating companies being requested to give more detailed accounts of their performance. The reporting format recommended (the GRI G3 Guidelines) is not a prescript, but is in practice seen as the preferred choice. This makes commitment to the UNGC Principles more material and also easier to check for compliance, for those who would like to do so. The link through the GRI to the OECD Guidelines, mentioned above, represents an interesting development that contributes to making the UNGC Principles more substantial.

Expansion and Critique of the UN Global Compact

As of February 2008, there were over 5,000 companies and a total of about 6,500 participants in the UNGC (UNGC Annual Review 2008). This means that more than one company a day has joined the UNGC initiative since it was launched in 2000. This represents a remarkable growth from the 50 or so companies that took part in the launch of the initiative. Although this growth is impressive, when the number of member companies is compared to the total number of TNCs (79,000 companies), it only represents around 6 per cent of the total. However, should this increase continue, in a matter of years the number of companies participating could very well reach 10 per cent. And although this is still a small share of the total number of companies, it would no longer be quite so marginal.

It should also be noted that approximately 20 per cent of the 100 largest companies in 22 countries are participants in the UNGC (KPMG International 2008). This means that the largest companies are overrepresented among the UNGC companies and thus influential in their capacity as sector/market leaders. This could contribute to further enhancement of UNGC.

What is interesting to note is that this growth of interest in the UNGC has occurred in parallel with the launch and discussion of the UN Draft Norms, not least from the business community. The UNGC might appear to be a compromise or a preferable choice, in view of the reaction from business to the UN Draft Norms described above.

With the growth of the UNGC initiative, there is an apparent need to find ways to decentralize the process, if the initial concept of the UNGC as a platform and a network, and not an organization, is to be maintained. This has led to the development of local UNGC networks. As of December 2008, there were some 60 such local networks, with close to 30 additional networks on the verge of being developed (UNGC and Barcelona Center for the Support of the Global Compact 2007: 6). This should be compared to some 9 local networks in 2006 (UNGC 2007: 16). These local networks may play an important role in the future development of the UNGC in terms of bringing more participants into the network and expanding the importance of the initiative.

The UNGC initiative has consequently proven successful in certain regards, including obtaining support from individual companies and business associations. Support has also come from the heads of G8 countries, who in connection with their meeting in 2007 publicly offered support to the UNGC and the GRI (G8 2007). This represents an important statement of support for the UNGC and should contribute to further enhancement of the initiative. It should be noted that many civil society organizations from the G8 countries are opposed to the UNGC, and there is a division not only between civil society and business on this issue, but also between civil society and their governments. One can thus anticipate that additional transborder alliances between like-minded organizations will be forged as a consequence.

There is also great concern for the cooperation between TNCs and the UN. We can see that the UNGC mirrors the UN Draft Norms in several respects. Right from the start, there was strong opposition to the UNGC from certain NGOs. The opposition formed a coalition under the name Alliance for a Corporate-Free UN, with the purpose of monitoring the business-UN partnership, to pressure the UN to avoid such cooperation and instead develop UN instruments for accountability (CorpWatch 2001). According to these critics, the UNGC is undermining efforts by the UN and states to establish legal intergovernmental accountability frameworks, and companies are given undue influence in the UN that risks weakening the work of various UN organizations. The argument against the UNGC also points out that companies who have committed to the UNGC Principles are found to be violating them but still enjoy the public relations benefit of being seen as cooperating with the UN and using the UNGC logo, referred to as 'blue wash'.

The different goals and values represented in the UN and business, respectively, are also seen as a problem.[11]

The most serious argument involves the lack of monitoring and enforcement mechanisms.[12] The absence of monitoring and enforcement was stated implicitly as a condition for support by the business community, at least according to an opinion by the ICC published in the *International Herald Tribune* at the time of the launch of the UNGC (Livanos Cattaui 2000). From this perspective, one can interpret the UNGC as a tradeoff between the possibility of achieving efficient CSR standards and implementation, on the one hand, and involving TNCs in the process as a way to further the advancement of CSR, on the other. Although the UNGC might not satisfy its critics on various points, it may still be of importance for involving TNCs in activities relating to and discussions of CSR. This will have a constraining effect on their behaviour (to what extent can, of course, be debated) and, perhaps more importantly, change the general perception of the relationship between business and human rights in the long run.

Concluding Remarks on Consolidation and Internalization

As has been shown in the discussion in this chapter on norm internalization, this third stage of the CSR norm cycle is somewhat more ambiguous than the two earlier stages, discussed in previous chapters. Nevertheless, the cases of norm consolidation that have been considered here (as well as other such cases) show convergence around a number of CSR initiatives that have appeared coincident with norm cascading. This convergence is an important step towards norm internalization, which, if consolidated further, could lead to an internalization of CSR.

My argument is that norm consolidation is necessary for the transformation from norm cascade to norm internalization, where the dominant social process of socialization is transformed into *institutionalization* with a concomitant change of actors – to agents of internalization – and motives – to conformity. Just as the stage of norm emergence required a change, norm tipping, as a catalyst for that

---

11   See, e.g., letter from the Alliance for a Corporate-Free UN to Secretary General Kofi Annan, 29 January, 2002 entitled *Letter to Kofi Annan Recommending Redesign of Global Compact*, letter from the UN Global compact Office to the Alliance for a Corporate-Free UN, 21 February 2002, entitled *UN Response to the Alliance for a Corporate-Free UN*, and the response from the Alliance for a Corporate-Free UN entitled *Alliance for a Corporate Free UN Rebuts Global Compact Letter*, 7 March, 2002. The letters can be found on the Internet website of CorpWatch, www.corpwatch.org.

12   Critical publications were also issued such as 'Greenwash +10: The UN's Global Compact, Corporate Accountability and the Johannes Earth Summit', January 2002 by CorpWatch and 'Tangled Up in Blue: Corporate Partnerships at the United Nations', September 2000, by TRAC-Transnational Resource & Action Center. See also critical comment by Kahn (2000).

stage to transform into norm cascading, norm consolidation performs the same role in the transition from norm cascade to norm internalization.

If norm cascading is dominated by multiple actors and the dominant motive is legitimacy, the transformation through norm consolidation is slower and less conspicuous, and relies on actors of a different type than the earlier stages. The agents of internalization are found in the law, bureaucracy and professions. A new motive is also involved: conformity. In this transition there are, however, traces of both norm cascading and norm internalization, which can be seen in the cases discussed above.

The three cases that have been discussed, in my opinion, provide empirical support for the existence of consolidation. The case of Fairtrade labelling involves an attempt at market reform in an initiative that during its 20 years of existence has managed to become accepted in trade and on the market. Although Fairtrade products are fairly marginal in terms of sheer numbers (with the exception of certain products like bananas), they show a continuous high growth rate and have been ever more widely embraced by institutions and other market actors. The Fairtrade label has thus achieved a considerably greater importance in its symbolic value than it has in terms of market share, which may actually help increase future market share.

The two cases involving the UN (the UN Draft Norms and the UN Global Compact) are interesting for their differences and yet their mutual constitution. As was seen in the discussion above, they are in certain respects opposites – i.e., where one has a more binding character, the other is voluntary; support from NGOs is given primarily to one and not the other; business prefers one over the other; and the arguments against one are simultaneously the arguments for the other. Even though key representatives of businesses and states reject the codification seen in the UN Draft Norm, the initiative has had the indirect effect of mobilizing its opponents to adopt the voluntary UN Global Compact as an alternative. As the UN Global Compact is formalizing its procedures, it may turn into a not-so-voluntary option after all. The two UN initiatives also point to a kind of competition and low intensity struggle within the UN, but without the direct involvement of key institutions of the UN, the World Bank and the IMF (nor the WTO). What the outcome might be, due to the higher profile of human rights resulting from the establishment of the new Human Rights Council, is yet to be seen.

To conclude this discussion on norm internalization and norm consolidation, I would like to recapitulate briefly the key elements that indicate norm internalization: the agents of internalization, conformity and institutionalization. Although the presence of these elements cannot claim to give evidence of anything more than incipient norm internalization, I nevertheless argue that they are not insignificant indications of the development of CSR. As far as the agents of internalization are considered, we have seen that when law and regulations are involved, there is a development of international agreements, like the very early examples of the WHO Code and the ILO Principles, and the more recent revision of the OECD Guidelines, that are complemented by other international standards found in, e.g., the Global Framework Agreements and model codes of conduct seen in the CCC

Model Code, the Fair Labor Association Workplace Code of Conduct, and others. On a national basis, we have also seen the development of national regulation and policies in examples like the disclosure regulations regarding pension funds, amendments to the GSP system and lawsuits.

In all the CSR initiatives regarding standards and monitoring, there is a bureaucratization of the activities relating to CSR, and a number of such 'bureaucracies' were mentioned above. They include the procedures needed to screen for inclusion in or exclusion from socially responsible investments and investment indexes, and the development and maintenance of various monitoring or reporting schemes (Fair Labor Association, Global Reporting Initiative, the Social Accountability International SA8000 standard, the ISO26000 among others).

With this development, new professions are emerging to handle the new issues being raised. As mentioned earlier, they can be found within targeted TNCs and also in companies that provide services to TNCs (notably accounting and consulting companies) or other sectors closely connected to TNCs (such as the financial sector), as well as other organizations. What further augment the development of new professions are the growth of CSR education and the establishment of associations for professionals.

This development in turn encourages the conformity not only of TNCs but also other actors, as well as the institutionalization of various aspects of CSR. Many companies adopt codes of conduct, devote staff and resources to work on CSR, publish social reporting, and engage in multi-stakeholder organizations or even in Business Initiatives Organizations. The initiative undertaken by the EU to address the issue of CSR in the late 1990s and early 2000s requires member countries to report on their activities in the area of CSR (regardless of whether CSR is a prioritized policy area), and the reports are made public. Another example of conformity is the OECD decision to revise and strengthen the OECD Principles. The many different actors that have become involved create, intentionally or unintentionally, an expectation that others will follow.

Chapter 10
Summary and Concluding Discussion

This is the time to close the circle and conclude the discussion of the CSR norm cycle, answering the questions initially posed regarding the revival of interest in CSR in the 1990s and the processes involved. With regard to early developments, this will be an account of the role of the NGOs – i.e., their establishment, aims and activities as norm entrepreneurs and, therefore, important driving forces in making CSR a global concern. However, as CSR developed, other actors have also come to influence this development and led to changes in the process. The initial stage of norm emergence, which was dominated by the new CSR organizations, shifted into a norm cascade, with a proliferation of both CSR organizations and initiatives. Lately this development began transforming into norm internalization, through a suggested norm consolidation, when CSR is no longer as controversial.

As was seen in the previous chapter, CSR cannot be argued to have become fully internalized. However, this should not be taken as an argument against either the norm cycle model approach or the status of CSR itself. The ideas involved in the arguments for norm cycles do not claim that all norms necessarily end up 'internalized'; the focus of the approach is rather on the process and the different elements involved in norm construction, rather than on the end result itself. This concluding discussion will review each stage of the development of CSR up to the present. The chapter will discuss the implications of each stage and close with a brief look at prospective research issues.

Emergence of Corporate Social Responsibility as an International Issue

The idea that TNCs are responsible for human and labour rights violations began to surface in the 1970s and 1980s (discussed in Chapters 3 and 4). This new way of thinking had been preceded by the establishment of the ILO and international labour standards, a successful norm cycle that was achieved through advocacy by the labour rights movement acting as the main norm entrepreneurs. However, the developments of the 1970s point to a break with the existing standard of appropriateness, i.e., the reconfiguration of the international system began to transform some fundamental principles. The system of international labour rights was not well suited to the developments in international production that followed, creating disorder and discontent in various parts of society within both home and host countries. Workers in developed countries experienced unemployment and loss of bargaining power due to competition from low wage countries, whereas workers in developing countries often faced uncertain employment and harsh working conditions. Not only had changing industrial relations become an issue when production was relocated abroad, in addition, the implications of TNCs operating in countries with human rights violations began to surface as an issue. This issue became even more pronounced as the concept of human rights acquired greater legitimacy in the international system and was institutionalized to almost the same extent as labour rights. This transformation brought on new actors and raised new issues that started to shape the international agenda to a greater extent than before, including the question of CSR.

Initial Phase: Questioning the Existing Order

The discussion of the three major events of the 1970s in Chapters 3 and 4 illustrated how standards of appropriateness at the time were questioned. An initial faith in the benefits of industrialization was complemented by issues that were not purely economic issues. This development coincided with a major change in the political landscape – the Cold War, decolonialization and the appearance of newly independent states in the international system, not least as members of the UN as well as of other IGOs.

The *UN Code Case* pinpoints the transformation in the international system. Although one of the key goals was simply negotiation of a code of conduct for TNCs, these negotiations in fact revealed and reflected contention resulting from decolonialization and the Cold War. This contention was due in part to shifts in power in the international system with the entry of newly independent states, which began claiming rights to self-determination, in particular with regard to the management of natural resources and control of the operations of TNCs – claims that were supported by the socialist countries. These negotiations mainly involved governments with a certain amount of consultation with business and major trade unions and did not attract much attention from other parts of the society. In comparison, the present discussion of CSR, particularly in relation to the initiatives within the UN, engages broad segments of society.

Although the UN Code negotiations did not succeed in arriving at a common agreement, other negotiations did, as can be seen in positions taken in response to the UN and other initiatives at the time. Of these, the OECD Guidelines on Multinational Corporations (OECD Guidelines) and the ILO Tripartite Declaration of Principles concerning Multinational Enterprises and Social Policy (ILO Declaration) are the agreements that have maintained their importance to date and are referred to in the discussion of CSR.

Whereas the UN Code Case was mostly an intergovernmental affair, two other events of this period point to increasing involvement by NGOs (apart from the trade unions) in the international system and in world politics. This involvement is most apparent in the *Anti-apartheid Case*, where TNCs were targeted by NGOs before the issue was taken up by the international system as a whole. Unlike the Nestlé Boycott Case, the Anti-apartheid Case was characterized by two parallel civil rights struggles, one taking place in South Africa and one in the US. The

NGOs here had a frame of reference for their activities, particularly in the US. It should be emphasized that above all, this issue highlighted changing norms in views of racial discrimination in the international system as well as highlighting ideas of sovereignty, as international actors began to interfere in the internal affairs of the apartheid state of South Africa. Like the Nestlé Boycott Case, this was a unifying cause for the entire NGO community, not just for international trade unions. In spite of this unification, there was disagreement between those who believed that the only solution was complete withdrawal of corporate activities, investments and trade, and those who advocated for companies to contribute to ameliorating the situation by adopting responsible policies. The roles and responsibilities of institutional investors, who initially were restricted to church organizations, later expanded to include universities and university pension funds. Two initiatives evolved during this time that are still used in the development of CSR: shareholder activism and the adoption of codes of conduct as exemplified by the Sullivan Principles (today the Global Sullivan Principles). The development of socially responsible investment and multi-stakeholder monitoring schemes has resulted from these early anti-apartheid activities.

The *Nestlé Boycott Case* involved a combination of WHO experts and NGOs. In fact, the experts in the field were the first to bring up the issue of the negative impact of artificial infant formula in developing countries. However, this was done without explicitly targeting TNCs. Here we see experts on both sides of the controversy, those representing the industry and experts as development workers. Yet it was the NGOs who framed the issue and mobilized public opinion against Nestlé's marketing practices. In later negotiations over the WHO Code, the importance of WHO (and its secretariat) as a venue for the negotiations and drafting of the WHO Code, in combination with the activities of the NGOs, points to the importance of IGOs, not just as extensions of government authority but also as arenas for policy making. The Nestlé Boycott Case questioned a product not only for inappropriate use in developing countries (consumer safety) but also as an intrusion of Western lifestyles on 'natural' cultures (and former colonies), questioning that was also combined with a more conventional view on breast-feeding in general. Although the various NGOs had different perspectives on the issue, they could find a unifying cause in the targeting of Nestlé. This case also highlights different perspectives on the belief in what industry can achieve for development and indicates how new issues entered the international agenda, perceived by some as the politicization of the WHO.

While the Nestlé Boycott and the anti-apartheid cases differ from each other, they are both distinguishable from the UN Code Case. The UN Code Case represents a manifestation of standards of appropriateness that were in place at the time, incorporating a remnant of a de facto colonial system and a traditional view of the international system as a system of sovereign states. The Nestlé Boycott and the anti-apartheid cases point to a new development in the international system with the emergence of new issues and actors, including CSR.

Second Phase: Emergence and Advocacy by Norm Entrepreneurs

Parallel to, and partly overshadowed by the three events of the 1970s, was the emergence in the late 1980s of new organizations addressing various issues related to what we now label CSR. These organizations constituted the norm entrepreneurs that persuaded other segments of society of the need to change perceptions of the responsibility of TNCs. As Chapters 5 and 6 showed, these organizations can be distinguished by specific characteristics and assigned to different categories – i.e., Activists, Business Initiatives and Multi-stakeholders. The different categories and characteristics of the particular CSR organizations involved at the time influenced the development of CSR. The organizations mainly reflected concern over the negative effects of globalization and focused on the activities of TNCs in the context of the urban North (their home countries), although affected organizations in host countries provide necessary information describing the situation on the ground. At the same time, there is some heterogeneity, due to the variety of different organizations involved; in the case of the later Business Initiatives and Multi-stakeholders organizations, the targeted companies themselves were involved. This heterogeneity provided the process with competing definitions of CSR that extended the reach of the process to other portions of society. This implies the existence of a dynamic already among the initial norm entrepreneurs themselves.

General Characteristics of the Emerging CSR Organizations

The number of CSR organizations that emerged during this time mushroomed after the late 1980s, and, in particular, around the mid-1990s. These norm entrepreneurs believed it was necessary to make the general public aware of the changing aspects of the economic and political systems and the effects that followed this transformation. This manifestation of a growing concern over the effects of the transformation of the international system also focused on the role of TNCs.

Another feature of this group of CSR organizations is that they are predominately based in North America or Europe, in the political or financial capitals of the world. A number of reasons may explain this pattern. One obvious reason is the political opportunity structure of many of the host countries, which constrains dissidents from openly establishing organizations that publicly criticise the policies of their government or other elite groups. Even if such organizations are allowed, their activities may be severely constrained, making it difficult to achieve real improvements to society. Trade unions might not even exist or be weakened due to low membership or corruption, not be representative of the workforce (e.g., male trade union structure and female workforce) or be partisan. Even if they existed, the political opportunity structure might not permit them to have any real impact.

When other characteristics of CSR organizations (apart from time and location of establishment) are concerned, the organizations prove to be more heterogeneous than initially expected. The largest group of CSR organizations and the first to emerge, *Activist Organizations*, is the group that best corresponds to the traditional idea of activists. Their aims relate mainly to trade union and worker's rights, inequality and injustice, empowerment of and solidarity with workers, and the accountability of companies. They engage in partly 'inappropriate' behaviour such as spectacular or disturbing street actions, demonstrations and other activities such as mass letter campaigning, although more mainstream campaigning activities, including lobbying and general awareness-raising activities, dominate.

The second category of CSR organizations is identified as *Business Initiatives Organizations*, which appeared somewhat after the Activists. Their aims and activities are quite different than those of the Activists in many respects, although they share an overall support for CSR. This support is expressed in very different terms, often through the concept of sustainable development and other, similar concepts that incorporate economic aspects as well as responsibilities. Their advocacy is presented as positive campaigning, in which the negative aspects of TNC activities are emphasized less. Similarly, their activities concentrate on how to work with CSR and provide a closed arena for members, as well as how to involve other stakeholders and partners in what is explicitly stated as a shared responsibility. Whereas Activists attempted to place responsibility on companies, Business Initiatives strive for shared responsibility.

The Business Initiative Organizations are somewhat controversial. One can question whether they should be considered NGOs in the first place; because of the paradox of having companies themselves engaged in organizations that in one way or another advocate for CSR. Although their perspectives are different, and self-interest may constitute a more or less important part of a member's reasons for participation (which may be true also for Activists NGOs), in my opinion, it is possible to view them as NGOs and CSR advocates. It is not necessarily the case that organizations made up of companies or business leaders are only profit maximizers, trying their utmost to externalize costs and avoid regulation. It is possible that business leaders and companies actually may diverge in their views on the best way to conduct business and therefore be interested in advocating alternatives to the traditional view of business, 'the bottom-line' or making a profit notwithstanding. I also see the influence of business in norms that define how business leaders should behave and the proper conduct of business, which in large part involve a conventional view of a predominately male and highly competitive environment. The Social Venture Network (SVN) and the European Baha'I Business Forum are examples of two Business Initiative Organizations that include companies and business leaders with objectives that combine 'the bottom-line' with social responsibility. One can furthermore consider the advocacy of CSR on the whole as a challenge to the conventional views of business leaders and business.

The third group of CSR organizations, *Multi-stakeholder Organizations*, combines organizations with different stakes in the issue at hand. Most of the organizations in this category were established after the mid-1990s and can be viewed as a reaction to the activities of both the Activists and the Business Initiatives. The goals and activities of these organizations generally concentrate on developing specific schemes or mechanisms for CSR, which, together with their mixed membership, affect the character of the organization. This means that if Multi-stakeholder organizations engage in awareness-raising or membership mobilization, these activities will involve positive campaigning. In this context, Multi-stakeholders resemble Business Initiatives in that they do not focus on the negative aspects of TNC activity, i.e., TNCs are not to be targeted in naming and shaming campaigns. As is true for Business Initiatives, questions are raised about whether the Multi-stakeholder organizations should be defined as NGOs at all. The concept of hybrid organizations has been applied to define this new form of an organization of organizations involving non-governmental and sometimes governmental and for-profit organizations. This form of organizing around standardization and accountability also points to the development of new forms of global governance that blurs the traditional public-private, national-international, governmental-non-governmental distinctions.

Selected Focus Organizations

The five focus organizations that were selected from the three categories mentioned above for in-depth study are regarded as norm entrepreneurs and advocates for CSR, and therefore share certain similarities. There are also certain features that set them apart, which are particularly noticeable when the Activists are compared to organizations in the other two categories, Business Initiatives and Multi-stakeholders. The Activists (CCC, Global Exchange and the ILRF) all share a concern for and explicitly criticise TNCs, whereas the Business Initiative (IBLF) and the Multi-stakeholder (FLO) Organizations focus on combining market mechanisms with social aspects. The IBLF and the FLO also express concerns over globalization, although in different ways, but their concerns are downplayed or presented as general problems without targeting TNCs in particular. These differences in strategy are probably necessary due to the distinctive contexts in which the organizations are working. However, these differences serve to make the strategies mutually supportive. Whereas the FLO and the IBLF may, for various reasons, choose not to criticise TNCs, the other organizations most certainly will, and thus fill a gap in the image of CSR that FLO and IBLF would like to portray. Conversely, cooperating directly with companies and the market on their own terms and from their own perspectives is not something that the ILRF, Global Exchange and the CCC are doing. Hence, the FLO and the IBLF are able to involve TNCs in the process, which might not otherwise occur.

When looking at the *background to the creation of the focus organizations*, the IBLF is the odd man out, originating as it did in concerns over social unrest in urban areas in the UK and based as it was on the initiative of a royal person. The IBLF worked in part on social unrest in addressing the transition economies in East Europe in the early 1990s. However, other issues were also addressed at that time, such as sustainable development and globalization. This agenda was somewhat similar to the agendas of the other focus organizations only in that the issues were addressed from a business perspective and it was assumed that business would make a positive contribution. The other focus organizations share more or less similar backgrounds, in that they were developed by individuals or organizations involved with issues of development in the third world, human and labour rights (e.g., anti-apartheid), unequal benefits of globalization, solidarity movements, and alternative trade. Some of the focus organizations were initially founded on specific ideas or ideology, such as a partly religious context for some of the individual founders of the FLO and the ILRF (although other NGOs also participated and influenced these organizations). Global Exchange includes the socialist ideology and ideas of internationalism. The CCC initially grew out of spontaneous street actions that eventually formalized into an organization consisting of independent national CCC organizations and was therefore less influenced by the convictions of particular founding individuals.

The *aims of the focus organizations* in the initial years concentrate mainly on certain issue-areas. The CCC and the ILRF are mainly concerned with labour rights and standards. The ILRF initially intended to reform US legislation, trade policy and regional trade agreements through legislative amendments and social clauses, whereas the CCC developed a voluntary code of conduct for the clothing industry to make TNCs responsible for working conditions at their subcontractors. Global Exchange also focuses on US foreign policy, but works to create alternative channels of exchange (Fairtrade, citizen's diplomacy, information), and links US citizens with people in other countries (grassroots internationalism) as a countermeasure. In addition, Global Exchange focuses not only on labour rights, but also on a wide range of progressive issues and values, which follow from its stronger focus on 'internationalism' in general. This is illustrated by its support of the practical solidarity of Fairtrade, i.e., in creating alternative channels and adjusting the unequal terms of trade for small farmers. The IBLF stands out for its initial focus on sustainable development and support for the transformation of the transition economies of Eastern Europe. In the initial years of the IBLF, one can also discern support for the market economy and expectations for future market opportunities, rather than a concern about CSR as perceived by the other focus organizations.

It is important to note that the two US-based focus organizations target US foreign policy and the US general public. The other focus organizations do not target their respective national governments, although they do address their general public. There is clearly a different context within which the focus organizations operate, which makes the work of the US-based focus organizations very much in contention with their own government (although this partly depends on the administration in power).

Like their aims, the *activities undertaken by the focus organizations* are also both similar and different. Here the distinction between the Activists category and the Business Initiative and Multi-stakeholder categories once again becomes obvious. The CCC, Global Exchange and the ILRF share more or less the same action strategies, i.e., general public awareness-raising, mass letter campaigns, street actions, etc., whereas the other organizations work in a slightly different way. The IBLF establishes business-leader forums in other countries or supports the establishment of sister organizations, and acts as a catalyst for forming partnerships on different issues. One could label this elite mobilization, particularly when it involves the Prince of Wales. Another important activity for the IBLF is cooperation and partnership with different UN agencies, which is quite different from the other focus organizations, which seldom attend to the activities of IGOs apart from making occasional statements at meetings and receiving financial contributions. Even if one should be careful not to overestimate the impact a single organization can have, it is reasonable to conclude that in comparison, the influence of the IBLF with certain IGOs is disproportionate. The FLO also takes a different path, focusing its activities entirely on the development of the Fairtrade labelling system and soliciting support from various parts of the society, not least of all the consumers who make a political statement through their choice of product.

Similarities are also found among the focus organizations in that most engage in general campaigning activities, including producing and disseminating publications, influencing decision-makers, etc., – important activities in the framing of the issues advocated by the different organizations.

One can conclude from the aims and activities of the focus organizations that the strategies of persuasion used vary considerably, both in content and in the target. Some organizations are concerned with providing the general public with new information, either of a provocative or a matter-of-fact character, to mobilize the public for traditional activist activities and acquire support for the issue, which also gives legitimacy to the norm entrepreneurs themselves. The general public can also be addressed by spectacular actions that draw attention to the demonstrators and get their message across. Among the other strategies used to persuade others of the necessity of CSR are strategies that involve creating alternatives and working outside the system and through alternative methods, such as the establishment of the CCC Model Code, which was not only a standard with which companies were expected to comply but was also used as a petition and a way to frame the issue in general.

Whereas some organizations focused mostly on the general public, the IBLF directed its attention to companies, 'elites' and international forums with the purpose of acting as a catalyst, assisted by the Prince of Wales as an 'instrument' of persuasion. The FLO had to convince both companies and society in general to establish the Fairtrade labelling system, achieve legitimacy for the new idea of Fairtrade labelled coffee, and then make it work on the market. The two US-based focus organizations both criticized their national government policies, but only the ILRF attempted to work within the system.

One strategy of the ILRF, in fact, stands out from the other persuasion strategies and is in part a form of leverage politics making use of the coercive powers of other actors rather than persuasion. The focus of the ILRF on amending the GSP and other legislation as well as achieving the side agreement to NAFTA meant persuading (mainly) politicians to include social aspects in trade policies and legislation. However, once these goals were achieved, the resulting legislation is coercive, although we can also see weaknesses in the side agreement to NAFTA. And while the legislation became effective, someone still needs to take the initiative to file complaints through the complaints mechanisms. Here, the ILRF has created a platform through the state for action that may result in processes that are more coercive than persuasive.

Proliferation, Fragmentation and 'Dialogue'

As the persuasion practiced by the CSR organizations began affecting other segments of society, including individual consumers, other NGOs, companies, governments and IGOs, the process changed – a norm tipping paved the way for the CSR norm cascade that has been a feature of the international system since the mid-1990s. CSR began to proliferate more easily and became a justifiable activity in which to engage, as it provided the participating actors with legitimacy. The process became fragmented, as more and different actors joined in. The proliferation of CSR organizations and initiatives also meant that the actors by necessity began to interact in various ways and were socialized into adopting and advocating CSR. This socialization process sometimes focused on particular companies, as is seen in the targeting of Nike, but was also part of the development of different standards and monitoring schemes and measures taken to achieve other forms of accountability, discussed in Chapters 7 and 8.

Turning Point: Corporate Social Responsibility Goes Mainstream

The advocacy of the early norm entrepreneurs was successful in bringing attention to the issue of CSR, as other actors were drawn into the process. When one surveys the activities of the other actors, one sees that apart from the establishment and activities of CSR organizations, there is an apparent influx of CSR initiatives from the mid-1990s onwards (listed in Appendix 3). It is not possible to pinpoint the exact year at which the turning point occurred, but from the combined change in the activities of the focus organizations and the involvement of other actors, the mid-1990s appear to be a particularly intense period.

In Chapters 6–8, we saw how different kinds of actors began adopting CSR policies of various kinds on a broad scale. In particular, companies themselves and their trade and industry associations began adopting codes of conduct or other policies supporting CSR. Companies targeted by Activists, or belonging to the same industry sector as targeted companies, have most certainly shown interest in adopting such codes of conduct. The same is true for industry associations in those industry sectors that have been specially targeted as a whole, such as the extractive industries.

Governments and IGOs also began addressing the issue in the mid-1990s. This study has shown that at that time, individual governments began to adopt policies and undertake other measures on CSR, as in the case of the US and the establishment of the Fair Labor Association. Among the initiatives undertaken by IGOs, one could mention the OECD Guidelines, which were revised and strengthened, and the work within the UN and the EU. Attempts to link trade with labour rights in the so-called social clauses in trade agreements proved less successful. The social clauses were heavily criticized as protectionism and have not been a major focus for CSR organizations lately.

Contributing to the success of the norm entrepreneurs are also so-called 'world events', which help highlight the issues advocated by these organizations. These world events do not always occur by chance, but sometimes result from the strategic work of the CSR organizations themselves, although the events are not completely controlled by them. One of the world events that augmented the development of CSR is, in particular, the exposure of the use of child labour in the production of footballs 'occurring' at the time of the football championships. Similar conditions have been exposed in other industry sectors (hand-knotted carpets, well-known clothing brands, etc.). Child labour had of course been used well before these revelations, but suddenly such use became known worldwide. Similar events can be other, more dramatic and tragic events, such as factory fires with many casualties, or the exposure of inhumane working conditions among illegal immigrants.

The effect of the proliferation of CSR internationally, the entrance of new actors and the establishment of new CSR organizations and initiatives mean a change in the activities of the norm entrepreneurs as well as a change in the process itself. Before the norm tipping occurred, the norm entrepreneurs had been more or less on their own. There had either been little interest in the issues advocated by the norm entrepreneurs or outright resistance to and rejection of their arguments in favour of CSR. As the process changed, CSR suddenly became a trend and a legitimate activity, to be undertaken by any kind of actor, not just by progressive or radical activists. In fact, it not only became more legitimate, there was a general pull towards engaging in CSR for various reasons. This proliferation had both a constituting and socializing effect; it created both new actors and new initiatives that in turn influenced existing actors to engage in the social practices involved in CSR.

Instances of Socialization

The norm cascading of the 1990s manifested itself in many different ways. Chapters 7 and 8 discussed some of the more important ones involving focus organizations. The targeting of Nike was a case that focused attention on the issue of CSR at an individual company, demonstrating the process of interaction between Activists and a single TNC. The development of standards, including monitoring schemes or what from a business perspective is labelled best practice, is another striking feature of norm cascading. More formal accountability systems also appeared in the form of national legislation and lawsuits. These can all be seen as instances of socialization, i.e., the social process that characterizes this stage of the norm cycle.

A Company of Mark Becomes a Marked Company

The targeting of Nike is one case where we can see how, over a period of time, a company is socialized to adopt CSR policies. Targeting Nike was not centrally planned or coordinated by the CSR organizations; the campaign developed instead through a loosely connected informal network of organizations that exchanged information on Nike and on their individual campaign activities. This was a strategy that empowered the otherwise not materially resourceful NGOs. Despite the lack of material resources, or perhaps because the action was so disorganized, wherever Nike turned, the company was met with criticism from a different organization.

The range of strategies used to pressure Nike involved every imaginable activist action, from matter-of-fact information to ridicule and fierce criticism, such as the staged 'court hearing' by the CCC, which Nike did not attend, but nevertheless found it necessary to respond to with a written statement. Almost all of the focus organizations participated directly (or indirectly in the case of the IBLF), apart from FLO, with its restricted mandate. Global Exchange took a central role in the campaign, conducting the most intense campaigning with its own Director, Medea Benjamin, at the forefront.

This growing pressure led Nike to new and expanded CSR measures, apart from the initial adoption of codes of conduct. These measures included devoting staff and other resources within the company to the problem, engaging external expertise from an accounting firm and a high profile individual, and joining CSR initiatives such as Business for Social Responsibility, the Fair Labor Association (Nike is a founding member) and the Vietnamese Business Link Initiative. Today, Nike has even disclosed the names and locations of all its subcontractors.

The IBLF can be said to have engaged indirectly in the campaign on Nike in two ways: by being instrumental in the establishment of the Vietnamese Business Link Initiative partnership (relating to hazardous chemicals in the production process), and developing advice in the case of 'brand-jacking' discussed in Chapter 8. Both activities were linked to Nike's operations, with Nike being a partner in the first case. In the second case, Nike is a clear example of what brand-jacking means and how not to respond.

Media also played an important part in the Nike campaign. Yet key mainstream media had to run articles on the issue before the issue really reached a broad audience and the campaign gained legitimacy. Once *The New York Times* had taken up the issue, it became an appropriate issue and no longer just the voice of some radical activists. This was, of course, a strategy among the NGOs (to draw attention to various actions in order to publicize the associated issue), which proved to be a successful strategy. The media were not only important in the campaign against Nike, but also in the development of CSR in general, contributing to continuous news reporting on CSR organizations and initiatives, the failure of individual companies to comply with certain commitments and the like.

Standards and Accountability Systems

One effect of the growing attention to CSR was the demand for more specific recommendations on what should actually be expected from the TNCs who were being criticized. The development of standards as well as corresponding systems of accountability was an activity in which several of the focus organizations were engaged. This represented another way of socializing companies and others, either by their direct involvement in the system or by framing the issue and using the standards as a compliance check.

One example is the Fairtrade labelling standards and monitoring system, in which the different actors (small farmers' cooperatives, NGOs and companies) cooperated and negotiated the content of the system. Once the system was in place and working, particularly after the different national labelling initiatives were able to agree on a common international system and Fairtrade logo, it became a fairly non-controversial initiative, and Fairtrade products are becoming more and more accepted. This was not the case at first. The difficulties involved not only persuading coffee companies and retailers to join the labelling scheme, but also assembling the various national initiatives into the FLO and agreeing on a common Fairtrade logo. The basic motivation for coordination of the different national labelling initiatives was to obtain a clear profile in the market and society at large, i.e., to create a well-known label that could be recognized and used to identify the product, not only by consumers, but also other actors of interest to the movement (e.g., financial contributors). Here we see how the development of Fairtrade not only meant an adjustment for the coffee companies and retailers, but also for the Fairtrade movement itself. The Fairtrade organizations had to relinquish their national identities and different goals for Fairtrade and adapt to the market mechanisms. That was the price for introducing Fairtrade on the market. This seems to have been a successful strategy, as sales figures keep increasing every year.

Other standards besides Fairtrade labelling were also developed, with or without accountability systems. Chapter 8 discussed the CCC Model Code, the Voluntary Principles on Security and Human Rights, and the Fair Labor Association, among other similar initiatives. A common feature of these initiatives is that almost all have developed as a consequence of a 'world event', pressure on an industry for an extended period or other crises. They point to the motive for participation to be found in the need of the companies for legitimation, achieved through adherence to a particular standard and accountability system.

The ideas of good practice and partnership advocated by the IBLF correspond in part quite well with the ideas of standards, accountability and multi-stakeholder organizations. However, a distinction can be made between these standards and the standards expressed through the concept of good practices. Companies that adopt good practices, show leadership and act as role models for other companies. This resonates with the traditional idea in business of being a market leader. Furthermore, good practices are not external obligations with which companies have to comply. On the contrary, these market leaders come across as enlightened executives or board directors who have made the right choices. It is possible to understand the idea of partnership in a somewhat similar fashion, as focusing on pressing global issues that cannot be solved individually by any individual or organization, not even a TNC. Partnership is the solution, where companies can contribute with their particular expertise – in other words, where their knowledge and resources are in demand. There is also the argument that companies need to participate in order to influence the process by which limits are imposed on the responsibility of companies. If they do not, someone else will create those limits for them. Partnerships are multi-stakeholder forums, but presented as cooperation among equals with benefits to all participants, not as a somewhat contentious interaction of stakeholders, each negotiating for their share.

Some strategies of persuasion used by the focus organization were more coercive or relied on the coercion of other actors, as was seen in the discussion of the initial years of activity by the ILRF in trying to amend legislation. After some years, the ILRF developed this strategy even further when it began filing the so-called ATCA lawsuits. Like the idea of suggesting an amendment to the GSP regulation, this represented an innovative interpretation of existing law. This approach can also be seen in the arguments made for a reinterpretation of international human rights law and CSR in relation to the UN Draft Norms. This effort provoked an outcry from certain US businesses and may have set in motion a countermovement that will influence the further development of CSR. The negative response to the ATCA lawsuits is paralleled in part by the strong reaction to the UN Draft Norms.

Internalization of Corporate Social Responsibility?

If the two previous stages in the norm cycle, i.e., norm emergence and norm cascade, have been quite obvious in CSR development, the third stage, norm internalization, is less evident. Therefore, it is more accurate to discuss indications of *incipient* norm internalization. Indications of this incipient norm internalization were seen in the discussion in Chapter 9 regarding agents of internalization (law, bureaucracy and professions), motives of conformity and the dominant social process, institutionalization. Here I have added the concept of norm consolidation to the norm cycle model. Norm consolidation becomes the link between norm cascade and norm internalization; it is the process necessary to transform one stage into another.

The concept of norm consolidation involves a convergence around specific standards of appropriateness, which are seen to provide the legitimacy, reputation or esteem that are demanded by the various actors involved in CSR in the norm cascade. There is thus a process of clustering around a limited number of CSR initiatives, in contrast to the process of proliferation that is involved in norm tipping and norm cascading. Actors gather around these limited numbers of initiatives and engage in repeated interaction, eventually leading to habits of trust. A consequence of this is that common life-worlds are produced (necessary for consolidation to occur), and from this follows conformity of behaviour. Chapter 9 discussed cases where the process just described can be discerned, i.e., social labelling of Fairtrade products, the two UN initiatives represented by the UN Draft Norm and the UN Global Compact.

Cases of Norm Consolidation

Fairtrade labelling has shown remarkable growth in the last 10 years, with an increase in the number of participants in the system itself (including the establishment of new national initiatives), expansion of the effects of the labelling to include dependents (an estimated 5 million individuals), inclusion of new products, and continued increases in sales. The very system itself manifests the elements of norm internalization in the 'bureaucracy' that the organization of the labelling system represents and in involving specific professions to carry out different tasks. One can also speak of a certain level of conformity in the continuous growth of Fairtrade, evidenced not least by the involvement of other companies and institutions. It is interesting to note that certain coffee roasters and/or coffee shops have found it necessary to develop schemes of their own similar to the Fairtrade labelling system that introduce social responsibility into their purchases of coffee. Although these schemes usually are not as elaborate as Fairtrade labelling (often lacking price guarantees), they show that companies conform to an expectation. Another example of conformity in this area is the interest that has been shown in Fairtrade by others, such as institutions that decide to provide Fairtrade products, wholly or partly; hotel chains, retailers, and IGOs.

One fact that undermines the argument for conformity is the small market share that the Fairtrade products represent. This is somewhat surprising, due to the seemingly widespread support for Fairtrade, but serves to sustain the arguments of Fairtrade labelling as a phenomenon that has an ideational impact greater than the present consumption behaviour. There is great symbolic value connected to the idea of Fairtrade and the Fairtrade label. However, one could still argue that the spectacular growth, in particular the growing demand from institutions and companies outside the labelling system itself, points to continued future conformity. The fact that even marginal changes in the market tend to have a large effect may also lend support to the argument that Fairtrade labelling is continuing to be an important factor in the development of CSR.

The other examples of convergence discussed occur within the UN, i.e. the *UN Draft Norm* and the *UN Global Compact (UNGC)*. These initiatives have attracted a considerable amount of international attention, but for different reasons. They demonstrate an interesting conflict within the UN itself, with CSR taking quite different turns within one and the same organization. The UN Draft Norm originated in a concern for indigenous peoples and an attempt to link development more closely with the realization of economic, social cultural rights. The UN Draft Norm initially incorporated concern over the policies of certain multilateral institutions and the advent of globalization; ultimately, the main concern was directed towards the negative effects of TNC activity. The UNGC developed partly along the same trajectory, but from a different perspective and with another strategy.

The two initiatives also illustrate the division that is seen within the development of CSR between voluntary initiatives and binding regulation. The division is not simply between progressive NGOs and free-trade-oriented business, but also includes some unexpected elements, with representatives from business expressing support or cautious appreciation for the UN Draft Norms, as seen in the cases of the Business Leaders Initiative on Human Rights and the French retailer CarreFour.

In a sense, the two UN initiatives are opposite images of each other. One is quite wide ranging and elaborate, while the other is brief. One is a far reaching (progressive?) interpretation of international law, the other more moderate and traditional. One is de facto binding in character, whereas the other is not, and factions that oppose one are usually supportive of the other. One could argue that they complement each other and are mutually constitutive, as the perceived inappropriateness of one leads to increased support of the other.

Taken together, these cases of consolidation are interesting in the way they bring up changing views on market exchange (including companies), international governance and international human rights law.

Norms, Corporate Social Responsibility and Future Research Agendas

The present study has effectively shown that CSR is a norm in development that has reached, if not norm internalization, at least a stage of 'incipient norm internalization'. This means that it has become fairly extensively accepted that, with reference to international law or other well-established international agreements and in situations of weak government, companies have responsibilities that go beyond what is stated in (national) law or practiced by custom. This norm has subsequently been partly internalized in the international system, through the establishment of new governance structures and international agreements within the multilateral forums of IGOs, adoption of government policies, changing behaviour of companies (although not full compliance), growing political consumerism of individuals and widespread advocacy among a large number of NGOs. The idea of CSR that is on the verge of being internalized appears to converge on at least the following themes: market-based solutions (social labelling and socially responsible investment), voluntary private or private-public regulations, and to some extent, hard law-oriented accountability, whether in national or international law.

However, some steps have yet to be taken before 'comprehensive' norm internalization will be reached, i.e., before CSR is perceived to be uncontroversial and hardly regarded as an issue at all. In practice, no norm can reach this ideal state, as there is probably not a norm in existence that exhibits total internalization. Even the most dominant norms in a society are questioned by someone. In relation to theories of norms and norm construction, it is important to provide further empirical studies for a better understanding of the working of norms in relationship to norm theory in the area of CSR. This is particularly important where social constructivist approaches are concerned, in order to develop our knowledge of the quite illusive ideas involved in concepts such as mutual constitution. In particular, where the norm cycle model is concerned, the concept of norm consolidation introduced in this study needs further development and application to other issues in international relations.

As has been seen in the case of CSR, contentious issues still surface as soon as CSR is specified. This is particularly true when hard law is considered. It seems as if any responsibility can be accepted provided that it is voluntary, which appears to be a paradox. The complete opposite goes for binding regulation, where no responsibility is acceptable. This is illustrated particularly in the discussion of the UN Draft Norms and the UN Global Compact. At present, the first round seems to have been won by the UN Global Compact, although this might only be preparation for more binding regulation. The formalization of the UN Global Compact initiative may be taken as support for such a development.

In the cases of the UN Draft Norms and the UN Global Compact, research by legal scholars and others is important to further understand the content and implications of various developments in the area of CSR and the roles of non-state actors. Both initiatives represent new developments in the areas of human rights and global governance that merit further attention, not least by IR scholars. The same can be said for other CSR initiatives.

Another area that needs further study is of course the practical implications and effects on the ground of the various CSR initiatives. Is there only 'talk', or are there also signs of CSR having a real effect? In that case, what are the effects, for example, on transnational civil society, local organization and mobilization and similar aspects? In this context, opposition to the development of more binding regulation in the area of CSR based on the claim that private (at times private-public), voluntary self-regulation is superior should be scrutinized. The effects of these kinds of CSR initiatives require study, as mere reference to the general benefit of economic development that TNC activity is said to provide in my opinion is insufficient.

Bibliography

A who's who of corporate responsibility action groups. 1972. *Business and Society Review*, 72–73(4), 81–86.

Addo, M.K. 1999. *Human Rights Standards and the Responsibility of Transnational Corporations*. The Hague: Kluwer.

Adler, E. 2002. Constructivism and international relations, in *Handbook of International Relations*, edited by W. Carlsnaes, T. Risse and B.A. Simmons. London: Sage, 95–118.

Alston, P. 2005. *Labour Rights as Human Rights*. Oxford: Oxford University Press.

Amnesty International and IBLF (International Business Leaders Forum). 2002. *Business and Human Rights: A Geography of Risks*. London: Amnesty International.

An-Na'im, A.A. 2005. The interdependence of religion, secularism and human rights: Prospects for Islamic societies. *Common Knowledge*, 11(1), 56–80.

Ascoly, N. and Zeldenrust, I. 1999. *The Code Debate in Context: A Decade of Campaigning for Clean Clothes*. [Online: Clean Clothes Campaign]. Available at: www.cleanclothes.org/codes/99-3-11.htm [accessed: 7 September 2004].

Athreya, B. 2003. Deputy Director, ILRF. Interview conducted in Washington, DC, US, April 2003.

Baade, H.W. 1980. Codes of conduct for multinational enterprises: An introductory survey, in *Legal Problems of Codes of Conduct for Multinational Enterprises*, edited by N. Horn. Deventer: Kluwer, 407–44.

Bakker, I. and Gill, S. 2003. *Power, Production and Social Reproduction. Human In/security in the Global Political Economy*. Basingstoke: Palgrave Macmillan.

Barnes, H. 2003. Collaborative Engagement Officer, United Kingdom Social Investment Forum (UKSIF). Interview conducted in London, UK, December 2003.

Barnett, M. and Duvall, R. 2005. *Power in Global Governance*. Cambridge: Cambridge University Press.

Basu, K., Horn, H., Román, L. and Shapiro, J. 2003. *International Labor Standards: History, Theory, and Policy Options*. Malden, MA: Blackwell Publishers.

Beauvais, E. 2003. SRI Program and Research Coordinator, Social Investment Forum (SIF). Interview conducted in Washington, DC, US, April 2003.

Beck, U. 1999. *World Risk Society*. Cambridge: Polity Press.

Bello, W. 2005. Director, Focus on the Global South. Interview conducted in Stockholm, Sweden, August 2005.

Benjamin, M. and Freedman, A. 1989. *Bridging the Global Gap: A Handbook to Linking Citizens of the First and Third Worlds*. Cabin John, MD: Seven Locks Press.

Bennett, C.J. 2004. Senior Research Associate, Global Corporate Citizenship, The Conference Board. Interview conducted in New York, US, July 2004.

Bielefeldt, H. 1995. Muslim voices in the human rights debate. *Human Rights Quarterly*, 17(4), 587–617.

Björkdahl, A. 2002a. *From Idea to Norm: Promoting Conflict Prevention*. Lund: Department of Political Science, Lund University.

Björkdahl, A. 2002b. Norms in international relations: Some conceptual and methodological reflections. *Cambridge Review of International Affairs*, 15(1), 9–23.

BLIHR (Business Leaders Initiative on Human Rights). 2004. *Submission to the Office of the UN High Commissioner for Human Rights relating to the 'Responsibilities of transnational corporations and related business enterprises with regard to human rights'*, 28 September 2004.

Boli, J. and Thomas, G.M. 1999. *Constructing World Culture: International Nongovernmental Organizations Since 1875*. Stanford, CA: Stanford University Press.

Bork, R.H. 2003. Judicial imperialism. *The Wall Street Journal*, 17 June, 16.

Bowen, H.R. 1953. *Social Responsibilities of the Businessman*. New York, NY: Harper & Brothers.

Braithwaite, J. and Drahos, P. 2000. *Global Business Regulation*. Cambridge: Cambridge University Press.

Bretcher, J. and Costello, T. 1991. *Global Village v. Global Pillage: A One-World Strategy for Labor*. Washington, DC: International Labor Rights Fund.

Brief for the National Foreign Trade Council, USA*Engage, The Chamber of Commerce of the United States of America, The United States Council for International Business, The International Chamber of Commerce, The Organization for International Investment, The Business Roundtable, the American Petroleum Institute, and the US–ASEAN Business Council as amici curiae in support of petitioner, No. 03-339, In the Supreme Court of the United States, Sosa v. Alvarez–Machain, et al., On Writ of Certiorari to the United States Court of Appeals for the Ninth Circuit. 23 January 2004.

Brysk, A. 2002. *Globalization of Human Rights*. Los Angeles, CA: University of California Press.

Buffle, J-C. 1986. *Dossier N comme Nestlé: Multinational et Infanticide, le Lait, les Bébés et la Mort*. Paris: Alain Moreau.

Buhle, M.J., Buhle, P. and Georgakas, D. 1992. *Encyclopaedia of the American Left*. Urbana, IL: University of Illinois Press.

Bulletin of the International Metalworker's Federation. 1959–1962.

Callinicos, A. 2002. Marxism and global governance, in *Governing Globalization: Power, Authority and Global Governance*, edited by A. McGrew and D. Held. Cambridge: Polity Press, 249–66.

Carrefour. 2005a. *Communiqué de Press, Le 14 novembre 2005, Carrefour s'engage en faveur des norms de l'ONU sur la responsabilité des enterprises en matière de droits de l'Homme.*

Carrefour. 2005b. *Groupe Carrefour: Sustainability Report 2005.* Paris: Carrefour Group.

Carroll, A.B. 1999. Corporate social responsibility: Evolution of a definitional construct. *Business and Society*, 38(3), 268–95.

Cavanagh, J., Compa, L., Ebert, A., Goold, B., Selvaggio, K. and Shorrock, T. 1988. *Trade's Hidden Costs: Worker Rights in a Changing World Economy.* Washington, DC: International Labor Rights Education and Research Fund.

Cavanagh et al. 2002. *Alternatives to Globalization: A Better World is Possible.* San Francisco, CA: Berrett-Koehler.

CCC (Clean Clothes Campaign). 1993a. *The Clean Clothes Campaign*, April 1993.

CCC (Clean Clothes Campaign). 1993b. *Clean Clothes Newsletter*, No. 1, November 1993.

CCC (Clean Clothes Campaign). 1995a. *Reports of Meetings of the European Project on Clean Clothes: March to July 1995.*

CCC (Clean Clothes Campaign). 1995b. *Clean Clothes Newsletter*, No. 5, November 1995.

CCC (Clean Clothes Campaign). 1995c. Nike: Hot air or a leader? *Clean Clothes Newsletter*, No. 5, November 1995.

CCC (Clean Clothes Campaign). 1995d. Negotiations with Retailers Started On Garments … and On Toys. *Clean Clothes Newsletter*, No. 5, November 1995.

CCC (Clean Clothes Campaign). 1996a. *Clean Clothes Newsletter*, No. 6, July 1996.

CCC (Clean Clothes Campaign). 1996b. Clothing industry summit, July 16 in DC. *Clean Clothes Newsletter*, No. 6, July 1996.

CCC (Clean Clothes Campaign). 1996c. Linking the source to the buyer: Research in the garment sector in Asia. *Clean Clothes Newsletter*, No. 6, July 1996.

CCC (Clean Clothes Campaign). 1997a. Nike: Fair play? *Clean Clothes Newsletter*, No. 7, February 1997.

CCC (Clean Clothes Campaign). 1997b. Nike: Is just *not* doing it. *Clean Clothes Newsletter*, No. 7, February 1997.

CCC (Clean Clothes Campaign). 1998a. International forum on clean clothes! Make sure you don't miss it! *Clean Clothes Newsletter*, No. 9, February 1998.

CCC (Clean Clothes Campaign). 1998b. International forum on clean clothes brings new perspectives for campaigns. *Clean Clothes Newsletter*, No. 10, August 1998.

CCC (Clean Clothes Campaign). 2000a. The clean clothes communities. *Clean Clothes Newsletter*, No. 12, May 2000.

CCC (Clean Clothes Campaign). 2000b. *Clean Clothes Newsletter*, No. 13, November 2000.

CCC (Clean Clothes Campaign). 2000c. Some background for the CC strategy debate. *Clean Clothes Newsletter*, No. 13, November 2000.

CCC (Clean Clothes Campaign). 2001. Nike and Reebok in Mexico. *Clean Clothes Newsletter*, No. 14, July 2001.

CCC (Clean Clothes Campaign). 2002. *Clean Clothes Newsletter*, No. 15, June 2002.

CCC (Clean Clothes Campaign). 2003. Lawsuits and legislation. *Clean Clothes Newsletter*, No. 16, February 2003.

CCC (Clean Clothes Campaign). 2004. *Frequently Asked Questions*. [Online: Clean Clothes Campaign]. Available at: www.cleanclothes.org/faq/faq02.htm [accessed: 2 September 2004].

CCC (Clean Clothes Campaign). 2005. *Looking For a Quick Fix*. Amsterdam: Clean Clothes Campaign.

CEBC (Center for Ethical Business Cultures). 2005a. *Our History.* [Online: Center for Ethical Business Cultures]. Available at: www.cebcglobal.org/Overview/History.htm [accessed: 6 September 2005].

CEBC (Center for Ethical Business Cultures). 2005b. *The Minnesota Principles: Toward An Ethical Basis For Global Business.* [Online: Center for Ethical Business Cultures]. Available at: www.cebcglobal.org/KnowledgeCenter/Publications/Principles/MinnesotaPrinciples.htm [accessed: 6 September 2005].

Charnovitz, S. 1987. The influence of international labour standards on the world trading regime: A historical overview. *International Labour Review*, 126(5), 565–84.

Chatfield, C. 1997. Intergovernmental and nongovernmental associations to 1945, in *Transnational Social Movements and Global Politics: Solidarity Beyond the State*, edited by J. Smith, C. Chatfield and R. Pagnucco. Syracuse, NY: Syracuse University Press, 19–41.

Checkel, J.T. 1997. International norms and domestic politics: Bridging the rationalist-constructivist divide. *European Journal of International Relations*, 3(4), 473–95.

Checkel, J.T. 1998. The constructivist turn in international relations theory. *World Politics*, 50(2), 324–48.

Chetley, A. 1979. *The Baby Killer Scandal: A War on Want Investigation into the Promotion and Sale of Powdered Baby Milks in the Third World*. London: War on Want.

Chetley, A. 1986. *The Politics of Baby Foods: Successful Challenges to an International Marketing Strategy*. London: F. Pinter.

Clapham, A. 2006. *Human Rights Obligations of Non-state Actors*. Oxford: Oxford University Press.

Clark, I. 2007. *International Legitimacy and World Society*. Oxford: Oxford University Press.

Colás, A. 2002. *International Civil Society: Social Movement in World Politics*. Oxford: Polity Press.

Collingsworth, T. 2003. *The Alien Tort Claims Act: A Vital Tool for Preventing Corporations from Violating Fundamental Human Rights.* Washington, DC: International Labor Rights Fund.

Commission draft resolution. 1997. *The relationship between the enjoyment of economic, social and cultural rights and the right to development, and the working methods and activities of transnational corporations. Cuba, Iran (Islamic Republic of)*, Morocco*, Nigeria*: draft resolution.* Commission on Human Rights, Report of the Sub-Commission on prevention of discrimination and protection of minorities on its forty-eighth session. E/CN.4/1997/L.44, 7 April 1997.

Commission note. 1997. *Question of the realization in all countries of the economic, social and cultural rights.* Note by the Secretariat. Commission on Human Rights, E/CN.4/Sub.2/1997/110, 31 January 1997.

Commission report. 2005. *Report of the Sub-Commission on the promotion and protection of human rights. Report of the United Nations Commissioner on Human Rights on the responsibilities of transnational corporations and related business enterprises with regard to human rights.* Summary. Commission on Human Rights, E/CN.4/2005/91, 15 February 2005.

Commission resolution. 1997. *Question of the realization in all countries of the economic, social and cultural rights.* Commission resolution 1997/17, 11 April 1997. Commission on Human Rights, Report on the Fifty-Third Session, E/1997/23, E/CN.4/1997/150, 10 March–18 April 1997

Commission resolution. 2004. *Responsibilities of transnational corporations and related business enterprises with regard to human rights.* Commission resolution 2004/116, 20 April 2004. Commission on Human Rights, Report on the Sixtieth Session, E/2004/23, E/CN.4/2004/127, 15 March–23 April 2004.

Commission resolution. 2005. *Human rights and transnational corporations and other business enterprises.* Commission on Human Rights, resolution 2005/69, 20 April 2005.

Commission written support. 1997. *Question of the realization in all countries of the economic, social and cultural rights. Written statement submitted by Human Rights Advocates, a nongovernmental organization in special consultative status* [in support for the Sub-Commission resolution 1996/39]. Commission on Human Rights, E/CN.4/1997/NGO/48, 17 March 1997.

Commission on Global Governance. 1995. *Our Global Neighbourhood: The Report of the Commission on Global Governance.* Oxford: Oxford University Press.

Commission for Labor Cooperation. 1996. *Annual Report 1996.* [Online: Commission for Labor Cooperation]. Available at: http://new.naalc.org/index.cfm?page=626 [accessed: 1 August 2009].

Compa, L. and Vogt, J.S. 2001. Labor rights in the generalized system of preferences: A 20-year review. *Comparative Labor Law & Policy Journal,* 22(2–3), 199–238.

Connor, T. 2001. *Still Waiting For Nike To Do It: Nike's Labor Practices in the Three Years Since CEO Phil Knight's Speech to the National Press Club*. San Francisco, CA: Global Exchange.

COPEC (Conference on Christian Politics, Economics, and Citizenship). 1924. *Commission on Industry and Property, Industry and Property: Being the Report Presented to the Conference on Christian Politics, Economics and Citizenship at Birmingham, April 5–12, 1924*. London: Longmans, Green.

CorpWatch. 2001. *CorpWatch Campaign Profile: Alliance for a Corporate–Free UN, March 2001*. [Online: CorpWatch]. Available at: http://www.corpwatch. org/article.php?id =927 [accessed: 1 August 2009].

Craddock, S. 1983. *Retired, Except on Demand: The Life of Dr Cicely Williams*. Oxford: Green College.

CRT (Caux Round Table). 2002. *Who are We?* [Online: Caux Round Table]. Available at: www.cauxroundtable.org/Whoarewe.HTM [accessed: 10 October 2002].

Derbyshire, D. 2005. Fairtrade criticised over Nestlé approval. *The Daily Telegraph*, 7 October. [Online: LexisNexis Academic]. Available at: http:// www.lexisnexis.com/us/lnacademic/search/homesubmitForm.do [accessed: 1 August 2009].

Donnelly, J. 2003. *Universal Human Rights in Theory and Practice*. Ithaca, NY: Cornell University Press.

Donnelly, J. 2007. *International Human Rights*. Boulder, CO: Westview Press.

Dunning, J. 1997. *Alliance Capitalism and Global Business*. London: Routledge.

ECOA (Ethics & Compliance Officer Association). [Online: Ethics & Compliance Officer Association]. Available at: www.theecoa.org//AM/Template. cfm?Section=Home [accessed: 1 August 2009].

ECOSOC (Economic and Social Council). 1972. *ECOSOC Resolution 1721(LIII)*, adopted 28 July 1972, meeting 1836.

Ehrenberg, J. 1999. *Civil Society: The Critical History of an Idea*. New York: New York University Press.

Engerman, S.L. 1981. Introduction, in *The Abolition of the Atlantic Slave Trade: Origins and Effects in Europe, Africa and the Americas*, edited by D. Eltis and J. Walvin. Madison, WI: University of Wisconsin Press.

Enloe, C. 1995. The globetrotting sneaker. *Ms.* 5(March/April), 10–15.

Enterprise IG and the IBLF. 2004. *Brand-jacking and How to Avoid it. Issues: A Publication for Brand and Identity Decision Makers, No. 2*. London: Enterprise IG.

Equal Exchange. 2004a. *Welcome to Equal Exchange*. [Online: Equal Exchange]. Available at: www.equalexchange.com [accessed: 19 May 2004].

Equal Exchange. 2004b. *Fair Trade, Organic and Shade Grown*. [Online: Equal Exchange]. Available at: www.equalexchange.com/intro/eeintro9.html [accessed: 19 May 2004].

Eshuis, F. and Harmsen, J. 2003. *Trade on Condition: 15 Years of Coffee with the Max Havelaar Label*. Utrecht: Max Havelaar Foundation.

Ethical Corporation. 2006. *Ethical Corporation: Special Report. May 2006.* [Online: Ethical Corporation]. Available at: http://www.ethicalcorp.com/special-issues/docs/EC%20-%20Special%20Report%20Education.pdf [accessed: 20 March 2007].

Ethical Corporation. 2007. *Ethical Corporation: Business Education Special Report 2007.* [Online: Ethical Corporation]. Available at: http://www.ethicalcorp.com/edu/docs/EC-EducationReport2007.pdf [accessed: 1 September 2009].

European Commission. 2001. *Green Paper: Promoting a European Framework for Corporate Social Responsibility*, 18 July 2002, COM(2001)366 final. Brussels: European Commission.

European Commission. 2002. *Communication from the Commission Concerning Corporate Social Responsibility: A Business Contribution to Sustainable Development*, 2 July 2001, COM(2002)347 final, 2002. Brussels: European Commission.

European Commission. Undated a. *Compendium on national public policies on CSR in the European Union (2003)*. [Online: Directorate General on Employment and Social Affairs]. Available at: http://ec.europa.eu/employment_social/emplweb/csr-matrix/csr_matrix_en.cfm [accessed: 20 March 2007].

European Commission. Undated b. *Corporate Social Responsibility: National public policies in the European Union (2007)*. [Online: European Commission, Enterprise and Industry, Policy Areas, CSR]. Available at: http://ec.europa.eu/enterprise/csr/documents/stakeholder_forum/Compendium_MS_updated_Portugal_2212.pdf [accessed: 1 August 2009].

European Parliament. 2006. *Report on Corporate Social Responsibility: A New Partnership* (2006/2133(INI)), A6-0471/2006, 20 December 2006. Rapporteur: Richard Howitt. Luxemburg: Committee on Employment and Social Affairs.

Eyskoot, M. 2004. European Coordinator, International Secretariat, Clean Clothes Campaign. Interview conducted in Amsterdam, The Netherlands, September 2004.

Fair Wear Foundation. 2003. *Annual Report 2003*. Amsterdam: Fair Wear Foundation.

Finlayson, J.A. and Zacher, M.W. 1983. The GATT and the regulation of trade barriers: Regime dynamics and functions, in *International Regimes*, edited by S. Krasner. Ithaca, NY: Cornell University Press, 273–314.

Finnemore, M. 1996. *National Interests in International Society*. Ithaca, NY: Cornell University Press.

Finnemore, M. 2003. *The Purpose of Intervention: Changing Beliefs About the Use of Force*. Ithaca, NY: Cornell University Press.

Finnemore, M. and Sikkink, K. 1998. International norm dynamics and political change. *International Organization*, 52(4), 887–917.

FLO (Fairtrade Labelling Organization International). 2003. *Annual Report 2002/2003*. Bonn: Fairtrade Labelling Organization International.

FLO (Fairtrade Labelling Organization International). 2004. *Annual Report 2003/2004*. Bonn: Fairtrade Labelling Organization International.

FLO (Fairtrade Labelling Organization International). 2005a. *Annual Report 2004/2005*. Bonn: Fairtrade Labelling Organization International.

FLO (Fairtrade Labelling Organization International). 2005b. *About FLO: FLO's Structure; About FLO: Frequently Asked Questions; About FLO: How is the system financed?; About FLO: FLO's Main tasks; About FLO: Why does FLO exist?; Certification; Impact: Facts & Figures; Standards: Fairtrade Standards in General; Standards: Procedure for Standard Setting; Standards: Sets of Standards for All Products; Standards.* [Online: Fairtrade Labelling Organization International]. Available at: www.fairtrade.net/sites/aboutflo/structure.html; www.fairtrade.net/sites/aboutflo/faq.html; www.fairtrade.net/sites/aboutflo/financed.html; www.fairtrade.net/sites/aboutflo/tasks.html; www.fairtrade.net/sites/aboutflo/why.html; www.fairtrade.net/sites/certification/certification.html; www.fairtrade.net/sites/impact/facts.html; www.fairtrade.net/sites/standards/general.html; www.fairtrade.net/sites/standards/procedure.html; www.fairtrade.net/sites/standards/set.html; www.fairtrade.net/sites/standards/standards.html [accessed: 24 February 2005].

FLO (Fairtrade Labelling Organization International). 2006. *Annual Report 2005/2006*. Bonn: Fairtrade Labelling Organization International.

FLO (Fairtrade Labelling Organization International). 2007. *Annual Report: An Inspiration for Change*. Bonn: Fairtrade Labelling Organization International.

Florini, A.M. 1996. The evolution of international norms. *International Studies Quarterly*, 40(3), 363–89.

Florini, A.M. 2000. *The Third Force: The Rise of Transnational Civil Society*. Washington, DC: Japan Center for International Exchange and Carnegie Endowment for International Peace.

Forsyth, D. 2006. *Human Rights in International Relations*. Cambridge: Cambridge University Press.

Fortune. 2008. *Fortune 500 2008*. [Online: Fortune]. Available at: www.money.cnn.com/magazines/fortune/global500/2008/index.html [accessed: 30 August 2009].

Frankental, P. and House, F. 2000. *Human Rights: Is it Any of Your Business?* London: Amnesty International and The Prince of Wales Business Leaders Forum.

Freeman, R.E. 1984. *Strategic Management: A Stakeholder Approach*. Boston: Pitman Publishing.

Freeman, R.E. and Phillips, R. 2002. Stakeholder theory: A libertarian defense. *Business Ethics Quarterly*, 12(3), 331–49.

Friedman, M. 1970. The social responsibility of business is to increase its profits. *The New York Times Magazine*, 13 September, 173–78.

Friedrichs, J. 2001. The meaning of new medievalism. *European Journal of International Relations*, 7(4), 475–94.

Funkhouser, D. 2004. Strategic Outreach Coordinator, TransFair USA. Interview conducted in San Francisco, US, June 2004.

G8 Summit. 2007. *G8 Summit 2007 Heiligendamm. Growth and Responsibility in the World Economy, Summit Declaration (7 June 2007).* [Online: UN Global Compact]. Available at: http://www.unglobalcompact.org/docs/about_the_gc/government_support/G8_Summit_2007_Heiligendamm_Declaration.pdf [accessed: 1 August 2009].

Ghébali, V–Y. 1989. *The International Labour Organisation: A Case Study on the Evolution of U.N. Specialised Agencies.* Dordrecht: M. Nijhoff.

Giddens, A. 1984. *The Constitution of Society.* Berkeley, CA: University of California Press.

Gilpin, R. 2001. *Global Political Economy. Understanding the International Economic Order.* Princeton, NJ: Princeton University Press.

Giovannucci, D. 2003. *The State of Sustainable Coffee: A Study of Twelve Major Markets.* [Online: International Institute for Sustainable Development]. Available at: http://www.iisd.org/pdf/2003/trade_state_sustainable_coffee.pdf [accessed: 1 August 2009].

Global Exchange. 1989a. *Global Exchanges* [Newsletter]. Fall 1989.

Global Exchange. 1989b. A new spirit of internationalism. *Global Exchanges* [Newsletter], Fall 1989.

Global Exchange. 1989c. The internationalist movement … The year in review. *Global Exchanges* [Newsletter], Fall 1989.

Global Exchange. 1990a. Appalachia tour creates media stir. *Global Exchanges* [Newsletter], Spring 1990, Issue No. 3.

Global Exchange. 1990b. Global Exchange opens third world crafts center. *Global Exchanges* [Newsletter], Spring 1990, Issue No. 3.

Global Exchange. 1990c. Ways to build partnerships. *Global Exchanges* [Newsletter], Spring 1990, Issue No. 3.

Global Exchange. 1991. *Annual Report 1991.* San Francisco, CA: Global Exchange.

Global Exchange. 1992. *Annual Report 1992.* San Francisco, CA: Global Exchange.

Global Exchange. 1994. *Annual Report 1993–94.* San Francisco, CA: Global Exchange.

Global Exchange. 1997a. *Global Exchanges* [Newsletter], Fall 1997, Issue No. 32.

Global Exchange. 1997b. *Nike: Just* Don't *Do It, Stop Sweatshops! Special Report.*

Global Exchange. 1997c. Nike campaign continues. *Global Exchanges* [Newsletter], Spring 1997, Issue No. 30.

Global Exchange. 1997d. Update on Nike campaign. *Global Exchanges* [Newsletter], Summer 1997, Issue No. 31.

Global Exchange. 1997e. What's new at Global Exchange. *Global Exchanges* [Newsletter], Fall 1997, Issue No. 32.

Global Exchange. 1997f. Clinton task force leaves sweatshop intact. *Global Exchanges* [Newsletter], Summer 1997, Issue No. 31.

Global Exchange. 1998. *Annual Report 1997–98*. San Francisco: Global Exchange.

Global Exchange. 2001. Nike: Just doing nothing to protect workers' rights in Mexico. *Global Exchanges* [Newsletter], Spring 2001, Issue No. 46.

Goldman, R. and Papson, S. 1998. *Nike Culture: The Sign of the Swoosh*. London: Sage.

Goldstein, J. and Keohane, R.O. 1993. Ideas and foreign policy: An analytical framework, in *Ideas and Foreign Policy: Beliefs, Institutions and Political Change*, edited by J. Goldstein and R.O. Keohane. Ithaca, NY: Cornell University Press, 3–30.

Government Offices of Sweden. 2008. *From the Budget Bill for 2008: Budget Statement and Summary*. [Online]. Available at: www.sweden.gov.se/content/1/c6/09/05/18/d44289fd.pdf [accessed: 30 August 2009].

GRI (Global Reporting Initiative). 2004. *Synergies between the OECD Guidelines for Multinational Enterprises (MNEs) and the GRI 2002 Sustainability Reporting Guidelines: A Guide to help Organisations Communicate Their Use of the OECD MNE Guidelines for Multinational Enterprises (MNEs), June 2004*. Amsterdam: Global Reporting Initiative.

Gumbrell-McCormick, R. 2000a. Facing the multinationals, in *The International Confederation of Free Trade Unions*, edited by A. Carew and M. van der Linden. Bern: Lang.

Gumbrell-McCormick, R. 2000b. South Africa: The fight for freedom, in *The International Confederation of Free Trade Unions*, edited by A. Carew and M. van der Linden. Bern: Lang.

Gunter, B.G. and van der Hoeven, R. 2004. The social dimension of globalization: A review of the literature. *International Labour Review*, 143(1–2), 7–43.

Gurney, C. 2000. A great cause: The origins of the anti-apartheid movement, June 1959–March 1960. *Journal of Southern African Studies*, 26(1), 123–44.

Hahn, C. and Dunn, E. 1996. *Civil Society: Challenging Western Models*. London: Routledge.

Hall, B.L. 2000. Global civil society: Theorizing a changing world. *Convergence*, 33(1–2), 10–32.

Hamlyn, J. 2003. Programme Co-Ordinator, Corporate Partnership Development, International Business Leaders Forum (IBLF). Interview conducted in London, UK, December 2003.

Harmsen, J. 2004. Product Specialist Coffee, Max Havelaar Foundation. Interview conducted in Utrech, The Netherlands, September 2004.

Harvey, D. 1989. *The Condition of Postmodernity: An Enquiry Into the Origins of Cultural Change*. Oxford: Blackwell.

Harvey, P.J. 1999. Letters to the editor. Nike's certification no means guaranteed. *Financial Times*, 2 February, 16.

Harvey, P.J. 2004. Director and former Executive Director of ILRF. Telephone interview conducted in June 2004.

Heald, M. 1970. *The Social Responsibilities of Business: Company and Community, 1900–1960*. Cleveland, OH: Press of Case Western Reserve University.

Held, D. and McGrew, A. 2003. *The Global Transformations Reader: An Introduction to the Globalization Debate*. Cambridge: Polity Press.

Held, D., Goldblatt, D., McGrew, A. and Perraton, J. 1999. *Global Transformations: Politics, Economics and Culture*. Cambridge: Polity Press.

Henderson, D. 2001. *Misguided Virtue: False Notions of Corporate Social Responsibility*. London: Institute of Economic Affairs.

Hilowitz, J. 1997. Social labelling to combat child labour: Some considerations. *International Labour Review*, 136(2), 216–32.

Hirschland, M. 2004. Senior Manager, Member Communications, Business for Social Responsibility. Interview conducted in San Francisco, US, May 2004.

Holton, R.J. 1998. *Globalization and the Nation-state*. Basingstoke: Macmillan.

Hufbauer, G.C. and Mitrokostas, N.K. 2003. *Awakening Monster: The Tort Aliens Claims Act*. Washington, DC: Institute for International Economics.

Human Rights Council. 2007. *Report of the Special Representative of the Secretary-General on the issue of human rights and transnational corporations and other business enterprises. Business and human rights: Mapping international standards of Responsibility and Accountability for Corporate Acts*. Summary. Human Rights Council, A/HRC/4/035, 9 February 2007.

Human Rights Council. 2008. *Report of the Special Representative of the Secretary-General on the issue of human rights and transnational corporations and other business enterprises. Business and human rights: Towards operationalizing the 'protect, respect and remedy' framework*. Summary. Human Rights Council, A/HRC/11/13, 22 April 2009.

Hurd, I. 1999. Legitimacy and authority in international politics. *International Organization*, 53(2), 379–408.

Hurrell, A. 2005. Norms and ethics in international relations, in *Handbook of International Relations*, edited by W. Carlsnaes, T. Risse and B.A. Simmons. London: Sage, 137–54.

IBLF (International Business Leaders Forum). Undated a. *Introduction to the International Business Leaders Forum*. London: International Business Leaders Forum.

IBLF (International Business Leaders Forum). Undated b. *The Partnership Initiative*. London: International Business Leaders Forum.

IBLF (International Business Leaders Forum). 2000. *A Decade of Difference*. London: International Business Leaders Forum.

IBLF (International Business Leaders Forum). 2001a. *The Challenge of Economic Inclusion: Annual Review 2001*. London: International Business Leaders Forum.

IBLF (International Business Leaders Forum). 2001b. *IBLF Local Guidelines/ Check-list for Implementation, January 2001*. London: International Business Leaders Forum.

IBLF (International Business Leaders Forum). 2002. *IBLF Statement of Support for UN Draft Human Rights Principles and Responsibilities for Transnational Corporations and other Business Enterprises, Frances House, IBLF, 24 July 2002.*

IBLF (International Business Leaders Forum). 2003a. *IBLF Statement of Support for UN Draft Human Rights Principles and Responsibilities for Transnational Corporations and other Business Enterprises, July 2003.*

IBLF (International Business Leaders Forum). 2003b. *Strategic Partners.* [Online: International Business Leaders Forum]. Available at: www.iblf.org/csr/ csrwebassis.nsf/content/flb2b3.html [accessed: 4 December 2003].

IBLF (International Business Leaders Forum). 2004. *Annual Review 2004. Risks, Values, and Business Reputation. Addressing Societies' Expectations.* London: International Business Leaders Forum.

IBLF (International Business Leaders Forum). 2005. *A Statement on the Occasion of the Forum's 10th Anniversary, London, UK, June 2000.* [Online: International Business Leaders Forum]. Available at: http://www.iblf.org/iblf/csrwebassist. nsf/webprintview/fla2d3a2b4a5.html [accessed: 14 June, 2005].

IBLF (International Business Leaders Forum). 2006. *World Business Awards in support of the Millennium Development Goals, Invitation to nominate. The IBLF, ICC, and UNDP.*

IBLF (International Business Leaders Forum) and UNAIDS. 1997. *The Business Response to HIV/AIDS: Innovation and Partnership.* Geneva and London: International Business Leaders Forum and UNAIDS.

IBLF and UNEP. 1994. *Partnerships for Sustainable Development: The Role of Business and Industry.* London: The Prince of Wales Business Leaders Forum and UNEP.

ICC (International Chamber of Commerce). 2001. *ICC Comments on the European Commission Green Paper 'Promoting a European Framework for Corporate Social Responsibility', 20 December 2001.*

ICC (International Chamber of Commerce) and IOE (International Organization of Employers). 2003. Commission, Joint written statement submitted by the International Chamber of Commerce and the International Organization of Employers, non-governmental organizations in general consultative status, E/ CN.4/Sub.2/2003/NGO/44, 29 July 2003.

ICFTU (International Confederation of Free Trade Unions). 1959a. *ICFTU the First Ten Years: A Brief History of the Activities and Achievements of the ICFTU Since its Foundation.* Brussels: ICFTU.

ICFTU (International Confederation of Free Trade Unions). 1959b. *Foreign Investment in Economically Underdeveloped Countries: A Study Submitted to the ICFTU's Sixth World Congress.* Brussels: ICFTU.

ICFTU (International Confederation of Free Trade Unions). 1968. *ICFTU Economic and Social Bulletin*, 16(5).

ICFTU (International Confederation of Free Trade Unions). 1970. *ICFTU Economic and Social Bulletin. Special Number. The International Free Trade Union Movement and Multinational Corporations*, 18(5).

ICFTU (International Confederation of Free Trade Unions). 1972. *Address by Mr. Heribert Maier, Assistant General Secretary of the International Confederation of Free Trade Unions (ICFTU) to the Third Session of the United Nations Conference on Trade and Development, Santiago, Chile, April 24th.*

ILO (International Labor Organization). 1973. *Multinational Enterprises and Social Policy*. Geneva: International Labour Office.

ILRF (International Labor Rights Fund). 1986. *International Labor Rights Education & Research Fund.*

ILRF (International Labor Rights Fund). 1990. *Press Release. USTR Sued for Non-enforcement of Workers Rights, 29 March 1990.*

ILRF (International Labor Rights Fund). 1992. *International Labor Rights Education and Research Fund Summary of 1992 Activities.*

ILRF (International Labor Rights Fund). 1993. *Invitation to Join ILR Advocates, 8 June 1993.*

ILRF (International Labor Rights Fund). 1995a. *NEWS from ILRERF*, 11 April 1995.

ILRF (International Labor Rights Fund). 1995b. *Response of the International Labor Rights Education and Research Fund prepared by Jerome I. Levinson, 28 June 1995.*

ILRF (International Labor Rights Fund). 1999. *Child Labor in the Soccer Ball Industry: A Report on Continued Use of Child Labor in the Soccer Ball Industry in Pakistan.*

ILRF (International Labor Rights Fund). 2001a. *Reception to Honor Pharis J. Harvey, 12 July 2001.*

ILRF (International Labor Rights Fund). 2001b. *Workers in the Global Economy: Cornell University School of Industrial and Labor Relations*. New York: ILRF, Institute for Policy Studies, and Economic Policy Institute.

ILRF (International Labor Rights Fund). 2002. *Annual Report 2002*. Washington, DC: International Labor Rights Fund.

IOCU (International Organization of Consumers Union). 1986. *Milk and Murder: Address to the Rotary Club of Singapore in 1939 by Cicely Williams*. Penang, Malaysia: International Organization of Consumers Union. Regional Office for Asia and the Pacific.

Joseph, S. 2004. *Corporations and Human Rights Litigation*. Portland, OR: Hart Publishing.

Kahn, J. 2000. Multinationals sign UN pact on rights and environment. *The New York Times*, 27 July 2000, 3.

Katzenstein, P.J. 1996. *The Culture of National Security: Norms and Identity in World Politics*. New York: Columbia University Press.

Keck, M. and Sikkink, K. 1998. *Activists beyond Borders: Advocacy Networks in International Politics*. Ithaca, NY: Cornell University Press.

Keohane, R.O. and Nye, J.S. 1972. *Transnational Relations and World Politics*. Cambridge, MA: Harvard University Press.

Khagram, S., Riker, J. and Sikkink, K. 2002. *Restructuring World Politics: Transnational Social Movements, Networks, and Norms*. Minneapolis, MN: University of Minnesota Press.

King, P. 1972. *Multatuli*. New York: Twayne.

Klotz, A. 1995. *Norms in International Relations: The Struggle Against Apartheid*. Ithaca, NY: Cornell University Press.

Knudsen, K. 1988. The strike history of the First International, in *Internationalism in the Labour Movement 1830–1940*, edited by F. van Holthoon and M. van der Linden. Leiden: Brill.

Kocken, M. 2003. *Fifty Years of Fair Trade: A Brief History of the Fair Trade Movement*. [Online: NEWS (Network of European Worldshops)]. Available at: www.worldshops.org/Fairtrade/netw/2004_FinalHistory_of_FairTrade.doc [accessed: 6 December 2004].

Kohl Kaufmann, E. 2004. Executive Director, Social Accountability International (SAI). Interview conducted in New York, US, July 2004.

Kolk, A. and van Tulder, R. 2006. International responsibility codes, in *The Accountable Corporation: Corporate Social Responsibility*, Vol. 3, edited by M.J. Epstein and K.O. Hanson. Westport, CT: Praeger Publishers, 147–87.

KPMG International. 2005. *KPMG International Survey of Corporate Responsibility Reporting 2005*. [Online: KPMG International]. Available at: http://www.kpmg.com.au/Portals/0/KPMG%20Survey%202005_3.pdf [accessed: 1 September 2009].

KPMG International. 2008. *KPMG International Survey of Corporate Responsibility Reporting 2008*. [Online: KPMG International]. Available at: http://www.kpmg.com/SiteCollectionDocuments/International-corporate-responsibility-survey-2008_v2.pdf [accessed: 1 September 2009].

Krasner, S. 1983. *International Regimes*. Ithaca, NY: Cornell University Press.

Krasner, S. 1999. *Sovereignty: Organized Hypocrisy*. Princeton, NJ: Princeton University Press.

Kratochwil, F. 1989. *Rules, Norms and Decisions: On the Conditions of Practical and Legal Reasoning in International Relations and Domestic Affairs*. Cambridge: Cambridge University Press.

Kratochwil, F. and Ruggie, J. 1986. International organization: A state of the art or an art of the state. *International Organization*, 40(4), 753–75.

Krier, J-M. 2001. *Fair Trade in Europe 2001: Facts and Figures on the Fair Trade Sector in 18 European Countries*. [Online: European Fair Trade Association (EFTA)]. Available at: http://www.european-fair-trade-association.org/efta/Doc/FT-E-2001.pdf [accessed: 1 August 2009].

Krier, J-M. 2005. F*air Trade in Europe 2005: Facts and Figures on Fair Trade in 25 European Countries*. [Online: World Fair Trade Organization]. Available at: http://www.wfto.com/index.php?option=com_docman&task=cat_

view&gid=94&&Itemid=109 OCH FairTradeinEurope2005.pdf [accessed: 1 August 2009].

Lapid, Y. and Kratochwil, F. 1996. *The Return of Culture and Identity in IR Theory*. Boulder, CO: Rienner.

Leon H. Sullivan Foundation. 2005a. *Message from Hope Sullivan*. [Online: Leon H. Sullivan Foundation]. Available at: www.thesullivanfoundation.org/gsp/ print.asp [accessed: 24 July 2005].

Leon H. Sullivan Foundation. 2005b. *The Global Sullivan Principles*. [Online: Leon H. Sullivan Foundation]. Available at: www.thesullivanfoundation.org/ gsp/print.asp [accessed: 5 September 2005].

Livanos Cattaui, M. 2000. Yes to Annan's 'Global Compact' if it isn't a license to meddle. *International Herald Tribune*, 26 July, 2000, 8.

Magnusson, P. 2002. Making a federal case out of overseas abuses. *Business Week*, 25 November, 78.

Mark, J. 2004. Communications Manager, Global Exchange. Interview conducted in San Francisco, US, June 2004.

Massie, R. 1997. *Loosing the Bonds: The United States and South Africa in the Apartheid Years*. New York: Nan A. Talese/Doubleday.

McAdam, D., McCarthy, J.D. and Zald, M.N. 1996. *Comparative Perspectives on Social Movements: Political Opportunities, Mobilizing Structures, and Cultural Framings*. New York: Cambridge University Press.

McCarthy, J.D. 1997. The globalization of social movement theory, in *Transnational Social Movements and Global Politics: Solidarity Beyond the State*, edited by J. Smith, C. Chatfield and R. Pagnucco. Syracuse, NY: Syracuse University Press.

McLuhan, M. 1962. *The Gutenberg Galaxy: The Making of Typographic Man*. London: Routledge & K. Paul.

Meyer, M.K. and Prügl, E. 1999. *Gender Politics in Global Governance*. Lanham, MD: Rowman & Littlefield.

Moberg, J. 2003. Manager, Corporate Practices, International Business Leaders Forum. Interview conducted in London, UK, December 2003.

Moberg, J. 2005. Manager, Corporate Practices, International Business Leaders Forum. Interview conducted in London, UK, June 2005.

Nadelman, E.A. 1990. Global prohibition regimes: The evolution of norms in international society. *International Organization*, 44(4), 479–526.

Naidoo, K. 2000. The new civic globalism. *Nation*, 270(18), 34–6.

Nelson, D. 2004. Co-Executive Director, Social Venture Network (SVN). Interview conducted in San Francisco, US, July 2004.

Nelson, J. 1996. *Partnerships for Sustainable Development: The Role of Business and Industry*. London: Prince of Wales Business Leaders Forum in collaboration with the World Bank and the UNEP.

NetImpact. Undated. *Magnify Your Impact*. [Online: NetImpact]. Available at: http://www.netimpact.org/associations/4342/files/Net_Impact_Press_Kit_ 2009.pdf [accessed: 1 September 2009].

Nussbaum, M. 2003. Capabilities as fundamental entitlements: Sen and social justice. *Feminist Economics*, 9(2–3), 33–59.

O'Brian, R. 1999. NGOs, global civil society and global economic regulation, in *Regulating International Business: Beyond Liberalization*, edited by S. Picciotto and R. Mayne. New York: Palgrave Macmillan, 257–72.

O'Brian, R., Goetz, A.M., Scholte, J.A. and Williams, M. 2000. *Contesting Global Governance: Multilateral Institutions and Global Social Movements*. Cambridge: Cambridge University Press.

Oden, T.C. 1985. *Conscience and Dividends: Churches and the Multinationals*. Washington, DC: Ethics and Public Policy Center.

OECD (Organization on Economic Cooperation and Development). 2001. *Codes of Conduct: Expanded Review of their Contents*. Working Papers on International Investments Number 2001/6, May 2001. Paris: Organization on Economic Cooperation and Development.

Palmer, G. 2000. *Politics of Breastfeeding*. London: Pandora.

Pasha, M.K. and Blaney, D.L. 1998. Elusive paradise: The promise and peril of global civil society. *Alternatives: Social Transformation & Human Governance*, 23(4), 417–50.

Phillips, R. 2002. Approaching the organization of economic activity in the age of cross-border alliance capitalism, in *Global Political Economy: Contemporary Theories*, edited by R. Palan. London: Routledge.

Picciotto, S. and Mayne, R. 1999. *Regulating International Business: Beyond Liberalization*. New York: Palgrave Macmillan.

Porto, S. 2003. Membership Development Manager, Ethical Trading Initiative. Interview conducted in London, the UK, December 2003.

Price, R. 1995. A genealogy of the chemical weapons taboo. *International Organization*, 49(1), 73–103.

Price, R. 1998. Reversing the gun sight: Transnational civil society targets land mines. *International Organization*, 52(3), 613–44.

The Prince of Wales. 1992. *Address by HRH The Prince of Wales, President, The Prince of Wales International Business Leaders Forum, at the closing session of the World Economic Forum, in Davos, Switzerland, on 4th February 1992.*

The Prince of Wales. 2000. The business leaders' forum will reinforce the idea that companies should be global corporate citizens, says HRH The Prince of Wales. *Financial Times*, 27 June, 18.

Raynolds, L.T. 2002. Consumer/producer links in fair trade coffee networks. *Sociologia Ruralis*, 42(4), 404–24.

Renard, M-C. 1999. *Los Intersticios de la Globalización: Un Label (Max Havelaar) Para los Pequeños Productores de Café*. Lomas de Chapultepec, Mexico: Centre Français d'Éyudes Mexicaines et Centraméricaines.

Risse, T. 2000. 'Let's argue!': Communicative action in world politics. *International Organization*, 54(1), 1–39.

Risse, T., Ropp, S.C. and Sikkink, K. 1999. *The Power of Human Rights: International Norms and Domestic Change*. Cambridge: Cambridge University Press.

Rivera, S. 2003. Executive Director, Campaign for Labor rights. Interview conducted in Washington, DC, April 2003.

Robertson, R. 1992. *Globalization: Social Theory and Global Culture*. London: Sage.

Roozen, N. and van der Hoff, F. 2002. *L'Aventure du Commerce Équitable: Une Alternative à la Mondialisation par les fondateurs de Max Havelaar*. Paris: Jean-Claude Lattès.

Rosenau, J.N. and Czempiel, E-O. 1992. *Governance without Government: Order and Change in World Politics*. Cambridge: Cambridge University Press.

Rossi, I. 2007. *Frontiers of Globalization Research: Theoretical and Methodological Approaches*. New York: Springer.

Ruggie, J. 2006. *Human Rights Policies and Management Practices of Fortune Global 500 Firms: Results of a Survey, Harvard University, John F. Kennedy School of Government, September 2006*.

Sassen, S. 1998. *Globalization and its Discontents*. New York: New Press.

Scholte, J.A. 2000. *Globalization: A Critical Introduction*. Basingstoke: Palgrave.

Sen, A. 1997. *Human rights and Asian values. Sixteenth Morgenthau Memorial Lecture on Ethics and Foreign Policy*. New York: Carnegie Council on Ethics and International Affairs.

Sen, A. 1999. *Development as Freedom*. Oxford: Oxford University Press.

SERRV. 2004. *SERRV International*. [Online: SERRV]. Available at: www.serrv. org/index.php [accessed: 20 May 2004].

Servais, J-M. 2005. *International Labour Law*. The Hague: Kluwer Law International.

Sethi, P.S. 1974. *Up Against the Corporate Wall: Modern Corporations and Social Issues of the Seventies*. Englewood Cliffs, NJ: Prentice Hall.

Sethi, P.S. 1994. *Multinational Corporations and the Impact of Public Advocacy on Corporate Strategy: Nestlé and the Infant Formula Controversy*. Boston: Kluwer Academic.

Sethi, P.S. and Williams, O.F. 2000a. Creating and implementing global codes of conduct: An assessment of the Sullivan Principles as role model for developing international codes of conduct. Lessons learned and unlearned. *Business and Society Review*, 105(2), 169–200.

Sethi, P.S. and Williams, O.F. 2000b. *Economic Imperatives and Ethical Values in Global Business: The South African Experience and International Codes Today*. Boston: Kluwer Academic.

Shaw, R. 1999. *Reclaiming America: Nike, Clean Air, and the New National Activism*. Berkeley, CA: University of California Press.

Slater, A. 2004. Associate Director Communications, Global Reporting Initiative (GRI). Interview conducted in Amsterdam, The Netherlands, September 2004.

Smith, J. 1997. Characteristics of the modern transnational social movement sector, in *Transnational Social Movements and Global Politics: Solidarity Beyond the State*, edited by J. Smith, C. Chatfield and R. Pagnucco. Syracuse, NY: Syracuse University Press.

Smith, J., Chatfield, C. and Pagnucco, R. 1997. *Transnational Social Movements and Global Politics: Solidarity Beyond the State.* Syracuse, NY: Syracuse University Press.

Sub-Commission. 1992. *Summary Record of 31st Meeting*, Sub-Commission on Prevention of Discrimination and Protection of Minorities, E/CN.4/Sub.2/1992/SR.31, 31 August 1992.

Sub-Commission. 1993a. *Summary Record of 26th Meeting*, Sub-Commission on Prevention of Discrimination and Protection of Minorities, E/CN.4/Sub.2/1992/SR, 31 February 1993.

Sub-Commission. 1993b. *Summary Record of 22nd Meeting*, Sub-Commission on Prevention of Discrimination and Protection of Minorities, E/CN.4/Sub.2/1993/SR, 26 August 1993.

Sub-Commission resolution. 1994. *Measures towards the full realization of economic, social and cultural rights*. Sub-Commission resolution 1994/37. Report of the Sub-Commission on Prevention of Discrimination and Protection of Minorities on its forty-sixth session, Geneva, 1–26 August 1994. E/CN.4/1995/2, E/CN.4/Sub.2/1994/56, 28 October 1994.

Sub-Commission resolution. 1998. *The relationship between the enjoyment of economic, social and cultural rights and the right to development, and the working methods and activities of transnational corporations*. Sub-Commission resolution 1998/8, 20 August 1998. Sub-Commission on Prevention of Discrimination and Protection of Minorities, Report of the Sub-Commission on Prevention of Discrimination and Protection of Minorities on its Fiftieth Session, E/CN.4/1999/4, E/CN.4/Sub.2/1998/45, 30 September 1998.

Sub-Commission resolution. 2003. *Economic, social and cultural rights: Norms on the responsibilities of transnational corporations and other business enterprises with regard to human rights*. Sub-Commission on Prevention of Discrimination and Protection of Minorities, E/CN.4/Sub.2/2003/12/Rev.2, 26 August 2003.

SVN (Social Venture Network). 1999. *Social Venture Network: Standards of Corporate Social Responsibility*. San Francisco, CA: Social Venture Network.

SVN (Social Venture Network). 2002. *Social Venture Network: Report to Stakeholders*. San Francisco, CA: Social Venture Network.

Ten Thousand Villages. 2004. *Ten Thousand Villages Home*. [Online: Ten Thousand Villages]. Available at: www.tenthousandvillages.org [accessed: 19 May 2004].

Tharp, P.A. Jr. 1976. Transnational enterprises and international regulation: A survey of various approaches in international organizations. *International Organization*, 30(1), 47–73.

Thomas, D.C. 2001. *The Helsinki Effect: International Norms, Human Rights and the Demise of Communism.* Princeton, NJ: Princeton University Press.

Trade Unions of the World. 2001. London: John Harper.

TransFair USA. 2002. *Annual Report 2002.* San Francisco, CA: TransFair USA.

TransFair USA. 2004. *Annual Report 2004.* San Francisco, CA: TransFair USA.

TransFair USA. 2005. 2005 *Fair Trade Coffee Facts and Figures.* [Online: TransFair USA]. Available at: http://www.transfairusa.org/content/Downloads/2005Q2Factsand Figures.pdf [accessed: 1 August 2009].

UNCTAD (United Nations Conference on Trade and Development). 2006. *World Investment Report 2006. FDI from Developing and Transition Economies: Implications for Development.* New York: United Nations.

UNCTAD (United Nations Conference on Trade and Development). 2008. *World Investment Report 2008. Transnational Corporations, and the Infrastructure Challenge.* New York: United Nations.

UNGC (UN Global Compact). Undated. *After the Signature: A Guide to Engagement in the United Nations Global Compact.* [Online: UN Global Compact]. Available at: http://www.unglobalcompact.org/docs/news_events/8.1/after_the_signature.pdf [accessed: 1 August 2009].

UNGC (UN Global Compact). 1999. *Secretary-General Proposes Global Compact on Human Rights, Labour, Environment, in Address to World Economic Forum in Davos, Press Release SG_/SM/6881, 1 February 1999.*

UNGC (UN Global Compact). 2002a. *Overview.* [Online: UN Global Compact]. Available at: www.un.org/partners/business/gcevent/press/whatis_hd.htm [accessed: 10 October 2002].

UNGC (UN Global Compact). 2002b. *Issues Relating to the Global Compact.* [Online: UN Global Compact]. Available at: www.un.org/partners/business/gcevent/press/whatis_hd.htm [accessed: 10 October 2002].

UNGC (UN Global Compact). 2007. *UN Global Compact Annual Review: 2007 Leaders Summit.* [Online: UN Global Compact]. Available at: http://www.unglobalcompact.org/docs/news_events/8.1/GCAnnualReview2007.pdf [accessed: 1 August 2009].

UNGC (UN Global Compact). 2008. *Annual Review 2008.* [Online: UN Global Compact]. Available at: http://www.unglobalcompact.org/docs/news_events/9.1_news_archives/2009_04_08/GC_2008AR_FINAL.pdf [accessed: 1 August 2009].

UNGC (UN Global Compact). 2009. *Policy for the 'Communication on Progress' (COP) 3 April 2009.* [Online: UN Global Compact]. Available at: http://www.unglobalcompact.org/docs/communication_on_progress/COP_Policy.pdf [accessed: 1 August 2009].

UNGC (UN Global Compact) and Barcelona Center for the Support of the Global Compact. 2007. *Local Network Report: Deepening the Engagement of all Participants at the Local Level.* [Online: UN Global Compact]. Available at: http://www.unglobalcompact.org/docs/news_events/8.1/LNReport_FINAL.pdf [accessed: 1 August 2009].

UNGC (UN Global Compact) and GRI (Global Reporting Initiative). 2007. *Making the Connection: The GRI Guidelines and the global Compact Communication on Progress*. [Online: UN Global Compact]. Available at: http://www. unglobalcompact.org/docs/news_events/8.1/Making_the_Connection.pdf [accessed: 1 August 2009].

UIA (Union of International Association). 2003. *Yearbook of International Organizations 2003/2004*. Munich: KG Saur Verlag.

United Nations. 1972a. *Yearbook of the United Nations*. New York: United Nations.

United Nations. 1972b. *World Economic Survey 1971: Current Economic Developments*. New York: United Nations.

United Nations. 1973. *Multinational Corporations in World Development*. New York: United Nations.

United Nations. 1974a. *Summary of the Hearings before the Group of Eminent Persons to Study the Impact of Multinational Corporations on Development and on International Relations*. New York: United Nations.

United Nations. 1974b. *The Impact of Multinational Corporations on Development and on International Relations*. New York: United Nations.

United Nations. 1986. *The United Nations Code of Conduct on Transnational Corporations*. New York: United Nations.

United Nations. 1999. *Press Release SG/SM/7203. Good Corporate Citizenship, Business Reputations, Intimately Tied, Secretary-General Tells Corporation Leaders, 2 November 1999*.

Vernon, R. 1971. *Sovereignty at Bay: The Multinational Spread of US Enterprises*. London: Longman.

Voorhes, M. 1999. The US divestment movement, in *How Sanctions Work: Lessons from South Africa*, edited by N.C. Crawford and A. Klotz. Basingstoke: Macmillan.

Wapner, P. and Ruiz, L.E.J. 2000. *Principled World Politics: The Challenge of Normative International Relations*. Lanham, MD: Rowman & Littlefield.

Warkentin, C. and Mingst, K. 2000. International institutions, the state, and global civil society in the age of the world wide web. *Global Governance*, 6(2), 237–55.

Weissbrodt, D. and Kruger, M. 2005. Human rights responsibilities of businesses as non-state actors, in *Non-State Actors and Human Rights*, edited by P. Alston. Oxford: Oxford University Press, 315–50.

Wight, C. 2002. Philosophy of social science and international relations, in *Handbook of International Relations*, edited by W. Carlsnaes, T. Risse and B.A. Simmons. London: Sage, 23–51.

Wilkinson, R. and Hughes, S. 2002. *Global Governance: Critical Perspectives*. London: Routledge.

Willetts, P. 2002. *What is a Non-Governmental Organization?* [Online: UNESCO Encyclopaedia of Life Support Systems. Section 1. Institutional and Infrastructure Resource Issues. Article 1.44.3.7. Non-Governmental

Organizations]. Available at: http://www.staff.city.ac.uk/p.willetts/CS-NTWKS/NGO-ART.HTM [16 October 2002].

Zadek, S., Lingayah, S. and Forstater, M. 1998. *Social Labels: Tools for Ethical Trade.* Luxembourg: Office for Official Publications of the European Communities.

Zehfuss, M. 2002. *Constructivism in International Relations: The Politics of Reality.* Cambridge: Cambridge University Press.

Appendices

Appendix 1 Selected Corporate Social Responsibility Organizations

Activist Organizations	Location of main office	Year est.
International Confederation of Free Trade Unions (ICFTU)	Brussels, Belgium	1949
War on Want	London, UK	1951
Consumers International	London, UK	1960
Amnesty International	London, UK	1961
Interfaith Center on Corporate Responsibility	New York, USA	1971
Asia Monitor Resource Center (AMRC)	Hong Kong, China	1976
Baby Milk Action	Cambridge, UK	1978
Human Rights Watch	New York, USA	1978
Coalition against BAYER Dangers (CBG)	Dusseldorf, Germany	1978
International Baby Food Action Network (IBFAN)	(8 regional offices)	1979
National Labor Committee	New York, USA	1981
IRENE	Tillburg, The Netherl.	1981
Women Working Worldwide	Manchester, UK	1983
Third World Network (TWN)	Penang, Malaysia	1984
International Labor Rights Fund	Washington, DC, USA	1986
Global Exchange (GX)	San Francisco, USA	1988
Coalition for Justice in the Maquiladoras (CJM)	San Antonio, USA	1989
European Fair Trade Association	Maastricht, The Netherl.	1990
Clean Clothes Campaign	Amsterdam, The Netherl.	1990
Transnationals Information Exchange-Asia (TIE-Asia)	Kajang, Malaysia	1992
Coalition for the Charter of Safe Production of Toys	Hong Kong, China	1993
Global Witness	London, UK	1993
Transparency International	Berlin, Germany	1993
European Banana Action Network (EUROBAN)	Norwich, UK	1994
International Forum on Globalization (IFG)	San Francisco, USA	1994
Sweatshop Watch	San Francisco, USA	1995
Campaign for Labor Rights (CLR)	Washington, DC, USA	1995
Focus On The Global South	Bangkok, Thailand	1995
Oxfam International	Oxford, UK	1995
Maquiladora Solidarity Network (MSN)	Toronto, Canada	1995
Asia Pacific Workers Solidarity Links (APWSL)	Lahore, Pakistan	1996
Corporate Watch	Oxford, UK	1996
Banana Link	Norwich, UK	1996
CorpWatch	San Francisco, USA	1996
Oilwatch	Quito, Ecuador	1996
Global March against Child Labour	New Delhi, India	1997
Corporate Europe Observatory (CEO)	Amsterdam, The Netherl.	1997
United Students Against Sweatshops (USAS)	Washington, DC, USA	1998
Alliance for a Corporate-free UN	Washington, DC, USA	1999

Appendix 1   Continued

Activist Organizations	Location of main office	Year est.
Workers Rights Consortium (WRC)	Washington, DC, USA	2000
Institute of Contemporary Observation	Chegongmiao, China	2001
GATSwatch	Amsterdam, The Netherl.	2001
OECD Watch	Amsterdam, The Netherl.	2003
BankTrack	Utrecht, The Netherl.	2004
Business Initiatives Organizations		
Global Sullivan Principles, The	Scottsdale, USA	1977
Business in the Community (BITC)	London, UK	1982
Caux Round Table (CRT)	Minneapolis, USA	1986
Social Venture Network (SVN)	San Francisco, USA	1987
International Business Leaders Forum (IBLF)	London, UK	1990
European Baha'i Business Forum	Chambéry, France	1990
Business for Social Responsibility (BSR)	San Francisco, USA	1992
CSR Europe: Business Network for Corporate Social Responsibility	Brussels, Belgium	1995
World Business Council on Sustainable Development (WBCSD)	Geneva, Switzerland	1995
Future 500	San Francisco, USA, Tokyo, Japan	1996
Forum Empresa	Santiago, Chile	1997
Ethical Tea Partnership	London, UK	1997
World Cocoa Foundation (WFC)	Vienna, USA	2000
WRAP World Responsible Apparel Production	Washington, DC, USA	2000
International Council on Mining and Metals	London, UK	2001
Multi-stakeholder Organizations		
Rugmark Foundation	Washington, DC, USA	1994
Verité (Verification in Trade and Ethics)	Amherst, USA	1995
AccountAbility, Institute of social and ethical accountability	London, UK	1996
Social Accountability International (SAI)	New York, USA	1997
Global Reporting Initiative (GRI)	Amsterdam, The Netherl.	1997
Fairtrade Labelling Organization International (FLO)	Bonn, Germany	1997
Fair Labor Associations	Washington, DC, USA	1997
Ethical Trading Initiative (ETI)	London, UK	1998
Global Corporate Governance Forum (GCGF)	Washington, DC, USA	1999
Global Alliance for Vaccines and Immunization (GAVI)	Geneva, Switzerland	1999
Workers Rights Consortium (WCR)	Washington, DC, USA	2000
Center for Social Markets	London, UK, Kolkata, India	2000
UN Global Compact	New York, USA	2000
Ethical Shareholders of Europe	Cologne, Germany	2000
European Sustainable and Responsible Investment Forum (EUROSIF)	Culemborg, The Netherl.	2001
Association for Sustainable and Responsible Investment in Asia (ASrIA)	Hong Kong, China	2001

Source: Based on author's findings in this study.

Appendix 2 Focus Organizations

Organization*	Aims and Activities	Governance and Funding	Income and Expenditures	Number of Staff
Clean Clothes Campaign (CCC), Amsterdam, The Netherlands (1989)	*Aims* - Improve working conditions and empower workers in the global garment industry (incl. sports and foot wear) *Activities* - Putting pressure on major retailer and brands (incl. adoption of CCC model code), solidarity work, raising awareness and mobilization, exploring and lobbying for legal measures	*Governance* - Autonomous national CCC coalitions coordinated by an international secretariat - The International secretariat (and the Dutch CCC coalition) is governed by a Board supervising goal setting and functioning, annual planning, financial situation and annual reports *Funding* - Subsidies, member contributions	*Income* - Euro 393,000 (year 2004, international secretariat only) *Expenditure* - Campaign activities, staff salaries, office space and administration (international secretariat only)	Approx. 4 employees at the International Secretariat (year 2004, a back office with 3 employees provides administrative service to both the International and the Dutch CCC coalition) Staff at national CCC coalitions not included
Fairtrade Labelling Organizat ons International (FLO), Bonn, Germany (1997)	*Aims* - Improve the position of the poor and disadvantaged producers in developing countries by setting Fairtrade standards and creating a framework that enables trade to take place at conditions respecting their interests *Activities* - FLO: Guaranteeing the standards, business facilitation, and promoting producer support - National labelling organizations: to encourage industry and consumers to support Fairtrade and purchase Fairtrade products	*Governance* - Board of Directors elected by the FLO Fairtrade Forum (incl. producers and traders), and the Meetings of Members (composed of national labelling organizations) - Executive Board of Directors (operational board) - Separate systems for field inspections and auditing of retailers and traders - Multi-stakeholder committees for certification and standards *Funding* - Membership contributions, external grants for specific projects	*Income* - Euro 1.7 million (year 2002) *Expenditures* - International coordination, certification and inspection, standard setting, projects	27 employees (year 2003) National labelling initiatives not included

Appendix 2 Continued

Organization*	Aims and Activities	Governance and Funding	Income and Expenditures	Number of Staff
Global Exchange, San Francisco, USA (1988)	*Aims* - Promote political, social and environmental justice globally; increase global awareness among US public; build partnership worldwide *Activities* - Human rights campaigns (monitoring and reporting, support pro–democracy movements, responsibility of US companies, policies of WTO, WB and IMF, development of alternatives); Fairtrade stores and education, Reality Tours, public education (books, videos, articles, events, workshops, media, speakers bureau)	*Governance* - Board of Director (responsible for long range planning in dialogue with staff, appoints an Executive Committee of the Board responsible for current issues) *Funding* - Tour revenues, member contributions, foundation grants, sales, fiscally-sponsored projects, events and honoraria	*Income* - USD 4.5 million (fiscal year of 2002) *Expenditures* - Reality Tours, human rights campaigns, fundraising and management, Fairtrade, public education, grants given	Approx. 40 staff (as of 2004, not including interns and volunteers, an additional 10–12 persons are employed in the Fairtrade stores)
International Business Leaders Forum (IBLF), London, UK (1990)	*Aims* - Promote value-based leadership, develop cross-sector partnerships and collective-action, and provide practical assistance to company managers in the area of responsible business practices *Activities* - Building management capacity; regional partnerships; strategic policy dialogue and leadership; global programmes on information technology, health, tourism, young entrepreneurs and general exchange (ENGAGE); research and dissemination of publications; events and seminars; awards	*Governance* - Board of non-executive directors drawn from principal corporate supporters ('trustees', responsible for resources and overall strategy, Finance and General Purposes Sub-Committee (management performance and resource allocation), International Advisory Council drawn from corporate members *Funding* - Voluntary annual donations and programme support from members, grant support from found–ations and institutions (bilateral and multilateral agencies)	*Income* - GBP 3.7 million (fiscal year ending June 2002) *Expenditures* - Development work in developing and transitional countries, information and communication, policy and research, educational activities, fundraising and publicity, management and administration	42 employees at the London headquarter (as of June 2002), some additional 30 persons (as of June 2005) are on occasional assignment with the IBLF internationally

Appendix 2 Continued

Organization*	Aims and Activities	Governance and Funding	Income and Expenditures	Number of Staff
International Labor Rights Fund (ILRF), Washington DC, USA (1986)	*Aims* - Achieve a just and humane treatment for workers worldwide, promote the right to organize for workers' rights and interests (child labour, forced labour, and other abusive labour practices), and the enforcement of labour rights in general *Activities* - Public education and mobilization, research, litigation, legislation, and collaboration with labour, government and business groups	*Governance* - Board of Directors of academics, politicians, non-governmental organizations, policy institutes, financial entities, lawyers' associations and firms, trade unions - International Advisory Council *Funding* - Voluntary contributions from foundations, government grants, individuals, universities, and various groups (trade unions, churches, and companies)	*Income* - USD 1.05 million (year 2000) *Expenditures* - Programme services, support services (management and general, fundraising, etc.)	7 employees (as of 2004), not including interns, volunteers and ILR Advocates

Note: * Including location of main office and year of establishment. In the case of FLO the organization started as a national initiative, the Max Havelaar Foundation, in 1988.

Source: Annual reports and other printed material, interviews and Internet websites of the organizations.

Appendix 3   Listing of Corporate Social Responsibility Initiatives (by category of initiator and year of establishment)

Non-governmental Organizations	
European Charter on Child Labour in the Footwear Sector (European social partners)	1995
The Principles for Global Corporate Responsibility: Bench Marks for Measuring Business Performance (The Ecumenical Council for Corporate Responsibility of the United Kingdom (ECCR), the Interfaith Center on Corporate Responsibility of the USA (ICCR) and the Taskforce on the Churches and Corporate Responsibility of Canada (TCCR))	1995
ICFTU's/ITS's Basic Code of Labour Practice	1997
Amnesty International Human Rights Principles for Companies	1998
International Code of Conduct for the Production of Cut-Flowers	1998
Worker's Rights Consortium Model Code of Conduct	2000
European Coalition on Oil in Sudan (ECOS) Business Principles for the Interim Period	2002
Asia Monitor Resource Centre (AMRC): Asian Transnational Corporations Network	2002
ISEAL Alliance Code of Good Practice for Social and Environmental Standard Setting	2004
Earthworks and Oxfam America: No Dirty Gold Campaign's Golden Rules	2004
ISO26000 project	2004
International Dalit Solidarity Network: The Ambedkar Principles (on Employment and Economic and Social Exclusion relating to Caste Discrimination)	2005
Business Organizations	
International Federation of Pharmaceutical Manufacturers Associations (IFPMA) Code of Pharmaceutical Marketing Practices	1981
Canadian Chemical Producer's Association/International Council of Chemical Association Responsible Care	1985
Caux Round Table Principles for Business	1994
International Council of Toy Industries' Code of Business Practices	1995
International Code of Ethics for Canadian Business	1997
World Federation of the Sporting Goods Industry Model Code of Conduct	1997
US Chamber of Commerce's Business Civic Leadership Center (formerly the Center for Corporate Citizenship)	2000
Worldwide Responsible Apparel Production (WRAP) Apparel Certification Program (American Federation of Apparel Association)	2000
ICC and WBCSD Business Action for Sustainable Development	2001
World Economic Forum: Global Corporate Citizenship Initiative (working group on the contribution of corporations to society)	2001
World Economic Forum and former UN Secretary General Kofi Annan: Global Health Initiative (working group to engage businesses in public-private partnerships to fight HIV/AIDS, TB and Malaria)	2002
Foreign Trade Association (FTA): Business Social Compliance Initiative (BSCI)	2004
International Council of Chemical Association: Responsible Care Global Charter	2005
Global Business Coalition on HIV/AIDS, Tuberculosis and Malaria (GBC): Best Practice AIDS Standard (BPAS)	2005
Multi-stakeholder Organizations	
First Global Framework Agreement (Danone company)	1988
Bangladesh Garment Manufacturers and Exporters Association (BGMEA), the ILO and UNICEF: Joint programme on child labour in the Bangladesh's garment industry	1995
Second Global Framework Agreements (ACCOR Hotels company)	1995
European companies' Manifesto of Enterprises against Social Exclusion (in support of European Commission President Jacques Delors)	1995

Appendix 3 Continued

Fair Labor Association Workplace Code of Conduct	1996
Council on Economic Priorities/Social Accountability International: Social Accountability 8000 (SA8000) Standard	1997
Ethical Trading Initiative (ETI) Base Code and The Base Code Principles of Implementation	1998
ILO Declaration on Fundamental Principles and Rights at Work	1998
Flower Label Program (German trade associations and NGOs)	1998
Social Venture Network (SVN) Standards of Corporate Responsibility	1999
AccountAbility 1000 (AA1000)	1999
World Bank and Word Business Council on Sustainable Development: Business Ethics and Corporate Responsibility Internet-based Educational Project (in developing countries)	2000
Voluntary Principles on Security and Human Rights (extractive industry)	2000
Global Reporting Initiative (GRI) Sustainability Reporting Guidelines	2000
World Cocoa Foundation	2000
Industry Protocol (on cocoa)	2001
European Academy of Business in Society (EABIS)	2002
World Commission on the Social Dimension of Globalization (ILO)	2002
Extractive Industry Transparency Initiative (EITI)	2002
International Cocoa Initiative (Trade associations and NGOs)	2002
Kimberley Process (on diamonds)	2002
International Olympic Committee (IOC) and World Federation of the Sporting Goods Industry (WFSGI) Code of Conduct	2004
The Multi-Fiber Arrangement (MFA) Forum	2004
Business and Human Rights Resource Centre (Internet web portal)	2005
NGO and Business Partnerships for Sustainable Development in Asia and the Pacific (Asian Development Bank, NGO Center, GlaxoSmithKline Biologicals and the Populations and Community Development Association of Thailand)	2005
Governments	
US Model Business Principles	1996
The Copenhagen Centre	1998
Australian Government: The Prime Minister's Community Business Partnership	1999
UK Government Pension Funds Disclosure Regulation	2000
German Government Pension Funds Disclosure Regulation	2001
French Government Pension Funds Disclosure Regulation and mandatory 'triple bottom line' reporting for publicly listed companies	2001
UK Government Appointment of a minister for CSR	2002
UK Government Legislation on a voluntary Belgian Social Label	2002
Belgian Government Pension Funds Disclosure Regulation	2003
Intergovernmental Organizations	
OECD Principles for Corporate Governance	1999
Revision of the OECD Guidelines for Multinational Enterprises from 1976	2000
EU Green Paper on CSR	2001
UN Draft Norms on the Responsibilities of Transnational Corporations and Other Business Enterprises	2003
World Bank's first sustainability review report (using the GRI guidelines)	2004
World Bank International Financial Corporation (IFC) Environmental and Social Standards (for the finance of private sector projects in developing countries)	2006
Principles for Responsible Investment (UNEP, UN Global Compact and institutional investors)	2006

Appendix 3   Continued

Other Initiators (individuals, companies, etc.)	
Calvert Social Investment Fund	1982
Irish National Caucus of the US Congress: The MacBride Principles (on US companies practice with regard to anti-Catholic discrimination in Northern Ireland)	1984
Domini 400 Social Index (benchmark for equity portfolio)	1990
Domini Social Equity Fund (socially responsible investment fund)	1991
An Interfaith Declaration: A Code of Ethics on International Business for Christians, Muslims and Jews	1993
New Academy of Business (now the Association of Sustainability Practitioners, est. by Anita Roddick, the Body Shop)	1995
Calvert Foundation (for community investment, including Calvert Community Investment (CCI) Notes)	1995
Code of Labour Practice for the Production of Goods Licensed by the International Federation of the Football Association (FIFA)	1996
First US class action lawsuit relating to World War II war crimes and crimes against humanity (Swiss banks)	1996
Dow Jones Sustainability Indexes (1st global indexes for financial performance of sustainability-driven companies)	1999
Research Center: The Ramon V. del Rosario, Sr. Center for Corporate Social Responsibility	1999
Deadria Farmer-Paellmann: American Slave Case: Slavery Law Suit against US companies	2000
Bienestar International, Inc., Manufacturers of No Sweat Apparel (private company)	2000
Global e-sustainability Initiative (for the ICT industry)	2001
FTSE Group FTSE4Good Index Series (financial services industry benchmark)	2001
Business Leaders Initiative for Human Rights (BLIHR)	2003
Equator Principles (financial services industry benchmark)	2003
Electronic Industry Code of Conduct	2004

Source: Based on author's findings in this study.

Index

Note: References to figures and tables are given in *italics*; references to footnotes are indicated by the letter 'n', e.g. 143n2 is note 2 on page 143.